FLASH Review

for

Statistics

Julie Sawyer

Northeastern State University

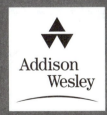
Addison
Wesley

Boston San Francisco New York
London Toronto Sydney Tokyo Singapore Madrid
Mexico City Munich Paris Cape Town Hong Kong Montreal

Acknowledgments

I would like to sincerely thank the following individuals at Addison-Wesley for their contributions to *Flash Review for Statistics*:

- Don Karecki for getting me started;
- Deirdre Lynch for her guidance, patience, encouragement, and professionalism;
- Anna Stillner for taking care of the details; and
- my hero, Joe Vetere, for providing an incredible education and solving myriad problems.

A very special thanks to my husband, Dr. Keith Sawyer, for spending hours listening, discussing, proofreading, and making suggestions that greatly enhanced the quality.

Heartfelt appreciation goes to my friend Denise, my father, and my horses for helping me maintain my sanity during the process.

Vice President and Publisher: Alison Pendergast
Acquisitions Editor: Deirdre Lynch
Associate Production Supervisor: Julie LaChance
Editorial Assistant: Anna Stillner
Project Coordination, Text Design, and Electronic Page Makeup: TechBooks
Cover Design Manager: Barbara Atkinson
Cover Design : Night & Day Design
Manufacturing Buyer: Evelyn Beaton
Printer and Binder: Phoenix Book Tech
Cover Printer: Phoenix Book Tech

Library of Congress Cataloging-in-Publication Data
Sawyer, Julie.
    Flash review for statistics/Julie Sawyer.
        p.cm.
    ISBN 0-201-77466-6
        1. mathematical statistics.   I. Title.
QA276.12.S285 2002
519.5--dc21   2001045859

Please visit our website at http://www. flashreview.com

12345678910-PHC-04030201

CONTENTS

FOREWORD

Dear College Student:

Congratulations on purchasing your *Flash Review*. The fact that you purchased it indicates that you know there's an easier way to make good grades in college—and that you have decided to pursue it. This is the first and most important step you can take to start excelling in your academic efforts.

You see, making good grades in college has more to do with your attitude, determination, and knowledge of how to excel academically than with your level of raw intelligence. I am living proof of that principle.

How a Struggling High School Student Became a College Star

As a high school senior, I had no desire to do well in school, and my grades reflected my bad attitude. As a freshman I had tried to study and make good grades, but my test scores were always disappointing. After my sophomore year I essentially gave up. After all, spending time with my friends was a lot more fun than staying home and studying. As a result, I graduated at the bottom of my class—497th in a class of 512 students. In fact, my poor academic performance almost kept me from graduating altogether.

My parents constantly reminded me how important my education was. They often told me it would determine what types of jobs I would get and how much money I would make. My education would even affect how happy I was, they said. Unfortunately, their advice fell on deaf ears. I was having fun with my friends, and homework seemed like a waste of time.

I underwent an attitude adjustment after high school. I took odd jobs such as shoveling asphalt to fill potholes, offloading semi trucks at a loading dock, flipping burgers at a fast-food joint, and delivering stacks of newspapers to paperboys on street corners. Now don't get me wrong—there's nothing wrong with good, honest hard work. I felt, though, that I was capable of doing more.

When I turned 27, I decided it was time to get a college education, so I took some refresher classes at a local community college to boost my grades. Eventually, I was accepted into a four-year college. Five years later I graduated at the top of my class with bachelor's and master's degrees in business. How did I do it? I learned how to be a smart student rather than a student who is smart.

Study the Habits of the Best Students

I knew I couldn't compete with the top students in terms of raw intelligence, so I started observing their study habits. Then I began to use all the tips, tool, and tactics they used to get straight A's. I asked a friend who was a great student to let me in on his secret. He said, "David, you need to look at your education as though it were a full-time job." He went on to ask, "Are you ever late for your regular job?" I wasn't. "Do you ever just skip work because you don't feel like going?" I didn't. Then he asked, "When your boss gives you an assignment, do you ever just blow it off?" Of course not—I'd get fired. "Exactly," he concluded. "You'd get fired. Why should your job be any different from your college education?"

That very day I decided I would take my education seriously and treat it as though it were a full-time job. I never skipped another class; I arrived on campus at 7:30 AM and didn't leave until I finished my work for the day; and I turned in every assignment that was given to me, even all the optional and extra-credit assignments.

I continued to gather information about study techniques from many other sources and started to figure out what worked for me and what didn't. Finally, I condensed all the advice into a few effective techniques, and I implemented them one by one. For example, I learned that studying in the same place at the same time every day helps one focus and get more done. So I found a spot in the corner of the campus library and made it my "office." Sure enough, I was able to concentrate better and get my work done faster.

Another powerful tip helped me boost my math and science scores. While most study-skills books tell you to stop studying a couple of hours before a test to clear your mind and help you relax, this technique had never worked for me. A friend advised me to do just the opposite—to spend the hour before the test memorizing the formulas. "Forget about how to apply them," he said. "Just organize them and write them down on paper several times. Keep studying them until the test starts. When the test begins, pull out a fresh piece of paper and write down all the formulas, just like you've been doing for the past hour." I tried this technique, and it worked. At the start of my next math exam, I had all the formulas I needed right in front of me—it was almost like an open-book test. That one tip increased my math and science test scores by a full grade.

Flash Review will help you put this tip into practice because it provides all the formulas in one compact, easy-to-study place. With *Flash Review*, you'll breeze through quick, comprehensive reviews before taking your tests.

Academic Success Is Mainly a Function of Knowing How to Make Good Grades

When my scores started to improve, I began to realize that academic success has more to do with knowing how to make good grades than with being a genius. Let me explain. When I started college I spent hours on end studying in the library. I tried to memorize information and cram for tests, but my grades were mediocre. I became frustrated and depressed.

Then a friend taught me some techniques for memorizing facts and figures using word-picture associations. I began to practice these and suddenly started to ace my daily quizzes. Then I bought an organizer and began to schedule my time and develop daily to-do lists. My productivity soared, and I was completing tasks in half the time they took previously. I formed a couple of study groups for some of my harder classes and found myself teaching others the material I was learning. My comprehension of the material improved dramatically. I started to visit my professors during office hours and developed trusting relationships. As a result, they always went the extra mile to help me when I had trouble. I went to the academic skills office and took a short course on taking tests. The course gave me a host of test-taking techniques, and my grades started to improve immediately.

Are you getting the picture? You must learn *how* to be a good student. Most of you will be in college for at least two years; some will be in college for more than eight years. That's a long time. Doesn't it make sense to invest some time in learning how to be an exceptional student?

Using *Flash Review* Will Help You Grasp Topics Quickly

Flash Review is an excellent study tool to help you learn your assigned topic quickly and easily. It is also an effective tool to use when preparing for exams. I'll never forget when I was assigned to do a report on Shakespeare's classic work *The Taming of the Shrew*. I read the first twenty pages and was completely lost. I kept trying to follow the story, but it was useless—I just wasn't getting it.

Finally, I decided to talk to the teacher's assistant, and he suggested that I buy a study guide similar to *Flash Review*. After reading the first few pages, the mystery unfolded, and I finally understood what the story was about. I went on to get an A in that class. After that experience, I purchased a study guide for every topic my classes covered.

Using *Flash Review* will help you grasp difficult and complex topics in record time. It will make you more productive, and when used in conjunction with your regular reading and homework assignments, it will help you master the material you are studying.

Flash Review has also developed a companion Web site that will dramatically improve your comprehension of the materials and shave time off your learning curve. The *Flash Review* Online Study Center (*http://www.flashreview.com*) is a fully interactive learning environment that allows you to take practice quizzes. It provides immediate feedback, enabling you to use your time wisely. Interactive quizzes are only one example of what the *Flash Review* Online Study Center offers to help you learn the material and become a top student. I urge you to visit Flashreview.com and start benefiting from its rich set of interactive learning tools.

I wish you success in your academic endeavors.

David Frey
Author, *Make Straight A's in School: 50 Proven Secrets for Making the Grade!*

INTRODUCTION

Welcome to the world of statistics! Many students begin an introductory statistics course with some trepidation; for some, the beginning of a journey through the world of statistics is much like the onset of a trip to a foreign country. You may find, however, that statistics are not as foreign as you think. In fact, statistics are incorporated into everyday life. For example:

1. The sports page in the local newspaper publishes the ERA of major league pitchers. An average is a commonly reported statistic.

2. A player rolls the dice in a game of Monopoly and calculates the chance of landing on Boardwalk. Probability is the basis on which many statistical methods are built.

3. During election years, a variety of opinion polls are conducted. How the results are interpreted relies on statistics.

4. A commercial on television explains that clinical studies show that a particular brand of aspirin relieves pain faster than the competition. The conclusions of the clinical study are based on statistics.

Any circumstance that involves the collection of data—observations or measurements on a person or thing—presents an opportunity to utilize statistical methods. A course in introductory statistics can help you become a more knowledgeable consumer of information.

Overview of Flash Review for Statistics

Flash Review for Statistics is a resource that can aid you in your understanding of statistical concepts. This resource was designed for students taking an introductory statistics course. It can be used as a companion to an assigned textbook, in distance-learning courses, or as a refresher for those who want to review concepts learned in a previous statistics course. The introduction contains a section of tips that may help you succeed in your statistics course. This is followed by a section on how *Flash Review for Statistics* can be used in relation to these tips for success. A table mapping the contents of *Flash Review for Statistics* to commonly used textbooks is located at the end of the introduction.

In addition to the introduction, *Flash Review for Statistics* contains five content units. The content units are organized into the following components:

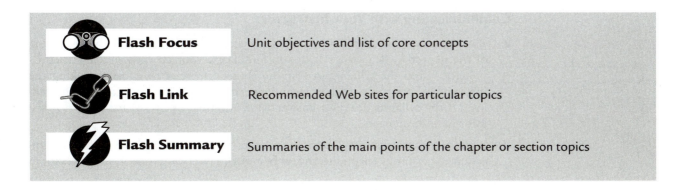

Flash Focus	Unit objectives and list of core concepts
Flash Link	Recommended Web sites for particular topics
Flash Summary	Summaries of the main points of the chapter or section topics

Flash Review Applications of core concepts to cases or practice; solutions follow the last Flash Review in the unit

Flash Test Practice test with true/false, multiple choice, short answer, and calculation problems, as well as solution explanations to the practice test

Content units begin with the Flash Focus and Flash Link components. The units are divided into chapters, often subdivided into sections, that include the Flash Summary and Flash Review components. Each unit ends with the Flash Test component.

The Flash Focus and Flash Link tables include space for you to add information provided by your instructor, your text, and your own exploration. The Flash Review and Flash Test components provide space to work the problems.

Tips for Success

Many factors affect the success of an individual in any course. These may include attitude, communicating with your instructor, class attendance, class preparation, note-taking, study habits, test preparation, and exam-taking strategies. Although these factors are discussed in relation to an introductory statistics class, the tips listed here can be helpful in any course.

Attitude:

✓ Keep it positive—It may seem odd that attitude is listed as the first factor in improving your chance for success in your introductory course in statistics. However, if you approach the course and the topic with a positive attitude, you will have a more positive experience.

✓ The course is not a waste of time—Learning statistical concepts and methods can be both interesting and useful. Have you ever taken a course that made you wonder why it was required because you don't think you will ever need the material again? If you will be involved in almost any kind of academic research, you will encounter statistics after you complete this course. As noted previously, you also encounter statistics constantly in your everyday life.

Communicating with Your Instructor:

✓ The syllabus—Most instructors provide a syllabus for the course at the beginning of the semester. Read the syllabus to familiarize yourself with your instructor's policies. Keep the syllabus in your notebook and refer to it before asking the instructor about topics such as attendance, homework, quizzes, exams, and grading. If the syllabus does not answer your question, ask your instructor for the information you need.

✓ Mode of communication—Determine your instructor's preferred mode of communication: in person, by telephone, and/or by e-mail. If you want to see your instructor in person, try to visit his/her office during posted office hours. If you have a conflict with those hours, make an appointment. When telephoning or e-mailing your instructor, identify yourself by name and by the course you are enrolled in at the beginning of the communication.

✓ Asking questions—Determine your instructor's preference for the timing of questions. Does he/she take questions only at the beginning or the end of the class period? Is it permissible to ask a question during the middle of a lecture? Ask questions as soon as it is feasible. Remember: The only stupid question is one you fail to ask. Failing to ask means you do not receive the information you need.

Class Attendance:

✓ Go to class—Information not contained in other sources, such as your text, may be covered in class; if you miss that lecture, you miss that information. While you should borrow notes if you must miss class, your own notes will generally make more sense to you than notes from a classmate. Class attendance is required by some instructors, thus missed classes may also affect your grade.

✓ Be on time—Students who are consistently late for class miss material and irritate the instructor. If you have a scheduling conflict that causes you to be tardy on a regular basis, discuss the problem with your instructor.

✓ Making up work—Your instructor's policies on making up homework assignments, quizzes, and exams are often included in the syllabus. If they are not, and you must miss class, contact your instructor **prior** to the missed class period to determine the make-up policy. If permissible, ask a classmate or friend to deliver homework assignments on time if you are unable to attend the class period when it is due.

Class Preparation:

✓ Read the text—Make an attempt to read the text prior to the class lecture on the topic. You may not understand all the material the first time you read it, but the topic will be familiar when you hear the instructor discuss it. When reading the text, pay particular attention to boxes and boldface print because these often contain important concepts, definitions, and formulas.

✓ Review your lecture notes—Read your lecture notes from the previous class, and make a list of questions about concepts you do not fully understand.

Note-Taking:

✓ Keep it organized—Keep a separate notebook for your statistics class or use dividers to keep your class notes separated if you have one notebook for several classes. Structure your notes sequentially in a manner that makes them easy to understand when you read them, such as outlining or listing definitions and formulas.

✓ Material—Many instructors write on the board or use overheads for major concepts. Much of this information should go into your notes. In addition, if the instructor works a sample problem, copy it into your notes to refer to it when you study. You may also want to include explanations that follow formal definitions.

✓ Incomplete notes—If you find that your notes are not as useful as you feel they should be due to missing information, ask your instructor if you may tape record the class. Leave blank space in your notes during class, and fill in missed material when you listen to the recording of the lecture. You might also compare your notes with those of a classmate to determine whether that student included material that you did not.

Study Habits:

✓ Time—Be sure you allot enough time in your schedule to study. A general rule of thumb is to spend an average of three hours per week studying for every hour of credit.

✓ Homework—It is particularly important in a statistics course to work homework problems. One of the major stumbling blocks for many statistics students is being unable to read an exercise and determine the appropriate statistical method to answer the question. The more problems you work, the more skilled you will become at this process. Start on homework problems as soon as the associated material is covered so that you will have time to work through difficult ones and ask questions about those you do not understand. Work all assigned exercises, and supplement those with additional problems on concepts that are troublesome for you.

✓ Read resource material—Read the text, both before a topic is covered in class and again after the instructor presents the topic in lecture. Compare your lecture notes to the text to help you decide what concepts to emphasize during your study time. Other sources of material can be utilized for topics that are particularly difficult for you and for those topics you find interesting.

✓ Work examples—Most textbooks and most instructors provide examples for material covered. Work through these examples without looking at the answers to help you determine if you understand the topic and the process. If you find yourself getting stuck at the same point in the process in similar problems, ask your instructor for assistance.

✓ Study groups—Studying with classmates can be very beneficial for all the students involved. Homework sessions work best if all participants have attempted all of the exercises before getting together to discuss solutions. Ask other students for help, but be sure you do your own work. Remember that you will not be able to rely on your study partner during an exam.

✓ Ask for help—If you are having difficulties with the material, try to identify the source of the problem. Providing you with assistance will be easier for your instructor if you can ask specific questions rather than just say, "I don't understand." If you continue to have difficulties, you may want to consider working with a tutor.

Test Preparation:

✓ Time—Be sure to allow plenty of time to study for an exam. A rule of thumb is to begin to review the oldest material to be covered on the exam one week prior to the exam date. Cramming the night before a test is not the most effective way to perform well; however, reviewing the night before (or earlier the same day if it is a late class) can be help you to remember material and feel less stressed.

✓ Rework problems—Rework homework exercises, quiz problems, and examples so that you are familiar with the problem-solving processes for different types of material. If you have difficulty with a particular exercise, find a similar one and work it as well.

✓ Review concepts—Make a list of important concepts, definitions, and formulas. Try to condense your notes for these topics onto one or two sheets of paper, and study from these sheets.

✓ Information from your instructor—Utilize any information your instructor provides such as study guides or sample tests. If your instructor schedules a review session, make a list of questions prior to attending.

✓ Chapter reviews—If your textbook includes a review section at the end of each chapter, read the information provided. Work any sample tests that are included.

✓ Ask for help—Make a list of any problem areas, and ask your instructor for help well in advance of exam time.

Exam-Taking Strategies:

✓ Be on time—Arriving late for an exam is disruptive to you and your classmates.

✓ Be prepared—Take all materials with you that you will need for the exam such as pencils, erasers, scantron sheets (if needed), and scratch paper (if allowed). If you are allowed to use a calculator, take extra batteries. Make sure you are very familiar with your calculator prior to exam time.

✓ You don't have to start with the first question—Look through the entire test to familiarize yourself with the types of questions included. Start with questions that you feel confident about being able to answer correctly. This will boost your confidence and keep you from using too much time at the beginning of the exam.

✓ Use available space—If writing on the exam is allowed, you may want to jot notes in the margins, underline pertinent information in problems, or draw appropriate pictures. If partial credit is available, show all your work. This will give your instructor more information on which to base points earned and may assist you in finding any errors you may have made.

✓ Pace yourself—Work as quickly and steadily as you can. Some types of problems will take longer than others. Don't rush, but don't spend an excessive amount of time on one problem.

✓ Don't panic—If you get stuck on a problem and start to panic, go on to another problem. Go back and finish that problem when you have completed the rest of the exam.

✓ Check your work—If you complete the exam before the allotted time is up, go back and check your work.

Try to remember that the purpose of an exam is to demonstrate your knowledge of statistical concepts and your skill in applying statistical methods in problem-solving. The more effectively you study, the more confidence you will have in your abilities.

Using Flash Review for Statistics *to Improve Success*

Flash Review for Statistics can be a valuable resource for improving your success—your knowledge, understanding and performance—in your introductory statistics course. The following suggestions may help you to utilize this resource effectively.

Flash Focus:

✓ Class preparation—Flash Focus provides definitions and explanations for core concepts discussed in the unit. Previewing these concepts prior to the lecture for a particular topic will familiarize you with the vocabulary.

✓ Study habits—Compare the concepts in the Flash Focus table to those in your text and lecture notes. Add any items from lectures or your text that you feel are important but are not included in the list. As you complete a unit, go back to the Flash Focus component and review the objectives. If you cannot meet any of the objectives, review the appropriate sections.

✓ Test preparation—The core concepts table in the Flash Focus component is an excellent resource for preparing for an exam. Use the objectives in the Flash Focus component to focus your test preparation time.

 Flash Link:

✓ Study habits—The recommended Web sites provided in the Flash Link table provide resources for additional material, including definitions, alternative explanations, and extra examples. In addition, some sites provide demonstrations of concepts to strengthen your understanding.

✓ Test preparation—Many of the Web sites listed in the Flash Link table include practice problems.

 Flash Summary:

✓ Class preparation—Summaries of the main points of the chapter or section topics provided in the Flash Summary component can be used as a preview of topics to be presented in future lectures.

✓ Note-taking—In some introductory statistics classes, it is possible to take class notes directly in the Flash Summary component of a chapter or section. These components include definitions, explanations, formulas, and examples. Use the margins to add concepts and examples.

✓ Study habits—The Flash Summary components are a useful study tool. If you take class notes in a separate notebook, compare your lecture notes with the information provided in Flash Summary. Work through the examples provided in these components. Use the graphs and figures for visualizing major concepts and the relationships between topics. Tables of the decision-making process for determining the appropriate statistical tool are provided when appropriate and can assist in solving homework exercises.

✓ Test preparation—Tables of formulas and decision-making processes can be particularly helpful when preparing for an exam.

 Flash Review:

✓ Study habits—Practice problems associated with core concepts are provided in the Flash Review components. The problems can be worked prior to attempting homework exercises to assess your understanding. After working the Flash Review problems, review the solutions that are provided after the last Flash Review in each unit. This can help you determine how well you understand the concepts and where you have made errors. If you have difficulty with the Flash Review problems, reread the Flash Summary component before attempting your homework.

✓ Test preparation—Rework the Flash Review problems in preparation for exams.

 **Flash Test:**

✓ Test preparation—The practice test in the Flash Test component is an excellent resource for preparing for exams. Since different instructors may ask that you demonstrate your knowledge in different ways on exams, the practice test includes true/false, multiple choice, short answer, and calculation questions. Detailed explanations of the correct answers are provided following the test. For any questions you miss, be sure to review the explanation carefully and reread the appropriate portion of the section to which the question applies. If you still do not understand the correct answer, review the concept in your text and/or ask your instructor for assistance.

Mapping Flash Review for Statistics *to Introductory Statistics Texts*

A table that maps the chapters and/or sections contained in *Flash Review for Statistics* to the analogous sections of five commonly used introductory statistics texts is provided on the next pages. The textbooks are listed in the table by author:

✓ Triola, M. *Elementary Statistics*. 8th ed. Boston: Addison-Wesley; 2001

✓ Moore, D. *The Basic Practice of Statistics*. 2nd ed. New York: Freeman; 2000

✓ Brase, C., Brase, C. *Understandable Statistics*. 6th ed. Boston: Houghton Mifflin; 1999

✓ Bluman, A. *Elementary Statistics: A Step by Step Approach*. 4th ed. Boston: McGraw-Hill; 2001

✓ Weiss, N. *Introductory Statistics*. 6th ed. Boston: Addison-Wesley; 2001

Flash Review for Statistics	Triola	Moore	Brase	Bluman	Weiss
Unit 1: Data and Descriptives					
Chapter 1—Statistics, Data, and Design of Experiments					
Section 1.1 Statistics as a Field of Study	1-1	Statistical Thinking	1.1, 1.3	1-1, 1-2	1.1
Section 1.2 Data Concepts	1-2	Ch.1, 3.1	1.1, 2.1	1-2, 1-3	1.3, 2.1
Section 1.3 Design of Experiments	1-4	3.2		1-4, 1-5	1.5
Chapter 2—Graphical Representations of Data	2-2, 2-3	1.1, 2.1	2.2, 2.3, 2.4, 10.1	2-2, 2-3, 2-4, 11-2	2.2, 2.3, 2.4
Chapter 3—Numerical Representations of Data					
Section 3.1 Measures of Central Tendency	2-4	1.2	3.1	3-2	2.5, 3.1, 3.2

(continued)

(*continued*)

Section 3.2 Measures of Variability	2-5	1.2	3.2	3-3	3.3
Unit 2: Probability					
Chapter 4—Basic Probability					
Section 4.1 Fundamentals of Probability	3-2	4.1	4.1	5-2	4.1, 4.2
Section 4.2 Probability Rules	3-3, 3-4, 3-5	4.2, 5.1	4.2	5-3, 5-4	4.3, 4.4, 4.5, 4.6
Section 4.3 Counting Rules	3-7		4.3	4-2, 4-3, 5-5	4.8
Chapter 5—Probability Distributions					
Section 5.1 Discrete and Continuous Probability Distributions	4-2, 4-3, 4-4, 5-2, 5-3, 5-4	1.3, 4.2, 5.2, 5.3	5.1, 5.2, 5.3, 6.1, 6.2, 6.3	6-2, 6-3, 6-4, 7-2, 7-3, 7-4	5.1, 5.2, 5.3, 6.1, 6.2, 6.3
Section 5.2 Sampling Distribution of the Sample Mean	5-5	4.3	7.1, 7.2	7-5	7.1, 7.2, 7.3
Unit 3: Inference Part I—Estimation					
Chapter 6—Fundamentals of Estimation	6-1	6.1		8-1	8.1
Chapter 7—One Population					
Section 7.1 Population Mean	6-2, 6-3, 6-4	6.1, 7.1	8.1, 8.2, 8.4	8-2, 8-3	8.1, 8.2, 8.3, 8.1
Section 7.2 Population Proportion	6-5	8.1	8.3	8-4	12.1
Section 7.3 Linear Relationships Between Two Variables	9-2, 9-3, 9-4	2.2, 2.3, 2.4	11-3, 10.2, 10.3	11-4, 11-5	14.1, 14.2, 14.3, 14.4, 15.3
Chapter 8—Two Populations					
Section 8.1 Difference Between Two Population Means	8-2, 8-3, 8-6	7.2	8.5	10-2, 10-4, 10-5	10.1, 10.2, 10.3, 10.5

(*continued*)

(continued)

Section 8.2 Difference Between Two Population Proportions	8-4	8.2	8.5	10-6	12.3
Unit 4: Inference Part II—Hypothesis Testing					
Chapter 9—Fundamentals of Hypothesis Testing	7-2	6.2, 6.3, 6.4	9.1, 9.3	9-2, 9-7	9.1, 9.2, 9.4, 9.5
Chapter 10—One Population					
Section 10.1 Population Mean	7-3, 7-4	6.2, 7.1	9.2, 9.4	9-3, 9-4	9.3, 9.6
Section 10.2 Population Proportion	7-5	8.2	9.5	9-5	12.2
Section 10.3 Linear Relationships Between Two Variables	9-2	11.1, 11.2	10.4	11-3	15.2, 15.4
Chapter 11—Two Populations					
Section 11.1 Difference Between Two Population Variances	8-5	7.3	11.4	10-3	11.2
Section 11.2 Difference Between Two Population Means	8-2, 8-3, 8-6	7.2	9.6, 9.7	10-2, 10-4, 10-5	10.1, 10.2, 10.3, 10.5
Section 11.3 Difference Between Two Population Proportions	8-4	8.2	11.5	10-6	12.3
Chapter 12—More Than Two Populations					
Section 12.1 One-Way Analysis of Variance	11-2	10.1, 10.2	11.5	13-2, 13-3	16.2, 16.3, 16.4
Section 12.2 Two-Way Analysis of Variance	11-3		11.6	13-4	Module C
Unit 5: Nonparametrics					
Chapter 13—Tests with Nominal Level Data	10-2, 10-3	9.1, 9.2	11.1, 11.2	12-2, 12-3	13.1, 13.2, 13.3, 13.4

(continued)

(continued)

Chapter 14—Tests with Ordinal Level Data	13-1, 13-3, 13-4, 13-5, 13-6	12.1, 12.2, 12.3	12.2, 12.3	14-4, 14-5, 14-6, 14-7	10.6, 16.5

Good luck with your course, and remember to enjoy the journey!

FLASH FOCUS

After completing this unit, you will be able to:

✓ Understand basic statistical terms
✓ Differentiate between a population and a sample; a parameter and a statistic; descriptive and inferential statistics; quantitative and qualitative data; discrete and continuous data; an observational study and an experiment
✓ Understand the steps in the design of experiments
✓ Identify different sampling methods
✓ Interpret graphical representations of data
✓ Determine appropriate graphical representations of data
✓ Calculate numeric representations of data
✓ Determine appropriate numeric representations of data

The following table lists the core concepts in this unit, along with definitions. Space is provided to add concepts discussed by your instructor.

Core Concepts in Unit 1

Chapter 1—Statistics, Data, and Design of Experiments	
Concept	**Definition**
Experimental unit	the individual or object on which measurements may be taken
Observation	the measurement attached to an experimental unit
Variable	a characteristic of interest being measured, which may vary
Population	the entire set of experimental units or observations
Sample	a subset of the population
Parameter	a numeric descriptive characteristic of a population
Statistic	a numeric descriptive characteristic of a sample
Descriptive statistics	methods for organizing, summarizing, and describing data sets
Inferential statistics	methods for drawing conclusions and making decisions regarding a population based on data from a sample
Quantitative data	data that are numeric
Qualitative data	data that can be placed in non-numeric categories

(continued)

(continued)

Discrete data	data that can take on a countable number of values
Continuous data	data that can take on any value in an interval
Levels of measurement	a method of classifying data according to the mathematical relationship between the measurements
Observational study	a study in which experimental units are measured, but no treatment is applied
Experiment	a study in which experimental units are treated or manipulated and then measured to observe the effect of the treatment by comparison with a control condition
Independent (explanatory) variable	the variable in an experiment being manipulated
Dependent (response) variable	the variable in an experiment being measured
Random sampling	a method of selecting experimental units for a sample in which each is equally likely to be chosen
Sampling error	the difference between the value of the sample statistic and the value of the population parameter

Chapter 2—Graphical Representations of Data

Frequency table	a table listing the possible values (usually grouped) in the data set and the frequency with which they occur
Relative frequency	the frequency of a value (or group of values) divided by the total number of values in the data set
Symmetric distribution	a data set in which the left half of the data is a mirror image of the right half
Right (positively) skewed distribution	a data set that has the majority of the data values grouped to the left and a long tail to the right
Left (negatively) skewed distribution	a data set that has the majority of the data values grouped to the right and a long tail to the left

Chapter 3—Numeric Representations of Data

Mean	the arithmetic average of a data set
Median	the center value of a data set when the observations are arranged in ascending (or descending) order
Mode	the most frequently occurring value in a data set
Range	the difference between the largest value and the smallest value in a data set
Variance	an index of the average squared deviation from the mean
Standard deviation	the positive square root of the variance
Percentile	the pth percentile the value for which p% of the data is less than or equal to that value

 FLASH LINK

The following table lists Web sites that may be helpful in studying the material in Unit 1. Space is provided to add other Web sites suggested in your text or by your instructor, or those you find on your own. Key to resource type: D, definitions; E, examples; X, exercises; C, calculation; M, demonstration.

Chapter	Resource Type	URL
1	D (data concepts)	http://davidmlane.com/hyperstat/intro.html
1	D, E (levels of measurement)	http://trochim.human.cornell.edu/kb/measlevl.htm
1–2	D, E (data concepts, graphs)	http://www.bmj.com/statsbk/1.shtml
1–2	D, E, X (data concepts, graphs)	http://www.stat.berkeley.edu/users/stark/SticiGui/Text/ch1.htm
1–3	D, E, X (data concepts, graphs, central tendency, variability)	http://www.anu.edu.au/nceph/surfstat/surfstat-home
1–3	D (data concepts, graphs, central tendency, variability)	http://library.thinkquest.org/10030/statcon.htm?tqskip=1

(continued)

1–3	X	http://occ.awlonline.com/bookbind/pubbooks/triola_awl/chapter1/deluxe.html (also chapter2)
1–3	X	http://occ.awlonline.com/bookbind/pubbooks/weiss2_awl/chapter1/deluxe.html (also chapter2 and chapter3)
2	D (graphs)	http://www.tufts.edu/%7Egdallal/plots.htm
2–3	D (graphs, central tendency, variability)	http://davidmlane.com/hyperstat/desc_univ.html
2–3	C	http://www.ruf.rice.edu/~lane/stat_analysis/descriptive
2–3	C	http://www.stat.uiuc.edu/~stat100/java/DataApplet.html
2–3	C	http://br109.math.tntech.edu/stats/stats.html
2–3	M	http://www.ruf.rice.edu/~lane/stat_sim/descriptive
3	D (central tendency, variability)	http://www.bmj.com/statsbk/2.shtml
3	D, E, X (central tendency, variability)	http://www.stat.berkeley.edu/users/stark/SticiGui/Text/ch2.htm
3	C	http://faculty.vassar.edu/~lowry/VassarStats.html
3	M	http://www.stat.uiuc.edu/~stat100/java/DataApplet.html

CHAPTER 1—Statistics, Data, and Design of Experiments

Section 1.1—Statistics as a Field of Study

FLASH SUMMARY

Statistics as a field of study deals with methods for organizing, summarizing, analyzing, and drawing conclusions from data. The vocabulary necessary for understanding these methods is presented in the preceding Flash Focus table.

A population is the entire set of units or observations of interest; a parameter is a numeric descriptive measure of the population. A sample is a subset of the population;

a statistic is a numeric descriptive measure of the sample. The size of the population is denoted by N, and the size of the sample is denoted by n.

For example, consider the average age of the students enrolled in your statistics class. The experimental unit is a student, the variable is age, the population is **all** the students in the class (or the ages of students in the class), and the average age is the parameter. The students sitting in the front row might be considered a sample from the population, and the average age of students in the front row would be a statistic.

Descriptive statistics refers to methods used to organize and summarize data from either a population or a sample. The two major areas of descriptive statistics are graphical representations (Chapter 2) and numeric representations (Chapter 3). Inferential statistics are tools for drawing conclusions about a population based on data from a sample. The two major areas of inferential statistics are estimation and hypothesis testing (Units 3–5).

Inferential Statistics

Random Sampling
(Step 4)

Population
(Steps 1 – 3)

Sample
(Steps 5 – 6)

Inference
(Step 7)

> ### INFERENTIAL STATISTICS: MAKING INFERENCES ABOUT A POPULATION
>
> Step 1: Define the population
>
> Step 2: Identify the variable(s) of interest
>
> Step 3: Determine how the variable(s) is to be measured
>
> Step 4: Use an appropriate method to randomly select experimental units for the sample
>
> Step 5: Measure the variable(s) of interest
>
> Step 6: Calculate the appropriate statistics from the sample data
>
> Step 7: Use the statistics to draw conclusions about the population

FLASH REVIEW

For each of the following situations, answer these questions:

a. Is the group a population or a sample?

b. What is the variable of interest?

c. What is the numeric descriptive measure of interest? Is it a parameter or statistic?

d. Is this an example of descriptive or inferential statistics?

1. A researcher wants to determine the average number of guns owned by all members of the National Rifle Association (NRA).

    a.

    b.

    c.

    d.

2. To determine whether females at Connor College have a higher grade point average (GPA) than the national average, an administrator randomly selects 100 female students and calculates the average GPA for this group.

    a.

    b.

    c.

    d.

Note: Solutions for Flash Review problems may be found following the last Flash Review in the unit.

Section 1.2—Data Concepts

 FLASH SUMMARY

Data can be described or classified in many different ways. Understanding the nature of the data is necessary to determine the appropriate statistical tools for description and analysis. Data may be quantitative (measured in a manner that produces numbers) or qualitative (measured in a manner that produces only labels). Age is an example of quantitative data, whereas gender is an example of qualitative data. Data may also be discrete (countable number of possible values) or continuous (infinitely many possible values). The number of students in your class is an example of discrete data, while the height of students in your class is an example of continuous data.

Data may also be classified by level of measurement. Nominal level measurement uses only categories or labels with no natural ordering among the possible values. Ordinal level measurement implies that there is a natural ordering among the values but that the distance between values is not necessarily equal. Interval level measurement requires a natural ordering, equal intervals between consecutive values and an arbitrary zero point. Ratio level measurement includes natural ordering, equal intervals, and an absolute zero, which is often described as an absence of the characteristic being measured. In using statistical tools, it is usually not necessary to distinguish between interval and ratio levels of measurement.

Level of Measurement	Data Characteristics	Mathematical Symbols	Examples
Nominal	qualitative discrete	$=, \neq$	hair color marital status
Ordinal	quantitative or qualitative discrete	$=, \neq, >, <$	military rank sizes (S, M, L, XL)

(continued)

Interval	quantitative discrete or continuous	$=, \neq, >, <, +, -$	IQ scores temperature in °F
Ratio	quantitative discrete or continuous	$=, \neq, >, <, +, -, \times, \div$	exam scores distance

FLASH REVIEW

For the following, determine if the data are quantitative or qualitative, discrete or continuous, and identify the level of measurement:

1. The number of guns owned by an NRA member

2. The weight of a gun (in grams) owned by an NRA member

3. The ethnicity of a student at Connor College

4. The classification of a student (freshman, sophomore, etc.) at Connor College

5. The GPA of a student at Connor College

Section 1.3—Design of Experiments
....

FLASH SUMMARY

To produce a data set that yields information that both answers the question under consideration and allows the researcher to accurately describe and analyze the variable(s) of interest, some issues in how the data are collected need to be considered. There are two basic methods of collecting data: (1) an observational study in which the experimental units are measured, and (2) experiments in which the experimental units are treated or manipulated and then measured to determine the effect of the treatment by comparison to a control condition. In an experiment, the treatment or variable being manipulated is called the independent or explanatory variable, and the variable being measured is called the dependent or response variable.

Suppose a researcher wants information on duration of headaches in college students. The researcher asks a sample of 20 college students how long a headache lasts on the average; this is an example of an observational study. Now suppose the researcher wants to determine if a certain brand of aspirin reduces the duration of headaches in college students. The researcher selects a sample of 20 college students, and randomly assigns 10 students to a treatment group in which each student receives the appropriate dose of aspirin and 10 students to a control group in which each student receives a placebo. The researcher then records the duration of the headache for each student and compares the average duration for the two groups. This is an example of an experiment.

The design of an experiment to collect data that will produce valid results involves three basic steps:

1. *Defining the problem*—This step involves determining what information is desired or what question is to be answered. The population and the variable(s) of interest must be carefully defined, and the method by which the characteristic of interest will be measured must be determined.

2. *Determining how the sample will be taken*—This step involves determining an appropriate method for taking a sample to avoid bias and to control for confounding variables. Bias in a sample is the under- or overrepresentation of a segment of the population. A confounding variable is a variable that has an effect on the response

variable that cannot be separated from the effect of the explanatory variable. Random sampling methods in which all experimental units have an equal chance of being selected help alleviate these problems. Common methods of random sampling include:

✓ Simple random sampling—All experimental units are placed in one large group, and a mechanical method (random number table, drawing numbers from a hat) is used to select the appropriate number of units for the sample. Each possible sample of size n has an equal chance of being selected for the sample. In the following example, a random number table was used to select units 2, 9, and 5.

Population

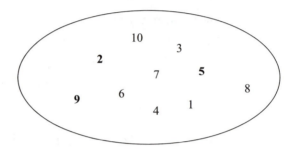

✓ Systematic random sampling—Experimental units are organized in an ordered list, an increment (denoted k) is selected, the starting point is randomly selected, and every k^{th} experimental unit is included in the sample. Each unit has an equal chance of being selected as the starting point. In the following example, the observations were put in numeric order, the increment $k = 5$ was selected, and unit 3 was the randomly selected starting point.

Population

1 2 *3* 4 5 6 7 *8* 9 10 11 12 *13* 14 15 16 17 *18* 19 20 21 22 *23* 24 25

✓ Stratified random sampling—Experimental units are divided into groups called strata, and units are randomly selected from every strata. Each unit within a strata has an equal chance of being selected for the sample. In the following example, the population was divided into two strata. A random number table was used to select units 1, 10, and 6 from Strata 1 and then the random number table was used to select units 8, 2, and 11 from Strata 2.

Population

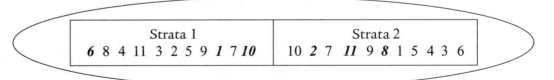

✓ Cluster sampling—Experimental units are divided into groups called clusters; clusters are randomly selected, and every unit within a cluster is measured. Every cluster has an equal chance of being selected for the sample. In the following example, a random number table was used to select clusters 7, 2, and 4.

Population

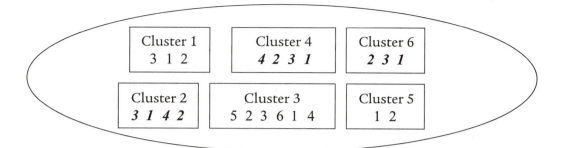

A convenience sample, for which the researcher uses readily available information that is not selected in a random manner, is sometimes used when it is not possible or is highly problematic to use a random method.

3. *Determining the appropriate statistical tool for describing and analyzing the data*—This step involves understanding the type of data collected (quantitative v. qualitative, discrete v. continuous), the level of measurement used, and the assumptions that must be met to select the appropriate statistical tool(s) to provide the information desired and/or to answer the question under consideration.

 FLASH REVIEW

1. Identify each of the following examples as an observational study or an experiment:

    a. A researcher surveys a sample of NRA members to determine their political party preference and the number of guns owned.

    b. A researcher divides a sample of freshmen from Connor College into two groups. The first group attends a seminar on study techniques, and the second group does not. At the end of the semester, the average GPAs of the two groups are compared.

    c. A sample of students from five different sections of Elementary Statistics at Connor College is selected, and the average scores on the first exam from the five different sections are compared.

2. For each of the following, determine which random sampling method is used:

    a. A researcher obtains an alphabetical listing of NRA members, randomly selects the 14th person as the starting point, and then selects every 20th member (14th, 34th, 54th . . .).

    b. A researcher obtains the names of all freshmen at Connor College and uses a random number table to select 100 students.

    c. A researcher obtains the class rosters for five sections of Elementary Statistics at Connor College and randomly selects 10 students from each section.

CHAPTER 2—Graphical Representations of Data

FLASH SUMMARY

Graphical representations of data are methods of organizing, summarizing, and presenting data in forms that describe the data without looking at every observation individually. These methods include tables, graphs, charts, and pictures. Some of the most common methods are frequency tables, histograms, bar graphs, pie charts, stem-and-leaf plots, and scatter plots. Graphical representations are used to depict the distribution of the data—the values in the data set and the frequency with which they occur. The shape, center or grouping, and spread of the distribution are commonly used descriptive characteristics that may be determined from graphical representations. The shape of the distribution is often described as symmetric (left and right halves are mirror images); left, or negatively skewed (majority of the data grouped to the right and a long tail to the left); or right, or positively skewed (majority of the data grouped to the left and a long tail to the right).

Left-Skewed	Symmetric	Right-Skewed

Mean ⌐ ⌐ Mode
Median

Mode = Mean = Median

Mode ⌐ ⌐ Mean
Median

Frequency tables can be used for quantitative data or qualitative data and for discrete or continuous data. These tables list the possible values in the data set and the frequency with which they occur. The values are usually grouped into classes (ranges of values). Histograms are used to represent quantitative, continuous data. The x-axis (abscissa) is labeled with the class boundaries, and the y-axis (ordinate) is labeled with the frequency. The width of the rectangle indicates the data values in the class, and the height represents the frequency (or relative frequency) of values within the class.

Bar graphs are similar to histograms but are used to represent discrete data. Bar graphs are often used for qualitative data and are sometimes used for a quantitative set of discrete data that have few possible values. The data values are listed on the x-axis and the frequency on the y-axis. The rectangles are centered over the data values, and the height of the rectangles indicates the frequency for the discrete value.

Pie charts are also used to represent discrete data, usually for a smaller number of categories. A "slice" of the pie indicates the percent of the values from the data set that fall into that category.

Stem-and-leaf plots are used for quantitative data and, unlike the other graphs described, retain all the data values. Observations are split into two parts—a stem and a leaf (such as the tens digit for the stem and the ones digit for the leaf). The stems are listed on the left, and the associated leaves are listed on the right in ascending order.

Graphical representations of a data set
Sample data set of exam scores: 48, 55, 64, 66, 68, 70, 71, 73, 74, 75, 75, 76, 77, 77, 77, 79, 80, 84, 85, 88, 89, 91, 94, 95, 97; Grades: 90-99, A; 80-89, B; 70-79, C; 60-69, D; below 60, F

Frequency Table for Scores

Score	Frequency	Relative Frequency
40–49	1	.04
50–59	1	.04
60–69	3	.12
70–79	11	.44
80–89	5	.20
90–99	4	.16
TOTAL	25	1.00

Stem-and-Leaf Plot of Scores

Stem	Leaves
4	8
5	5
6	4 6 8
7	0 1 3 4 5 5 6 7 7 7 9
8	0 4 5 8 9
9	1 4 5 7

Frequency Table for Grades

Grade	Frequency	Relative Frequency
A	4	.16
B	5	.20
C	11	.44
D	3	.12
F	2	.08
TOTAL	25	1.00

Bar Graph for Grades

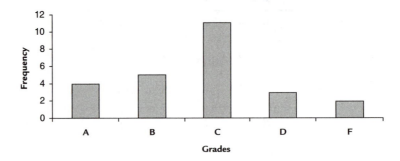

Scatterplots are used to depict the relationship between two quantitative variables. Two measurements are taken on each experimental unit, and a dot is used to represent each pair of observations. A positive relationship is characterized by an elliptical pattern from the lower left to the upper right, whereas a negative relationship is characterized by an elliptical pattern from the upper left to the lower right. A strong relationship is indicated by a narrow ellipse, and a weak relationship is indicated by a wider ellipse. A circular pattern represents a very weak or nonexistent relationship between the variables.

Relationships in scatterplots

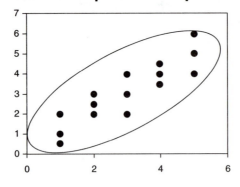

Moderate positive relationship

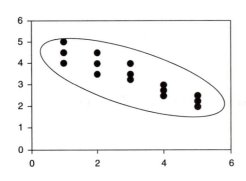

Strong negative or inverse relationship

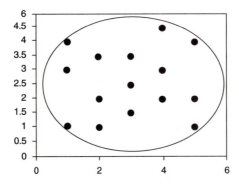

Very weak or no relationship

FLASH REVIEW

1. Which regular graphical representation would be most appropriate for each of the following?

   a. Political party affiliation for a random sample of NRA members

   b. GPA for a random sample of graduating seniors at Connor College

   c. The height and weight of students in your statistics class

2. If the pie chart below represents data from a sample of size 20, how many observations are in Class 1?

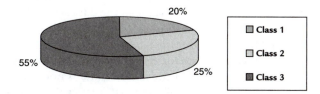

3. Use the histogram below to answer the following:

   a. How many observations are in Class 4? What is the total number of observations?

   b. Is the shape of the distribution symmetric, left-skewed, or right-skewed?

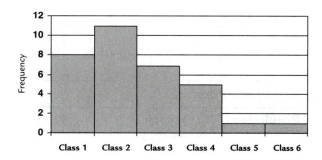

Section 3.1—Measures of Central Tendency

FLASH SUMMARY

Measures of central tendency are numeric values that describe the center or middle of a data set and give an indication of where the data are located on the number line. The mean, the arithmetic average, is the most commonly used measure of center. Other measures of central tendency include the weighted mean, the mean of grouped data, and the midrange. The mean exists for every data set of at least interval level measurement, uses every value in the data set, and is sensitive to extreme values.

The median is the value at which half of the data values are to the left and half of the data values are to the right when the observations are in ascending order. The median exists for every data set of at least ordinal level measurement, uses only values in the center of the data set, and is not affected by extreme values.

The mode is the most frequently occurring value in the data set. The mode exists for every data set, does not use every value in the data, and is not affected by extreme values. A data set can have only one mean and median but may have one (unimodal), two (bimodal), or many modes (multimodal). A data set in which all values are different is often described as having no mode, even though the mode exists by definition.

In selecting the appropriate measure of central tendency to use with a specific data set, you should determine the level of measurement and consider whether any extreme values (also called outliers) are present. The mean usually is used with data sets measured at the interval level and in which no extreme values are present. The median is often used with data sets measured at the interval level when the data set contains outliers (skewed distribution) and for data sets measured at the ordinal level. The mode is the only measure of center that can be used with nominal level data.

Measure	Notation		Formula or Other Calculation	
	Population	**Sample**	**Population**	**Sample**
Mean	μ	$\bar{x}$	$\mu = \dfrac{\sum x}{N}$	$\bar{x} = \dfrac{\sum x}{n}$
Median	$\tilde{\mu}$ or M_d	$\tilde{x}$ or m_d	1) Arrange the data in increasing order 2) If N is odd, use the value in the middle; if N is even, use the average of the two middle values	1) Arrange the data in increasing order 2) If n is odd, use the value in the middle; if n is even, use the average of the two middle values
Mode	M or M_o	m or m_o	find the value that occurs most frequently	find the value that occurs most frequently

FLASH REVIEW

1. The scores for a population of students in a statistics class on a 20-point quiz were 14, 14, 20, 15, 15, 9, 14, 16, 19, 17, 14, 15, 10, 14, 15, 12, 14, 17, 16, 15, 15, 16, 14, 13, 15.

a. Find the mean, median, and mode of the scores.

b. Which measure of center would be most appropriate as a description of the data? Justify your answer.

2. The following values are the annual salaries (in thousands of dollars) of a random sample of recent graduates with a master's degree in statistics: 40, 35, 31, 34, 37, 32, 68, 43, 39, 35.

    a. Find the mean, median, and mode of the salaries.

    b. Which measure of center would be most appropriate as a description of the data? Justify your answer.

Section 3.2—Measures of Variability

FLASH SUMMARY

Measures of variability (also called measures of dispersion) are numeric values that describe the spread of the data. The three most commonly used measures of variability are the range, the variance, and the standard deviation. All three measures require quantitative data measured at the interval or ratio level.

The range is the distance between the largest value and smallest value in the data set. The range uses only the most extreme values, thus it is highly influenced by outliers.

The variance and the standard deviation describe the spread in relation to the mean of the data. These measures are based on the deviation of each data point from the mean, or the distance between each data point and the mean. The population variance is the average squared deviation of the data points from the mean of the data set. The sample variance is a measure of the average squared deviation from the mean but is calculated using a divisor of $n - 1$ rather than n.

The standard deviation is defined as the positive square root of the variance and is the most commonly used measure of variability. The standard deviation is interpreted as the "typical" distance between observations in a data set and the mean of the values. The word "typical" is used to indicate an averaging type of measure because the standard deviation is not a true mathematical average. Larger values of the standard deviation indicate a more spread-out distribution. A value of zero for the standard deviation indicates that all values in the data set are equal.

Measure	Notation		Formula or Other Calculation	
	Population	**Sample**	**Population**	**Sample**
Range			largest − smallest value	largest − smallest value
Variance	σ^2 or σ_X^2	s^2 or s_X^2	Conceptual formula: $$\sigma^2 = \frac{\sum(x - \mu)^2}{N}$$ Calculation formula: $$\sigma^2 = \frac{\sum x^2 - \frac{(\sum x)^2}{N}}{N}$$	Conceptual formula: $$s^2 = \frac{\sum(x - \mu)^2}{n - 1}$$ Calculation formula: $$s^2 = \frac{\sum x^2 - \frac{(\sum x)^2}{n}}{n - 1}$$
Standard deviation	σ or σ_X	s or s_X	$\sigma = \sqrt{\sigma^2}$	$s = \sqrt{s^2}$

 **FLASH REVIEW**

1. The scores for a population of students in a statistics class on a 20-point quiz were 14, 14, 20, 15, 15, 9, 14, 16, 19, 17, 14, 15, 10, 14, 15, 12, 14, 17, 16, 15, 15, 16, 14, 13, 15. Find the range, variance, and standard deviation of the scores.

2. The following values are the annual salaries (in thousands of dollars) of a random sample of recent graduates with a master's degree in statistics: 40, 35, 31, 34, 37, 32, 68, 43, 39, 35. Find the range and standard deviation of the salaries.

Solutions to Flash Review Problems in Unit 1

Chapter 1—Section 1.1, Statistics as a Field of Study

1. **a.** population

   b. number of guns

   c. average number of guns, parameter

   d. descriptive statistics

2. **a.** sample

   b. GPA

   c. average GPA, statistic

   d. inferential statistics

Chapter 1—Section 1.2, Data Concepts

1. quantitative, discrete, ratio

2. quantitative, continuous, ratio

3. qualitative, discrete, nominal

4. qualitative, discrete, ordinal

5. quantitative, continuous, ratio

Chapter 1—Section 1.3, Design of Experiments

1. **a.** observational study

   b. experiment

   c. observational study

2. **a.** systematic

   b. simple

   c. stratified

Chapter 2—Graphical Representations of Data

1. **a.** Because the data are qualitative and there will be relatively few categories, either a bar graph or a pie chart would be appropriate.

   b. The data are quantitative and continuous, thus a histogram would be appropriate.

   c. Because there are two variables, a scatterplot would be appropriate.

2. There are four observations in Class 1 (20% of 20 observations).

3. **a.** 5, 33

   b. right-skewed

Chapter 3—Section 3.1, Measures of Central Tendency

1. **a.** $\mu = \dfrac{\sum x}{N} = \dfrac{368}{25} = 14.72;$

ordered scores: 9, 10, 12, 13, 14, 14, 14, 14, 14, 14, 14, 15, 15, 15, 15, 15, 15, 15, 16, 16, 16, 17, 17, 19, 20, and N is odd, thus $\tilde{\mu} = 15;$

$M = 14$ & 15 because each appears 7 times

b. Any of these three measures would be appropriate as a description of the center of this data set. Because there are no extreme values, the mean utilizes all the data values, and the mean is the most commonly used measure, the mean might be considered the *most* appropriate descriptor.

2. **a.** $\bar{x} = \dfrac{\sum x}{n} = \dfrac{394}{10} = 39.4;$

ordered scores: 31, 32, 34, 35, 35, 37, 39, 40, 43, 68 and n is even, so

$\tilde{x} = \dfrac{35 + 37}{2} = 36;$

$m = 35$ because it is the only value that appears more than once in the data set b. The value 68 appears to be an extreme value, thus the mean is not the most appropriate measure to describe the data set. Because this is a skewed distribution, the median would be the most appropriate descriptor.

Chapter 3—Section 3.2, Measures of Variability

1. Range = largest − smallest value = 20 − 9 = 11;

$$\sigma^2 = \dfrac{\sum x^2 - \dfrac{\left(\sum x\right)^2}{N}}{N} = \dfrac{5548 - \dfrac{(368)^2}{25}}{25} = 5.2416;$$

$$\sigma = \sqrt{\sigma^2} = \sqrt{5.2416} = 2.29$$

2. range = largest − smallest value = 68 − 31 = 37;

$$s = \sqrt{\dfrac{\sum x^2 - \dfrac{\left(\sum x\right)^2}{n}}{n - 1}} = \sqrt{\dfrac{16554 - \dfrac{(394)^2}{10}}{9}} = \sqrt{114.48} = 10.70$$

FLASH TEST

The following pages contain a practice test so that you may assess your understanding of the material presented in Unit 1. Answers and explanations follow the exam. For any questions you miss, be sure to review the explanation carefully and reread the appropriate portion of the section to which the question applies. If you still do not understand the correct answer, review the concept in your text, and/or ask your instructor for assistance.

TRUE/FALSE (3 points each)

_____ **1.** The rank of a student in a graduating class is an example of interval level data.

_____ **2.** A survey is an example of an observational study.

_____ **3.** A bar graph would be the most appropriate graphical representation for a data set containing the distance students in a statistics class commute between home and school.

_____ **4.** If the values in a data set are whole numbers and the median is 45.5, the data set has an even number of observations.

_____ **5.** A data set with a standard deviation of 25 is more spread out than a data set with a variance of 25.

MULTIPLE CHOICE (3 points each)

Use the following information to answer questions 6 through 12. The 50 students in a statistics class were asked to record the make of their automobile, their age, number of siblings, eye color, height, and classification (freshman, sophomore, etc.). Each student then wrote his or her name on a slip of paper and placed it in a box. The instructor drew the names of five students out of the box at random.

_____ **6.** The type of random sampling used is

    A. simple   B. systematic   C. stratified   D. cluster

_____ **7.** Number of siblings is an example of _____, _____ data.

    A. qualitative, discrete   C. quantitative, discrete

    B. qualitative, continuous   D. quantitative, continuous

_____ **8.** A _____ would be an appropriate method of graphing the height measurements from the entire class.

    A. bar graph   B. histogram   C. pie chart   D. scatterplot

_____ **9.** Make of automobile is measured at the _____ level.

    A. nominal   B. ordinal   C. interval   D. ratio

_____ **10.** Which of the following is an appropriate measure of center for eye color?

    A. mean   B. median   C. mode   D. none of these

_____ **11.** Which of the following is an appropriate measure of variability for classification?

    A. range   B. variance   C. standard deviation   D. none of these

_____ **12.** If the mean age of the sample is 25, what is the value of $\sum x$?

    A. 5   B. 25   C. 125   D. cannot determine from information given

_____ **13.** If a distribution is right-skewed, the measures of central tendency would most likely fall in which order on the number line from left to right?

    A. mean, median, mode   C. median, mean, mode

    B. mean, mode, median   D. mode, median, mean

_____ **14.** A random sample of size 30 is drawn from a population, and the standard deviation is found to be 16. Which of the following is a true statement?

    A. The typical distance between the data points and the mean is 16 units.

    B. The value of the variance is 4.

    C. The value of the range is 14.

    D. The value of the mean is 0.53.

_____ **15.** Students' scores on a 10-point quiz were 6, 5, 9, 9, 10, 7, 8, 10, 8, 10, 9, 8, 6, 9, 10, 8, 7, 9, 7, 8. A frequency table is to be constructed with classes of 5–6, 7–8, and 9–10. The values in the frequency column (in order) would be

A. 0.15, 0.40, 0.45   C. 3, 11, 20

B. 3, 8, 9   D. none of these

SHORT ANSWER (3 points each)

Use the following information to answer questions 16 through 20. A large company with branches in four cities has an employee health program. The company nutritionist wants to explore the effect of a nutritional supplement on weight loss in obese female employees who are 18 to 25 years of age. The nutritionist takes a random sample of 10 obese female employees in this age group from each of the four branches (a total of 40 experimental units). From each group of 10, five are assigned to a treatment group and given the supplement for one month; the other five are assigned to a control group and given a placebo. At the end of the one-month period, the weight loss for each experimental unit is recorded. The average weight loss for the treatment group is compared with the average weight loss for the control group.

16. Identify the population of interest.

17. Is this an observational study or an experiment? Justify your answer.

18. What sampling method is used? Justify your answer.

19. Identify the independent (explanatory) variable and the dependent (response) variable.

20. Is this an example of descriptive or inferential statistics? Justify your answer.

CALCULATIONS (5 points each)

Use the following information for questions 21 through 23. A teacher measured the time (in minutes) required for a random sample of kindergarten students to complete a jigsaw puzzle. The times were 2.4, 3.5, 3.7, 4.2, 4.5, 5.4, 5.6, 5.6, 5.8, 6.2.

21. Calculate the mean time to complete the puzzle. Give both the appropriate symbol and the value.

22. Find the median. Give both the appropriate symbol and the value.

23. Calculate the standard deviation. Give both the appropriate symbol and the value. Round to two decimal places.

Use the following information for questions 24 through 28. The manager of the bookstore at Connor College wants to determine if keeping the bookstore open after 5 PM on weeknights (Monday through Friday) is cost-effective. He randomly selected four weeks and recorded the number of students who entered the bookstore after 5 PM on the weeknights of those four weeks (a total of 20 observations). The values were 15, 23, 7, 9, 36, 18, 21, 25, 23, 29, 32, 17, 22, 25, 27, 20, 12, 19, 24, 30.

24. Calculate $\sum x$.

25. Calculate $\sum x^2$.

26. Find the mode.

27. Calculate the range.

28. Calculate the variance. Round to two decimal places.

Answers to practice test begin on the next page.

TRUE/FALSE

1. F; the observations are ranks, thus the data are ordinal.

2. T; the experimental units are not treated or manipulated, just measured.

3. F; a histogram would be the most appropriate because the data are continuous.

4. T; because the measurements are whole numbers, if the number of observations was odd, the median would be a whole number.

5. T; a data set with a variance of 25 has a standard deviation of 5, and a standard deviation of 5 indicates a smaller spread than a standard deviation of 25.

MULTIPLE CHOICE

6. A; all experimental units were put in one group and had an equal chance of being selected.

7. C; the data type is quantitative. It is a count and discrete because the number of siblings is a whole number.

8. B; height is quantitative and continuous, thus a histogram is appropriate.

9. A; makes of vehicles (Chevrolet, Ford, etc.) are categories with no natural order.

10. C; the mode is the only appropriate measure of center for nominal level data.

11. D; classification is measured at the ordinal level and at least interval level, data are needed to calculate the range, variance, and standard deviation.

12. C; $\bar{x} = \dfrac{\sum x}{n}$ thus $25 = \dfrac{\sum x}{5}$ and $\sum x = 25 \cdot 5 = 125$

13. D; a right-skewed distribution has a long tail to the right, which implies that the mean will be the largest of the three values (remember, the mean is sensitive to extreme values).

14. A; this is the interpretation of the standard deviation; the value of the variance is 256, and the value of the range and mean cannot be determined from the information given.

15. B; order the data: 5, 6, 6, 7, 7, 7, 8, 8, 8, 8, 8, 9, 9, 9, 9, 9, 10, 10, 10, 10; there are three values of 5 and 6, eight values of 7 and 8, and nine values of 9 and 10.

SHORT ANSWER

16. The population of interest is obese female employees of the company who are between the ages of 18 and 25.

17. This is an experiment. A treatment is being applied to the experimental units, and the effect of the treatment is being explored.

18. Stratified random sampling is used. The four branches are the strata, and experimental units are randomly selected from each.

19. The administration of the nutritional supplement (supplement versus control) is the explanatory variable, and weight loss is the response variable.

20. This is an example of inferential statistics. Information from the sample is being used to draw a conclusion about the effect of the supplement on weight loss in the population.

CALCULATIONS

21. $\bar{x} = \dfrac{\sum x}{n} = \dfrac{46.9}{10} = 4.69$

22. The values are already in ascending order, and the two center values are 4.5 and 5.4 thus $\tilde{x} = \dfrac{4.5 + 5.4}{2} = 4.95$

23. $s = \sqrt{\dfrac{\sum x^2 - \dfrac{(\sum x)^2}{n}}{n - 1}} = \sqrt{\dfrac{233.55 - \dfrac{(46.9)^2}{10}}{9}} = \sqrt{1.509\overline{8}} = 1.23$

24. $\sum x = 434$

25. $\sum x^2 = 10{,}472$

26. Order the data: 7, 9, 12, 15, 17, 18, 19, 20, 21, 22, 23, 23, 24, 25, 25, 27, 29, 30, 32, 36. The modes are 23 and 25 because both occur twice, and all other values occur once.

27. The range is the largest minus the smallest value, thus $36 - 7 = 29$.

28. $s^2 = \dfrac{\sum x^2 - \dfrac{\sum x}{n}}{n - 1} = \dfrac{10472 - \dfrac{(434)^2}{20}}{19} = 55.48$

FLASH FOCUS

After completing this unit, you will be able to:

✓ Understand basic probability terms
✓ Calculate probabilities of simple and compound events
✓ Calculate the number of outcomes in a sample space and an event
✓ Find the mean and standard error of discrete probability distributions
✓ Identify the probability distribution appropriate for a given situation
✓ Use probability tables to determine probabilities

The following table lists the core concepts in this unit, along with definitions and/or explanations. Space is provided to add concepts discussed by your instructor.

Core Concepts in Unit 2

Chapter 4—Basic Probability	
Concept	**Definition and/or Explanation**
Experiment	an experiment in the context of probability is a procedure that generates observations
Trial	one iteration of the procedure in an experiment
Outcome	the result of an experiment
Sample space	all the possible outcomes of an experiment
Event	a subset of the sample space
Probability	a number describing the likelihood that a given event will occur
Simple event	an event that cannot be reduced further
Compound event	a combination or two of more events
Union	the union of two events consists of all outcomes in the first event or the second event, or both
Intersection	the intersection of two events consists of all outcomes in both events
Relative frequency probability	the ratio of the number of outcomes in an event and the number of outcomes in the sample space for an actual experiment

(continued)

Classical probability	the ratio of the number of possible outcomes in an event and the number of possible outcomes in the sample space where the outcomes are equally likely to occur
Subjective probability	a "best guess" of the probability of an event
Law of large numbers	as an experiment is repeated a large number of times, the relative frequency probability approaches the classical probability
Complementary event	the complement of an event consists of all the outcomes in the sample space that are not included in the event
Mutually exclusive events	two events are mutually exclusive if they share no outcomes
Independent events	two events are independent if the occurrence of the first event does not affect the probability that the second event will occur.
Conditional probability	the conditional probability of event is the probability of the event given that another event has already occurred
Basic probability rules	the basic probability rules give the values for the probability of the sample space, an impossible event, and simple events
Complement rules	the complement rules give formulas for finding the probability of a complement if the probability of the event is known and vice versa
Addition rules	the addition rules give formulas for finding the probability of the union of two events
Multiplication rules	the multiplication rules give formulas for finding the probability of the intersection of two events
Permutations	the number of sequences of x objects chosen from n objects
Combinations	the number of groups of x objects chosen from n objects

Chapter 5—Probability Distributions

Probability distribution	gives the possible values of a random variable and the associated probabilities
Discrete distribution	a probability distribution for a discrete random variable
Continuous distribution	a probability distribution for a continuous random variable

(*continued*)

Expected value	the value expected when an experiment is repeated a large number of times (average value)
Binomial random variable	the number of successes in n trials of a binomial experiment
Sampling distribution	a probability distribution for a sample statistic
Standard error	the standard deviation of the sampling distribution
Central Limit Theorem (CLT)	gives the approximate distribution, mean, and standard error of the sampling distribution of the sample mean for large samples

FLASH LINK

The following table lists Web sites that may be helpful in studying the material in Unit 2. Space is provided to add other Web sites suggested in your text or by your instructor or those you find on your own. Key to resource type: D, definitions; E, examples; X, exercises; C, calculation; M, demonstration.

Chapter	Resource Type	URL
4	D, E, X (basic concepts, rules)	http://www.mathgoodies.com/lessons/ toc_vol6.shtm
4	D, E, X (basic concepts)	http://www.stat.berkeley.edu/users/stark/SticiGui/ Text/ch9.htm (also ch8.1)
4	D, E, X (basic concepts, rule, binomial)	http://davidmlane.com/hyperstat/probability.html
4-5	D (basic concepts, rules, discrete distributions)	http://stat.tamu.edu/stat30x/notes/node50.html
4-5	D, E (basic concepts, rules, distributions, CLT)	http://www.anu.edu.au/nceph/surfstat/ surfstat-home
4-5	D, E, X (basic concepts, rules, distributions)	http://cne.gmu.edu/modules/dau/prob/ probability_frm.html
4-5	X	http://occ.awlonline.com/bookbind/pubbooks/triola_awl/ chapter3/deluxe.html (also chapter4 and chapter5)

(*continued*)

4-5	X	http://occ.awlonline.com/bookbind/pubbooks/ weiss2_awl/chapter4/deluxe.html (also chapter5, chapter6 and chapter7)
5	D (binomial)	http://www-stat.stanford.edu/~naras/jsm/ example5.html
5	D, E (binomial)	http://huizen.dds.nl/~berrie/binomial.html
5	D, E, X (binomial, discrete distributions, normal)	http://www.stat.berkeley.edu/users/stark/SticiGui/ Text/ch11.htm (also ch12 and ch16.1)
5	C	http://www-stat.stanford.edu/~naras/jsm/ examplebot.html
5	C	http://faculty.vassar.edu/~lowry/VassarStats.html
5	D (distributions)	http://stat.tamu.edu/stat30x/notes/node73.html
5	D, E, X (sampling distributions)	http://davidmlane.com/hyperstat/sampling_dist.html
5	D, E (sampling distributions)	http://trochim.human.cornell.edu/kb/sampstat.htm
5	D, E, M (CLT)	http://faculty.vassar.edu/~lowry/central.html
5	M	http://www.ruf.rice.edu/~lane/stat_sim/ sampling_dist
5	D, E, X (CLT)	http://www.stat.berkeley.edu/users/stark/SticiGui/ Text/ch16.1.htm
5	M	http://www.stat.berkeley.edu/users/stark/Java/ SampleDist.htm

CHAPTER 4—Basic Probability

Section 4.1—Fundamentals of Probability

FLASH SUMMARY

Most of the methods used in inferential statistics are based on probability. Probability as a field is the study of randomness; a probability is a number that describes the likelihood that a particular result will be obtained when an experiment is conducted.

In the context of probability, an experiment is a procedure that produces observations. One iteration of the procedure is called a trial. The result of an experiment is called an outcome, and the sample space (S) is the collection of all possible outcomes for the experiment. An event is a subset of the sample space. A simple event cannot be further reduced; a compound event consists of some combination of two or more simple events. Events are labeled with capital letters such as A or B.

The union of event A with event B consists of all outcomes in A or B or both, whereas the intersection consists of all outcomes in both A and B at the same time. Note that the intersection is a subset of the union. The word "or" indicates a union; notationally, the union is often denoted as $A \cup B$.

The word "and" indicates an intersection and is denoted $A \cap B$. If events A and B are mutually exclusive, they have no outcomes in common, and the intersection is the empty set. Another way of defining two mutually exclusive events is to understand that if one of the events occurs, the other event cannot occur.

The complement of an event A—denoted $\overline{A}$, A', or A^C—consists of all the outcomes in the sample space that are not included in the event A. All of these ideas can be extended to more than two events.

Suppose you are going to toss a balanced coin three times and record the side of the coin facing you (head or tail). The procedure is flipping the coin, thus a trial would be one flip. The experiment would be the three tosses of the coin; the sample space would consist of all the possible combinations of heads (H) and tails (T) on tosses 1, 2, and 3. The sample space would be written as:

S = {HHH, HHT, HTH, HTT, THT, TTH, THH, TTT}.

Define the simple event A = a head on the first flip and B = a tail on the third flip. Then:

A = {HHH, HHT, HTH, HTT} and B = {HHT, HTT, THT, TTT}.

The union of the two events, a head on the first flip or a tail on the third flip, is:

$A \cup B$ = {HHH, HHT, HTH, HTT, THT, TTT};

and the intersection, a head on the first flip and a tail on the third, is:

$A \cap B$ = {HHT, HTT}.

Because the intersection is not the empty set, A and B are not mutually exclusive events. The complement of event A is:

A' = {THT, TTH, THH, TTT}

and the complement of event B is:

B' = {HHH, HTH, TTH, THH}.

A tree diagram can be useful to determine the outcomes of a particular experiment. The base column of the tree diagram lists the possible outcomes for the first trial of the experiment. Branches are drawn from each of these outcomes, and the possible outcomes on the second trial form the next column. This process continues through the last trial.

Tree diagram for coin toss

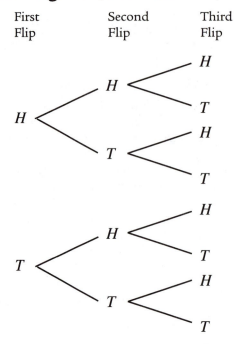

First
Flip

Second
Flip

Third
Flip

A Venn diagram can be used to represent the relationships between events, depict the outcomes in each event, or calculate probabilities of events. A rectangle is used to represent the sample space, and circles represent the events. Circles may be shaded to show relationships, or outcomes or probabilities of events may be listed within (or outside of) the appropriate circles.

Venn diagrams for coin toss

$A \cup B$ $A \cap B$ A'

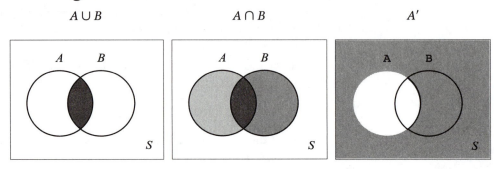

Basic probabilities are assigned in one of three ways. The classical approach considers all possible outcomes of an experiment without actually conducting the experiment. Using the classical approach requires assuming that all possible outcomes are equally likely to occur.

The probability of event A, denoted P(A), is then calculated by taking the ratio of the number of outcomes in event A to the number of outcomes in the sample space:

$$P(A) = \frac{number\ of\ outcomes\ in\ event\ A}{number\ of\ outcomes\ in\ S}.$$

The relative frequency approach is used when an actual experiment is conducted. The probability of event A is estimated by the ratio of the number of times event A occurs in the experiment to the number of times the experiment is repeated:

$$P(A) = \frac{number\ of\ times\ event\ A\ occurs}{number\ of\ times\ the\ experiment\ is\ repeated}.$$

Note that the classical approach considers the theoretical aspect of the experiment (what **can** happen), whereas the relative frequency approach considers the practical aspect of the experiment (what **did** happen). The law of large numbers states that when the experiment is repeated a large number of times, the relative frequency probability gets very close to the classical probability. The subjective approach is based on the researcher's "best guess" at the probability of an event and is usually based on prior knowledge.

In the coin toss example, you can assume each outcome is equally likely because a balanced coin is used. Using the classical probability approach:

$$P(A) = \frac{4}{8} = 0.5;$$

$$P(B) = \frac{4}{8} = 0.5;$$

$$P(A \cup B) = \frac{6}{8} = 0.75;$$

$$P(A \cap B) = \frac{2}{8} = 0.25;$$

$$P(A') = \frac{4}{8} = 0.5; \text{ and}$$

$$P(B') = \frac{4}{8} = 0.5.$$

FLASH REVIEW

At an intersection, a car can turn right (R), turn left (L), or go straight (S). Consider the next two cars that pass through the intersection. (For each part below, be sure to include appropriate notation.)

1. Determine the sample space.
2. Give the set of outcomes for event A if A = the second car turns left.
3. Give the set of outcomes for event B if B = the first car turns right.
4. What is the probability that the first car will turn right and that the second car will turn left?
5. What is the probability that the first car will turn right or that the second car will turn left?
6. What is the probability that the first car will not turn right?
7. What is the probability that both cars will go in the same direction?

Section 4.2—Probability Rules
....

FLASH SUMMARY

There are a number of probability rules that define possible values for probabilities and provide ways of calculating probabilities of events without listing all possible outcomes. The basic rules of probability state that (1) the total probability of the sample space is equal to one; (2) the probability of an impossible event (the null set) is equal to zero; and (3) probabilities of all events are between zero and one inclusive.

The complement rules are based on the fact that all the outcomes in event A and all the outcomes not in event A together make up the entire sample space. The addition rules provide formulas for calculating the probability of unions, whereas the multiplication rules provide methods for calculating the probability of intersections. All of these rules are listed in the following table.

Type of Rule	Formula
Basic	1) $P(S) = 1$
	2) P(impossible event) $= 0$; $P(\phi) = 0$
	3) $0 \le P(A) \le 1$
Complement	1) $P(A) + P(A') = 1$
	2) $P(A) = 1 - P(A')$
	3) $P(A') = 1 - P(A)$
Addition	1) $P(A \cup B) = P(A) + P(B)$ if events A and B are mutually exclusive
	2) $P(A \cup B) = P(A) + P(B) - P(A \cap B)$ if events A and B are not mutually exclusive For three events: $P(A \cap B \cap C) = P(A) + P(B) + P(C) - P(A \cap B) - P(A \cap C) - P(B \cap C) + P(A \cap B \cap C)$
Multiplication	1) $P(A \cap B) = P(A)P(B)$ if events A and B are independent
	2) $P(A \cap B) = P(A)P(B \mid A) = P(B)P(A \mid B)$ if events A and B are dependent

To use these rules, you must first understand the concepts of independent events and conditional probability. Events A and B are independent if the probability that event A occurs is in no way influenced by the probability that event B has already occurred (or vice versa). If the occurrence of one event affects the occurrence of the other event, the events are said to be dependent.

Conditional probability deals with calculating the probability of an event "given" that another event has already occurred. The notation for the probability that event A occurs given that event B has already occurred is $P(A \mid B)$. This probability is calculated by taking the ratio of the probability of the intersection of events A and B to the probability of event B:

$$P(A \mid B) = \frac{P(A \cap B)}{P(B)}.$$

Note that $P(A \mid B)$ and $P(B \mid A)$ are not necessarily equal because the divisors may be different. If $P(A \mid B) = P(A)$ and $P(B \mid A) = P(B)$, then events A and B are independent. Events A and B are also independent if $P(A \cap B) = P(A)P(B)$.

In the coin toss example, A and B are independent events because getting a head on the first toss does not affect the probability of getting a tail on the third toss. Using the formulas:

$$P(A \mid B) = \frac{0.25}{0.5} = 0.5 = P(A);$$

$$P(B \mid A) = \frac{0.25}{0.5} = 0.5 = P(B); \text{ and}$$

$$P(A \cap B) = 0.25 = (0.5)(0.5) = P(A)P(B).$$

 FLASH REVIEW

1. Let $P(A) = 0.24$, $P(B) = 0.35$, and $P(A \cap B) = 0.17$. Round probabilities to three decimal places.

a. Find the probability that event *A* will occur given that event *B* has already occurred.

b. Find the probability that event *B* will occur given that event *A* has already occurred.

c. Find the probability that event *A* will occur or that event *B* will occur.

d. Find the probability that event *A* will not occur.

e. Are events *A* and *B* independent? Justify your answer.

2. Let $P(A) = 0.2$, $P(B) = 0.25$, $P(C) = 0.5$, $P(A \cap B) = 0.1$, $P(A \cap C) = 0.1$, $P(B \cap C) = 0.15$, and $P(A \cap B \cap C) = 0.05$.

a. Find the probability of event *A* or event *B* or event *C*.

b. Draw a Venn diagram that represents the probabilities of the listed events.

Section 4.3—Counting Rules

FLASH SUMMARY

The counting rules provide a means for determining the number of outcomes in a sample space or an event without writing out all the possible outcomes. Two questions should be asked to decide which counting rule is appropriate for a given situation: (1) "Does order matter?" and (2) "Are all of the objects (or outcomes) being considered?"

The fundamental counting rule (also called the multiplication rule of counting) gives the number of outcomes for two successive events by multiplying the number of outcomes for the first event by the number of outcomes for the second event. This can also be extended to more than two events. All objects are used and order matters. In the coin toss example, the first event (first flip) has two outcomes (H and T), the second event has two outcomes, and the third flip has two outcomes. Therefore, the total number of outcomes in the sample space is $(2)(2)(2) = 8$.

The factorial rule calculates the number of orderings for a particular number of objects (denoted *n*) by multiplying the number of objects available for the first position by the number of objects available for the second position and so on down to the last position:

$$n \cdot (n - 1) \cdot (n - 2) \cdots 1 = n!$$

For example, if five students are to be seated on the front row, the number of orderings from seat 1 to seat 5 would be

$$5! = (5)(4)(3)(2)(1) = 120.$$

All of the objects are used and order matters.

Permutations and combinations are used in situations in which some of the objects are selected from the group of objects under consideration. Permutations are the number of orderings of *x* objects selected from *n* objects, and combinations are the number of groups of *x* objects selected from *n* objects (order does not matter). Consider selecting two numbers from the numbers 1, 2, and 3. There are six possible orderings (permutations) for the two selected: 12, 13, 21, 23, 31, and 32. However, because 12 and 21 contain the same objects as do 13 and 31, and 23 and 32, there are only three possible groupings (combinations). The notations and formulas for permutations and combinations are given in the following table.

Rule	Does Order Matter?	Are All Objects Considered?	Calculation
Fundamental counting	Yes	Yes	$n_1 \cdot n_2$ for two events $n_1 \cdot n_2 \cdots n_k$ for k events
Factorial	Yes	Yes	$n!$
Permutations	Yes	No	$_nP_x = \dfrac{n!}{(n-x)!}$
Combinations	No	No	$_nC_x = \binom{n}{x} = \dfrac{n!}{(n-x)!x!}$

 FLASH REVIEW

1. The Connor College chapter of Mu Sigma Rho National Statistics Honor Society has 18 members.

   a. How many ways can three members of the group be selected to attend the annual national meeting?

   b. Three members of the group are to be selected for the Quiz Bowl Team. The team positions are captain, vice captain, and researcher. In how many ways can the Quiz Bowl Team be selected from the 18 members?

2. Students in a statistics class are asked to give the instructor a three-character code by which grades will be posted.

   a. If the three characters must be selected from the digits 0 through 9, how many codes are possible if digits can be repeated?

   b. If the first character must be a capital arabic letter and the second and third characters must be numbers, how many codes are possible if the digits cannot be repeated?

Section 5.1—Discrete and Continuous Probability Distributions

FLASH SUMMARY

In a probability context, a random variable may be thought of as a rule for assigning values to the outcomes in a sample space. In the coin toss example, the random variable X could be defined as the number of heads in three flips. A probability distribution gives the possible outcomes of the random variable and the associated probabilities for each. Probability distributions are often represented by tables or formulas. The basic rules of probability extend to probability distributions. Each probability in the distribution must be between zero and one inclusive, and the total of the probabilities must equal one.

Discrete probability distributions are used for discrete random variables, and continuous probability distributions are used for continuous random variables. Discrete random variables have non-zero probabilities only on the possible values. Probabilities for continuous random variables are associated with the area under the curve between two possible values and thus have non-zero probabilities only on intervals between possible values, not on the values themselves. For a continuous random variable, $P(X = x) = 0$ for any value of x.

The mean of a discrete probability distribution is found by multiplying each possible value of the random variable by the associated probability and adding those products together:

$$\mu = \sum x \mathrm{P}(x).$$

The variance is found by multiplying the squared deviation of each value from the mean by the associated probability and adding the products:

$$\sigma^2 = \sum (x - \mu)^2 \mathrm{P}(x).$$

As with the data sets in Chapter 1, a calculation formula exists for the variance:

$$\sigma^2 = \sum [x^2 \mathrm{P}(x)] - \mu^2$$

The standard deviation is then calculated by taking the square root of the variance. Finding the mean and variance of a continuous probability distribution involves the use of calculus, which is outside the scope of most introductory statistics courses.

The probability distribution for the coin toss example is discrete because there are only four possible values for the random variable. The possible values for X defined for the coin toss example would be 0, 1, 2, and 3. The probabilities associated with these values would be calculated as follows:

$$P(X = 0) = \frac{1}{8};$$

$$P(X = 1) = \frac{3}{8};$$

$$P(X = 2) = \frac{3}{8}; \text{ and}$$

$$P(X = 3) = \frac{1}{8}.$$

This probability distribution can be displayed in a table:

x	0	1	2	3
P(x)	0.125	0.375	0.375	0.125

Note that a capital X is used to denote a random variable, and a lower case x is used to denote a value of a random variable.

The notation P($X = 0$) denotes P($X = x$) where $x = 0$. Probabilities of compound events can be found using the probability distribution table. For example, the probability that the number of heads is between 0 and 2 inclusive is:

$$P(0 \leq X \leq 2) = P(X = 0) + P(X = 1) + P(X = 2) = 0.125 + 0.375 + 0.375$$
$$= 0.875$$

because there are no non-zero probabilities for quantities between these values. This probability may also be calculated using the complement rule:

$$P(0 \leq X \leq 2) = 1 - P(X = 3) = 1 - 0.125 = 0.875$$

because the total probability must equal one. The probability of getting more than one head in three coin tosses would be:

$$P(X > 1) = P(X = 2) + P(X = 3) = 0.375 + 0.125 = 0.5.$$

The mean and variance of the distribution would be calculated as follows:

$$\mu = \sum xP(x) = 0(0.125) + 1(0.375) + 2(0.375) + 3(0.125) = 1.5; \text{ and}$$

$$\sigma^2 = \sum[x^2P(x)] - \mu^2 = 0^2(0.125) + 1^2(0.375) + 2^2(0.375) + 3^2(0.125) - 1.5^2 = 0.75.$$

The expected value is E(X) $= \mu = 0.5$, and the standard deviation is $\sigma = \sqrt{0.75} = 0.866$ to three decimal places.

Certain discrete and continuous random variables and their associated probability distributions are frequently used in statistics. Tables displaying the probabilities are available for most of these distributions. For discrete distributions, the mean and standard deviation are usually expressed as formulas; for continuous distributions, the mean and standard deviation are usually given. The parameters of these distributions are the pieces of information necessary to determine which particular distribution applies to the random variable under consideration.

Discrete probability distributions commonly encountered in statistics include binomial, geometric, and Poisson distributions. Common continuous distributions in statistics include normal, t, F, and χ^2 ("chi-square") distributions.

Binomial random variables are among the most commonly used discrete random variables. A binomial random variable is often appropriate when the X can be defined as the number of successes in n trials. A binomial random variable is produced by a binomial experiment that has the following characteristics: (1) there are a fixed number of trials (n); (2) the trials are independent; (3) there are only two outcomes on each trial, which are labeled success and failure; and (4) the probability of a success (p) is constant across trials. Note that the probability of a failure is $1 - p$ by the complement rule and is denote q in many texts.

The coin toss example meets the criteria for a binomial experiment. A trial is a flip of the coin, so there are three trials. The trials are independent because one flip does not affect the outcome on the other two. The two outcomes are H and T; because X was defined to be the number of heads, H is a success. For a balanced coin, the probability of a success is 0.5 for every trial.

The parameters of a binomial distribution are n and p, which must be known to calculate probabilities associated with values of the random variable. This means that there are infinitely many binomial distributions, one for every possible combination of n and p. Probabilities may be found by using a binomial probability table or the binomial formula (given in the following table). Note that p is frequently given as a percent rather than in decimal form.

Probability Distributions for Discrete Random Variables

Name	Description and Characteristics	Formulas
Binomial	X = the number of successes in n trials Parameters: n, p Characteristics of a binomial experiment 1) fixed number of trials 2) trials are independent 3) only two outcomes on each trial 4) p is constant across trials	$P(X = x) = \binom{n}{x} p^x (1-p)^{n-x}$ $x = 0, 1, \ldots, n$ $\mu = np$ $\sigma = \sqrt{np(1-p)}$
Geometric	X = the number of trials until the first success Parameter: p 1) trials are independent 2) only two outcomes on each trial 3) p is constant across trials	$P(X = x) = p(1-p)^{x-1}$ $x = 1, 2, \ldots$ $\mu = \dfrac{1}{p}$ $\sigma = \sqrt{\dfrac{1-p}{p^2}}$
Poisson	X = the number of successes per unit time Parameter: λ 1) trials are independent 2) only two outcomes on each trial 3) p is constant across trials	$P(X = x) = \dfrac{e^{-\lambda}\lambda^x}{x!}$ λ = mean number of successes per unit time $x = 0, 1, 2, \ldots$ $\mu = \lambda$ $\sigma = \sqrt{\lambda}$

Normal random variables are very frequently encountered in statistical inference. Normal distributions are symmetric, bell-shaped curves that are defined by the function

$$f(x) = \frac{1}{\sqrt{2\pi\sigma^2}} e^{-\frac{(x-\mu)^2}{2\sigma^2}}$$

for any real number x. The parameters are μ and σ.

Normal random variables can be standardized to one distribution called the standard normal distribution, which has a mean of zero and a standard deviation of one. The standard normal random variable is denoted Z, and the standardization formula is:

$$z = \frac{x - \mu}{\sigma}.$$

These values are called z-scores and are interpreted as the number of standard deviation units the raw score falls above (if the sign is positive) or below (if the sign is negative) the mean of the original normal distribution.

Probabilities for intervals between two values of normal random variables are found by integrating the function. Because this is beyond the scope of most introductory statistics courses, standard normal probability tables are usually used. The values of the normal distribution are standardized and the probabilities found using the table(s). Be sure to check your textbook for which standard normal probability tables are available and instructions on how to use them.

Suppose X is a normal random variable with a mean of 10 and a standard deviation of 2. The probability that X is between the values of 9 and 12 would be found as follows:

$$P(9 < X < 12) = P\left(\frac{9 - 10}{2} < \frac{X - \mu}{\sigma} < \frac{12 - 10}{2}\right) = P(-0.5 < Z < 1) = 0.5328.$$

It can be very helpful to draw a picture when calculating normal probabilities. For the example above, an appropriate picture would be:

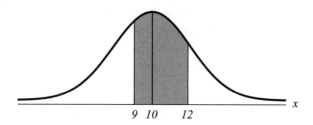

Probability Distributions for Continuous Random Variables

Name	Characteristics	Parameters
Normal	1) bell-shaped 2) symmetric about μ 3) asymptotic to X axis 4) $-\infty < X < \infty$	μ is given σ is given
Standard normal	1) bell-shaped 2) symmetric about $\mu = 0$ 3) asymptotic to X axis 4) $-\infty < Z < \infty$	$\mu = 0$ $\sigma = 1$
t	1) bell-shaped 2) symmetric about $\mu = 0$ 3) asymptotic to X axis 4) $-\infty < t < \infty$ 5) as $n \to \infty$, $t \to Z$	$df = n - 1$ (one sample)* $df = n_1 + n_2 - 2$ (two samples, pooled variance)* $df' = \dfrac{(n_1 - 1)(n_2 - 1)\left(\dfrac{s_1^2}{n_1} + \dfrac{s_2^2}{n_2}\right)^2}{(n_2 - 1)\left(\dfrac{s_1^2}{n_1}\right)^2 + (n_1 - 1)\left(\dfrac{s_2^2}{n_2}\right)^2}$ (two samples, nonpooled variance)*
F	1) right-skewed 2) $0 < F < \infty$ 3) $F = t^2$	$df_{\text{N}} = n_{\text{N}} - 1$ $df_{\text{D}} = n_{\text{D}} - 1$
χ^2	1) right-skewed 2) $0 < \chi^2 < \infty$	$df = (r - 1)(c - 1)$

*These concepts are explained in Unit 3.

FLASH REVIEW

1. Twenty students in a statistics class at Connor College were asked how many courses they were taking during the current semester. Two students were enrolled

in two courses, four students were enrolled in three, nine students were enrolled in four, three students were enrolled in five, and two students were enrolled in six.

    a. Construct a probability distribution table.

    b. Find the mean and standard deviation of the distribution.

    c. Find the probability that a randomly selected student is enrolled in at most four courses.

    d. Find the probability that a randomly selected student is enrolled in between three and five courses inclusive.

2. The ages of all students enrolled at Connor College form a normal distribution with a mean of 25 years and a standard deviation of 5 years.

    a. What is the probability that a randomly selected student is between 19 and 28 years old?

    b. What is the probability that a randomly selected student is at least 27.4 years of age?

    c. What age is the boundary between the youngest 10% and the oldest 90% of the students?

3. Fifty-five percent of the students at Connor College are female. A researcher takes a random sample of 10 students from the population of all students.

    a. What is the probability that seven of the students in the sample are female?

    b. What is the probability that none of the students in the sample are male?

    c. What is the expected number of females in the sample?

Section 5.2—Sampling Distribution of the Sample Mean

FLASH SUMMARY

Assume the numbers 1, 2, 3, and 4 are the values in a population, and suppose a random sample of size two is to be drawn. The value of the sample mean will depend on which sample of $n = 2$ is selected. The following table lists the possible samples and associated sample means.

Sample No.	1	2	3	4	5	6
Values	1, 2	1, 3	1, 4	2, 3	2, 4	3, 4
Mean	1.5	2	2.5	2.5	3	3.5

Because the value of the sample mean varies depending on which sample is actually selected, the sample mean is a random variable prior to drawing the sample.

A probability distribution for the sample means (the random variable $\bar{X}$) can be constructed. This distribution is called the sampling distribution of the sample mean. The mean and standard deviation of the distribution can be calculated in the same manner as the probability distributions described previously, and probabilities of events can be found. The probability distribution for the above example is

$\bar{x}$	1.5	2	2.5	3	3.5
$P(\bar{x})$	$\dfrac{1}{6}$	$\dfrac{1}{6}$	$\dfrac{1}{3}$	$\dfrac{1}{6}$	$\dfrac{1}{6}$

The mean of this distribution is:

$$\mu_{\bar{X}} = \sum \bar{x} P(\bar{x}) = 2.5$$

and the standard deviation is:

$$\sigma_{\overline{X}} = \sqrt{\sum [\overline{x}^2 P(\overline{x})] - \mu_{\overline{X}}} = 0.645 \text{ to three decimal places.}$$

The standard deviation of the sampling distribution is called the standard error.

Many statistical tools used in inference rely on the assumption that the sampling distribution of the sample mean is normally distributed. If the random variable X has a normal distribution with mean μ and standard deviation σ, then for random samples of size n, the random variable $\overline{X}$ has a normal distribution with mean $\mu_{\overline{X}} = \mu$ and standard error $\sigma_{\overline{X}} = \dfrac{\sigma}{\sqrt{n}}$. Notice that the standard error will never be larger than the standard deviation of the original random variable X, and $\sigma_{\overline{X}} = \sigma$ only when $n = 1$.

If the random variable X is not normally distributed, the central limit theorem (CLT) is a powerful result that describes the sampling distribution of the sample mean for large samples (usually $n \geq 30$). The CLT states that if X is a random variable with a probability distribution that has a mean of μ and standard deviation σ and repeated samples of size n are taken from the population, the random variable $\overline{X}$ has **approximately** a normal distribution with mean $\mu_{\overline{X}} = \mu$ and standard error $\sigma_{\overline{X}} = \dfrac{\sigma}{\sqrt{n}}$ for large n. The case in which X is **not** normally distributed and n is small is beyond the scope of most introductory statistics courses.

Suppose the random variable X is normally distributed with a mean of 30 and a standard deviation of 5. A random sample of size $n = 25$ is to be taken. The sampling distribution of the sample mean — the distribution for the random variable $\overline{X}$ for $n = 25$ — will be normally distributed with a mean of:

$$\mu_{\overline{X}} = \mu = 30$$

and a standard error of:

$$\sigma_{\overline{X}} = \frac{\sigma}{\sqrt{n}} = \frac{5}{\sqrt{25}} = 1.$$

Now suppose that the random variable X has a distribution that is left-skewed with a mean of 30 and a standard deviation of 5. A random sample of size $n = 50$ is to be taken. The random variable $\overline{X}$ for $n = 50$ is **approximately** normally distributed with a mean of:

$$\mu_{\overline{X}} = \mu = 30$$

and a standard error of:

$$\sigma_{\overline{X}} = \frac{\sigma}{\sqrt{n}} = \frac{5}{\sqrt{50}} = 0.707.$$

Describing the sampling distribution of the sample mean

Q: Is X normally distributed?	Yes	$\overline{X}$ normally distributed $\mu_{\overline{X}} = \mu$ $\sigma_{\overline{X}} = \dfrac{\sigma}{\sqrt{n}}$		
	No	Q: Is $n \geq 30$?	Yes	$\overline{X}$ approximately normally distributed $\mu_{\overline{X}} = \mu$ $\sigma_{\overline{X}} = \dfrac{\sigma}{\sqrt{n}}$
			No	beyond the scope of the course

FLASH REVIEW

1. The probability distribution of electric bills for the month of March for households in the small town of Perkins has a mean of $47.32 and a standard deviation of $17.57.

   a. Describe the sampling distribution of the sample mean for $n = 100$. (Give the name of the distribution, the mean, and the standard deviation.)

   b. Find the probability that a random sample of 100 households has an average electric bill less than $45.

2. The number of hours that statistics students study for a final exam is normally distributed with a mean of 6 hours and a standard deviation of 1.5 hours.

   a. Describe the distribution of $\overline{X}$ for samples of size 9.

   b. Find the probability that a random sample of nine students has an average study time between 5 and 7 hours.

Solutions to Flash Review Problems in Unit 2

Chapter 4—Section 4.1, Fundamentals of Probability

1. $S = \{RR, RL, RS, LR, LL, LS, SR, SL, SS\}$
2. $A = \{RL, LL, SL\}$
3. $B = \{RR, RL, RS\}$
4. intersection (**and**), $A \cap B = \{RL\}$,

   $$P(A \cap B) = \frac{1}{9} = 0.\overline{1}$$

5. union (**or**), $A \cup B = \{RL, LL, SL, RR, RS\}$,

   $$P(A \cup B) = \frac{5}{9} = 0.\overline{5}$$

6. complement (**not**), $B' = \{LR, LL, LS, SR, SL, SS\}$,

   $$P(B') = \frac{6}{9} = 0.\overline{6}$$

7. Let C = both cars go same direction = $\{RR, LL, SS\}$,

   $$P(C) = \frac{3}{9} = 0.\overline{3}.$$

Chapter 4—Section 4.2, Probability Rules

1. **a.** $P(A \mid B) = \dfrac{P(A \cap B)}{P(B)} = \dfrac{0.17}{0.35} = 0.486$

   b. $P(B \mid A) = \dfrac{P(A \cap B)}{P(A)} = \dfrac{0.17}{0.24} = 0.708$

   c. $P(A \cup B) = P(A) + P(B) - P(A \cap B) = 0.24 + 0.35 - 0.17 = 0.42$

   d. $P(A') = 1 - P(A) = 1 - 0.24 = 0.76$

   e. No, $P(A \mid B) = 0.486 \neq P(A) = 0.24$ or

   $P(A)P(B) = (0.24)(0.35) = 0.84 \neq 0.17 = P(A \cap B)$.

2. a. $P(A \cup B \cup C) = P(A) + P(B) + P(C) - P(A \cap B) - P(A \cap C) - P(B \cap C) + P(A \cap B \cap C) = 0.2 + 0.25 + 0.5 - 0.1 - 0.1 - 0.15 + 0.05 = 0.65$

b.

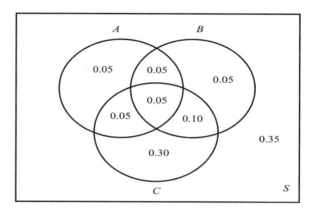

Chapter 4—Section 4.3, Counting Rules

1. a. Order does not matter and not all the members are selected, thus use combinations: $_{18}C_3 = \dfrac{18!}{(18-3)!3!} = 816.$

b. Order matters and not all members are selected, thus use permutations:

$_{18}P_3 = \dfrac{18!}{(18-3)!} = 4{,}896.$

2. a. Order matters and all digits are considered, thus use the fundamental counting rule: $(10)(10)(10) = 1{,}000.$

b. Order matters and all digits are considered (even though only nine digits are left for consideration for the third position), thus use the fundamental counting rule: $(26)(10)(9) = 2{,}340.$

Chapter 5—Section 5.1, Discrete and Continuous Probability Distributions

1. a. X is the number of courses and the possible values are $x = 2, 3, 4, 5, 6$

x	2	3	4	5	6
$P(x)$	0.1	0.2	0.45	0.15	0.1

b. $\mu = \sum x P(x) = 2(0.1) + 3(0.2) + 4(0.45) + 5(0.15) + 6(0.1) = 3.95$

$\sigma^2 = \sum [x^2 P(x)] - \mu^2 = 2^2(0.1) + 3^2(0.2) + 4^2(0.45) + 5^2(0.15) + 6^2(0.1) - 3.95^2 = 1.1475$, thus $\sigma = \sqrt{1.1475} = 1.071$

c. $P(X \le 4) = P(X = 2) + P(X = 3) + P(X = 4) = 0.1 + 0.2 + 0.45 = 0.75$

d. $P(3 \le X \le 5) = P(X = 3) + P(X = 4) + P(X = 5) = 0.2 + 0.45 + 0.15 = 0.8$

2. a. $P(19 < X < 28) = P\left(\dfrac{19-25}{5} < \dfrac{X-\mu}{\sigma} < \dfrac{28-25}{5}\right) = P(-1.2 < Z < 0.6)$

$= 0.6016$

b. $P(X \ge 27.4) = P\left(\dfrac{X-\mu}{\sigma} \ge \dfrac{27.4-25}{5}\right) = P(Z \ge 0.48) = 0.3156$

c. Because $z = \dfrac{x - \mu}{\sigma}$, $x = \mu + z\sigma$. $P(X < x) = P(Z < z) = 0.1$; find the value closest to 0.1 in the body of the standard normal table to determine that the approximate value for $z = -0.25$. Then $x = 25 + (-0.25)(5) = 23.75$.

3. This is a binomial experiment: 10 independent trials, two outcomes, $p = 0.55$.

   a. $P(X = 7) = \dbinom{10}{7}(0.55)^7(1 - 0.55)^{10-7} = 0.166$

   b. P (none male) $=$ P(all female) $=$ $P(X = 10) = \dbinom{10}{10}(0.55)^{10}(0.45)^0 = 0.003$

   c. $E(X) = \mu = np = (10)(0.55) = 5.5$

Chapter 5—Section 5.2, Sampling Distribution of the Sample Mean

1. a. Because X does not have a normal distribution but $n \geq 30$, apply the CLT so $\bar{X}$ is approximately normally distributed with a mean of $\mu_{\bar{X}} = \mu = \$47.32$ and a standard error of $\sigma_{\bar{X}} = \dfrac{\sigma}{\sqrt{n}} = \dfrac{17.57}{\sqrt{100}} = \$1.757$.

   b. $P(\bar{X} < 45) = \left(\dfrac{\bar{X} - \mu_{\bar{X}}}{\sigma_{\bar{X}}} < \dfrac{45 - 47.32}{1.757}\right) = P(Z < -1.32) = 0.0934$.

2. a. Because X has a normal distribution, $\bar{X}$ is normally distributed with a mean of $\mu_{\bar{X}} = \mu = 6$ and a standard error of $\sigma_{\bar{X}} = \dfrac{\sigma}{\sqrt{n}} = \dfrac{1.5}{\sqrt{9}} = 0.5$.

   b. $P(5 < \bar{X} < 7) = \left(\dfrac{5 - 6}{0.5} < \dfrac{\bar{X} - \mu_{\bar{X}}}{\sigma_{\bar{X}}} < \dfrac{7 - 6}{0.5}\right) = P(-2 < Z < 2) = 0.9544$.

FLASH TEST

The following pages contain a practice test so that you may assess your understanding of the material presented in Unit 2. Answers and explanations follow the exam. For any questions you miss, be sure to review the explanation carefully and reread the appropriate portion of the section to which the question applies. If you still do not understand the correct answer, review the concept in your text and/or ask your instructor for assistance.

FLASH TEST FOR UNIT 2

TRUE/FALSE (3 points each)

_____ 1. A coin is flipped three times and the number of heads is recorded. This procedure is repeated 1,000 times and a probability distribution for X = the number of heads in three flips is recorded. This is an example of the classical approach to probability.

_____ 2. The probability of event B can be found by dividing the probability of the intersection of events A and B by the probability of the event A given B.

_____ 3. If two events are mutually exclusive, they are also independent.

_____ 4. Let X be a continuous random variable with a normal distribution, and let x_1 and x_2 represent two values of the random variable. If A is the event that X lies between x_1 and x_2 inclusive, the complement of A is the event that X is greater than x_2.

_____ 5. The standard normal distribution has a mean equal to zero and a variance equal to one.

MULTIPLE CHOICE (3 points each)

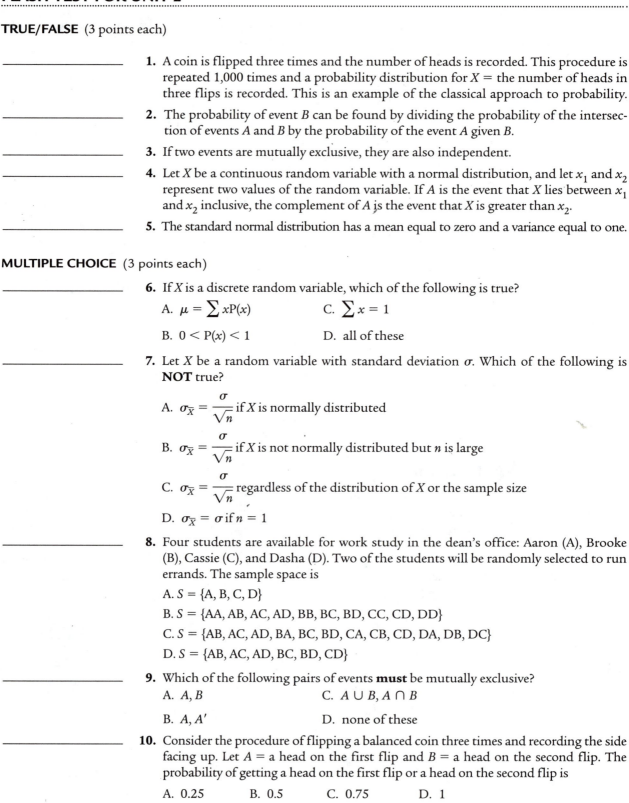

_____ 6. If X is a discrete random variable, which of the following is true?

A. $\mu = \sum xP(x)$ C. $\sum x = 1$

B. $0 < P(x) < 1$ D. all of these

_____ 7. Let X be a random variable with standard deviation σ. Which of the following is **NOT** true?

A. $\sigma_{\bar{X}} = \dfrac{\sigma}{\sqrt{n}}$ if X is normally distributed

B. $\sigma_{\bar{X}} = \dfrac{\sigma}{\sqrt{n}}$ if X is not normally distributed but n is large

C. $\sigma_{\bar{X}} = \dfrac{\sigma}{\sqrt{n}}$ regardless of the distribution of X or the sample size

D. $\sigma_{\bar{X}} = \sigma$ if $n = 1$

_____ 8. Four students are available for work study in the dean's office: Aaron (A), Brooke (B), Cassie (C), and Dasha (D). Two of the students will be randomly selected to run errands. The sample space is

A. $S = \{A, B, C, D\}$

B. $S = \{AA, AB, AC, AD, BB, BC, BD, CC, CD, DD\}$

C. $S = \{AB, AC, AD, BA, BC, BD, CA, CB, CD, DA, DB, DC\}$

D. $S = \{AB, AC, AD, BC, BD, CD\}$

_____ 9. Which of the following pairs of events **must** be mutually exclusive?

A. A, B C. $A \cup B, A \cap B$

B. A, A' D. none of these

_____ 10. Consider the procedure of flipping a balanced coin three times and recording the side facing up. Let A = a head on the first flip and B = a head on the second flip. The probability of getting a head on the first flip or a head on the second flip is

A. 0.25   B. 0.5   C. 0.75   D. 1

11. Twenty-five percent of the students at Connor College are married. Eight students are randomly selected and asked their marital status. The expected number of married students out of the eight students is

    A. 2   C. 8

    B. 4   D. not enough information to calculate

12. The Math Club at Connor College is conducting a contest and will allow the winner to select two prizes from the five available prizes. The number of possible prize packages is

    A. 10   B. 15   C. 60   D. 125

13. Let x_1 and x_2 be possible values for a random variable X. If $P(x_1 < X < x_2) = P(x_1 \le X \le x_2)$, then X

    A. has a discrete probability distribution

    B. has a continuous probability distribution

    C. can have either a discrete or a continuous probability distribution

    D. can have neither a discrete nor a continuous probability distribution

14. If a random variable X has a left-skewed distribution and $n = 50$, the sampling distribution of the sample mean is

    A. unknown   C. exactly normal

    B. left-skewed   D. approximately normal

15. Which of the following is true about the parameters of a normal distribution?

    A. $\mu = 0, \sigma = 1$

    B. $-\infty < \mu < \infty, -\infty < \sigma < \infty$

    C. $-\infty < \mu < \infty, \sigma > 0$

    D. $\mu > 0, \sigma > 0$

SHORT ANSWER (3 points each)

16. Is the following a valid probability distribution? Justify your answer.

x	1	5	10	17
$P(x)$	0.2	0.4	0.1	0.3

17. Thirty-five percent of the students at Connor College are freshmen. Twenty-five percent of students are married, and 7% of the students are married freshmen. Of the freshmen, 20% are married. Let the event F = freshman and the event M = married. Are the events F and M independent? Justify your answer.

18. A standard six-sided die is to be rolled and the number of spots on the top face recorded. This procedure will be repeated 20 times. Assume the die is balanced so that each side is equally likely to end up on top. Is this a binomial experiment? Justify your answer.

EA =

19. Studies have been conducted on the "handedness" of college students (left-handed, right-handed, ambidextrous). In a new study, the handedness of four students at Connor College will be determined. Explain two ways in which the number of outcomes in the sample space may be determined. **DO NOT** find the number of outcomes, just explain two methods you could use to do so.

20. One card is to be randomly selected from a standard deck of 52 cards. Let the event K = drawing a king and the event H = drawing a heart. Describe in words the events H', $K \cup H$, and $K \cap H$.

CALCULATIONS (5 points each)

21. Heights of male students at Connor College form a normal distribution with a mean of 70 inches and a standard deviation of 2 inches. What is the probability that the height of a randomly selected male student is between 65 and 68 inches?

22. The distribution of exam scores for statistics students at Connor College has a mean of 73 points with a standard deviation of 11 points. What is the probability that a random sample of 100 students has an average exam score of at least 75?

Use the following information for problems 23 and 24. The table below gives the probability distribution of the number of siblings for students in a statistics class.

x	0	1	2	3	4	5
$P(x)$	0.13	0.37	0.28	0.12	0.07	0.03

23. What is the probability that a randomly selected student has at least two siblings?

24. Find the mean and standard deviation for the distribution.

25. The lights in the hallway of the Taylor Towers building are already turned on when Mr. Taylor arrives early in the morning 62% of the time. Out of five randomly selected days, what is the probability that the lights will be on between one and three days inclusive?

26. Five of 12 photos are to be displayed in a frame in which the photos are placed in order from Photo 1 to Photo 5. In how many ways may five photos be displayed in the frame?

Use the following information for problems 27 and 28. Heather is going to go to the library on Monday and Friday of the coming week. She will select one book on each of these days from the categories of mystery (M), science fiction (F), western (W), and romance (R). She may select from the same category on both days.

27. Write out the sample space for the type of books she selects on Monday (first element) and Friday (second element).

28. Assuming each outcome is equally likely, what is the probability that she selects a western on Friday given that she selects a mystery on Monday?

Answers to the practice test begin on the next page.

SOLUTIONS TO FLASH TEST FOR UNIT 2

TRUE/FALSE

1. F; because the information relates to an actual experiment, this is an example of the relative frequency approach

2. T; because $P(A \mid B) = \dfrac{P(A \cap B)}{P(B)}$, $P(B) = \dfrac{P(A \cap B)}{P(A \mid B)}$

3. F; because the events are mutually exclusive, if A occurs, B cannot occur, thus the two events are dependent

4. F; $X > x_2$ is only part of the complement; the other part is $X < x_1$

5. T; the parameters of the standard normal are $\mu = 0$ and $\sigma = 1$, thus $\sigma^2 = 1$

MULTIPLE CHOICE

6. A; the signs in B should be $\leq$ rather than $<$, and the sum in C should be $\sum P(x) = 1$

7. C; A is true because X is normally distributed, B is true by the central limit theorem, C is true because $\sigma_{\overline{X}} = \dfrac{\sigma}{\sqrt{n}} = \dfrac{\sigma}{\sqrt{1}} = \sigma$

8. D; A is a sample space for choosing one student, B allows the same student to have both positions, C implies that order matters, which is not implied in the statement of the problem

9. B; A and A' are mutually exclusive because A' is defined as all the outcomes in S that are not in A

10. C; $A = \{HHH, HHT, HTH, HTT\}$,

    $B = \{HHH, HHT, THH, THT\}$,

    $A \cap B = \{HHH, HHT\}$,

    $P(A) = 0.5$, $P(B) = 0.5$, $P(A \cap B) = 0.25$,

    $P(A \cup B) = P(A) + P(B) - P(A \cap B) = 0.5 + 0.5 - 0.25 = 0.75$

    (or write out the event $A \cup B$)

11. A; this is a binomial experiment, thus $E(X) = \mu = np = (8)(0.25) = 2$

12. A; order does not matter and some items are considered, so use combinations

    $\dbinom{5}{2} = 10$

13. B; the statement $P(x_1 < X < x_2) = P(x_1 \leq X \leq x_2)$ implies that $P(X = x_1) = 0$ and $P(X = x_2) = 0$, which is true for continuous distributions but not for discrete distributions

14. D; apply the CLT

15. C; A gives the parameters for the standard normal distribution, B states that standard deviation can be negative, and D states that the mean cannot be equal to zero or a negative value

SHORT ANSWER

16. Yes, this is a valid probability distribution because $0 \leq P(x) \leq 1$ for all x and $\sum P(x) = 1$.

17. No, the events F and M are not independent. From the problem,
$P(F) = 0.35$, $P(M) = 0.25$, $P(F \cap M) = 0.07$, and $P(M \mid F) = 0.2$.
You can show the events are not independent by showing either
$P(F)P(M) = (0.35)(0.25) = 0.0875 \neq 0.07 = P(F \cap M)$ or
$P(M \mid F) = 0.2 \neq 0.25 = P(M)$.

18. No, this is not a binomial experiment. Although there are 20 independent trials and the probability for any value on the die is $\frac{1}{6}$ across trials, there are more than two possible outcomes on each trial.

19. 1) The fundamental counting rule may be used by considering the first student as the first event (three possible outcomes), the second student as the second event, etc. This may be the most efficient method of determining the number of possible outcomes because the outcomes do not need to be listed.

2) A tree diagram may be used to construct the possible outcomes and the total number of branches counted.

3) The outcomes could be listed in sample space notation, $S = \{RRR, RLA, \ldots\}$, and the number of outcomes counted.

20. $H' =$ not a heart = a club, a diamond, or a spade; $K \cup H =$ a king or a heart or the king of hearts; $K \cap H =$ a king and a heart = the king of hearts

CALCULATIONS

21. $P(65 < X < 68) = \left(\dfrac{65 - 70}{2} < \dfrac{X - \mu}{\sigma} < \dfrac{68 - 70}{2} \right) = P(-2.5 < Z < -1) = 0.1525$

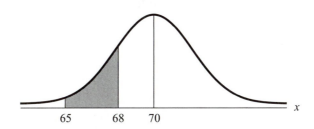

22. Because X is not normally distributed but $n \geq 30$, apply the CLT to get the sampling distribution of the sample means: $\overline{X}$ is approximately normally distributed with a mean of $\mu_{\overline{X}} = \mu = 73$ and a standard error of $\sigma_{\overline{X}} = \dfrac{\sigma}{\sqrt{n}} = \dfrac{11}{\sqrt{100}} = 1.1$.

Then $P(\overline{X} \geq 75) = P\left(\dfrac{\overline{X} - \mu_{\overline{X}}}{\sigma_{\overline{X}}} \geq \dfrac{75 - 73}{1.1} \right) = P(Z \geq 1.82) = 0.0344$.

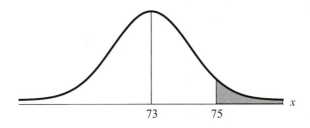

23. $P(X \geq 2) = P(X = 2) + P(X = 3) + P(X = 4) + P(X = 5) = 0.28 + 0.12 + 0.07$
$+ 0.03 = 0.5$

24. $\mu = \sum xP(x) = 0(0.13) + 1(0.37) + 2(0.28) + 3(0.12) + 4(0.07) + 5(0.03) = 1.72$

$\sigma^2 = \sum[x^2P(x)] - \mu^2 = 0^2(0.13) + 1^2(0.37) + 2^2(0.28) + 3^2(0.12) + 4^2(0.07)$

$+ 5^2(0.03) - 1.72^2 = 1.4816$, so $\sigma = \sqrt{1.4816} = 1.217$

25. This is a binomial experiment with $n = 5$ and $p = 0.62$. Then

$$P(1 \leq X \leq 3) = P(X = 1) + P(X = 2) + P(X = 3) = \binom{5}{1}(0.62)^1(0.38)^4$$

$$+ \binom{5}{2}(0.62)^2(0.38)^3 + \binom{5}{3}(0.62)^3(0.38)^2 = 0.620.$$

26. Order matters and some of the items are considered, so use permutations: $_{12}P_5 = 95{,}040.$

27. Elements are of the form (book selected on Monday)(book selected on Friday):

$S = \{$MM, MF, MW, MR, FM, FF, FW, FR, WM, WF, WW, WR, RM, RF, RW, RR$\}$

28. Let $A =$ a mystery on Monday and $B =$ a western on Friday. Then

$A = \{$MM, MF, MW, MR$\}$,

$B = \{$MW, FW, WW, RW$\}$,

$A \cap B = \{$MW$\}$, and

$$P(B \mid A) = \frac{P(A \cap B)}{P(A)} = \frac{\left(\dfrac{1}{16}\right)}{\left(\dfrac{4}{16}\right)} = \frac{1}{4} = 0.25.$$

Note that $P(B \mid A) = 0.25 = P(B)$ and $P(A)P(B) = (0.25)(0.25) = 0.0625 = P(A \cap B)$, thus A and B are independent events.

FLASH FOCUS

After completing this unit, you will be able to:

✓ Understand basic terms associated with estimation
✓ Determine and calculate the appropriate point estimate for a given parameter
✓ Determine the appropriate confidence interval for a given parameter
✓ Calculate and interpret the appropriate confidence interval for a given parameter
✓ Calculate and interpret a correlation coefficient
✓ Find the appropriate regression equation for two variables
✓ Use a regression equation to predict values

The following table lists the core concepts in this unit, along with definitions and/or explanations. Space is provided to add concepts discussed by your instructor.

Core Concepts in Unit 3

Chapter 6—Fundamentals of Estimation	
Concept	**Definition and/or Explanation**
Estimators	statistics used to estimate parameters
Estimates	values from samples used to estimate values of parameters
Point estimate	a single value from the sample used to estimate the value of a parameter
Interval estimate	a range of values from the sample used to estimate the value of a parameter
Confidence interval	an interval estimate based on a probability distribution
Confidence level	expressed as $(1 - \alpha)100\%$, the percent of intervals out of 100 that will contain the true value of the parameter
Critical value	a value from an appropriate probability distribution that separates probable values for the parameter from improbable values for the given confidence level
Margin of error	the largest distance between the point estimate and the parameter that is likely for the given confidence level
Confidence limits	the endpoints of a confidence interval

(continued)

(continued)

Standard error of the estimate	the standard deviation of the sampling distribution of the point estimate

Chapter 7—One Population	
Proportion	the ratio of the number of experimental units having the characteristic of interest to the number of experimental units under consideration
Correlation coefficient	a value that describes the strength and direction of the linear relationship between two variables
Explanatory variable	a variable whose value is used to predict the value of another variable
Response variable	a variable whose value covaries with the value of the explanatory variable
Coefficient of determination	the percent of variability in the response variable that is accounted for by the linear relationship of the response variable with the explanatory variable
Regression equation	a mathematical description of the linear relationship between two variables
Predicted value	the value of the response variable generated by the regression equation for a selected value of the explanatory variable
Residual	the distance between the predicted value and the observed value of the response variable

Chapter 8—Two Populations	
Dependent samples (paired samples)	two samples are dependent (or paired) if there is a reason to match a particular observation from sample one with a particular observation from sample two (often two measurements on one randomly selected group)
Independent samples	two samples are independent if there is not a reason to match a particular observation from sample one with a particular observation from sample two (usually two different randomly selected groups)

(continued)

(continued)

Pooled variance estimate	used when it is assumed that two population variances are the same, a pooled variance estimate uses a weighted combination of two sample variances to estimate a single population variance value

 FLASH LINK

The following table lists Web sites that may be helpful in studying the material in Unit 3. Space is provided to add other Web sites suggested in your text or by your instructor, or those you find on your own. Key to resource type: D, definitions; E, examples; X, exercises; C, calculation; M, demonstration.

Chapter	Resource Type	URL
7	D, E, M (μ)	http://www.ruf.rice.edu/~lane/stat_sim/conf_interval
7	D, E, X (correlation)	http://www.davidmlane.com/hyperstat/desc_biv.html
7	D, E, M (correlation)	http://www.ruf.rice.edu/~lane/stat_sim/comp_r
7	D, E (correlation)	http://trochim.human.cornell.edu/kb/statcorr.htm
7	D, E, X (correlation)	http://www.stat.berkeley.edu/users/stark/SticiGui/Text/ch4.3.htm
7	D, E, X (regression)	http://cne.gmu.edu/modules/dau/stat/regression/linregsn/nreg_3_frm.html
7	C	http://faculty.vassar.edu/~lowry/corr_stats.html
7	M	http://www.math.csusb.edu/faculty/stanton/m262/regress/regress.html
7–8	D (μ, $\mu_1 - \mu_2$, p, $p_1 - p_2$, correlation)	http://stat.tamu.edu/stat30x/notes/node98.html (also node101)
7–8	D, E (μ, $\mu_1 - \mu_2$, p, $p_1 - p_2$, correlation, regression)	http://www.anu.edu.au/nceph/surfstat/surfstat-home
7–8	D, E, X, M (μ, $\mu_1 - \mu_2$, p, $p_1 - p_2$, correlation)	http://www.davidmlane.com/hyperstat/confidence_intervals.html

(continued)

(continued)

7–8	X	http://occ.awlonline.com/bookbind/pubbooks/triola_awl/ chapter6/deluxe.html (also chapter8 and chapter9)
7–8	X	http://occ.awlonline.com/bookbind/pubbooks/ weiss2_awl/chapter8/deluxe.html (also chapter10, chapter12, chapter14, and chapter15)

CHAPTER 6—Fundamentals of Estimation

FLASH SUMMARY

As stated in Unit 1, two major areas of inferential statistics are estimation and hypothesis testing. The question under consideration for estimation is, "What is a reasonable value for the population parameter?" The question under consideration for hypothesis testing is, "Is this hypothesized value a reasonable value for the population parameter?"

If the value of the population parameter were known, inferential statistics would be unnecessary. It seems, then, that researchers should measure the population and find the exact value of the parameter of interest. Measuring the entire population is called a census. However, a census is rarely done and, in fact, sometimes cannot be done. Frequently, a researcher does not have the resources such as time, money, or personnel needed to conduct a census. Some populations are nonstatic, meaning they are constantly changing, thus it is impossible to measure all experimental units except, perhaps, at a given instant in time. In some cases, the experimental unit is destroyed when it is measured, such as in taste-testing a food product for quality control.

Because it is often extremely difficult to measure the whole population, a random sample is taken and measured. Using a random sample makes it more likely that the sample will be representative of the population. The information obtained from the sample is then used to draw conclusions about the value of the population parameter.

Parametric statistics are methods for data of at least interval level measure. These methods require that assumptions about the probability distribution of the random variable under consideration be met and are discussed in Units 3 and 4. Nonparametric statistics are methods used when data are measured at the nominal or ordinal level or when assumptions about the probability distribution cannot be met. These methods are discussed in Unit 5.

An estimator is a statistic used to estimate a parameter. An estimate is the value (or values) of the statistic used to estimate the parameter value. A point estimate is a single value, whereas an interval estimate is a range of values. For example, if an individual is going to buy a new car, he might ask two of his friends to estimate the average cost of a particular vehicle. The first friend might reply "$17,000," whereas the second might estimate "$15,000 to $20,000." The first response is a point estimate, and the second response is an interval estimate.

Point estimates are easy to calculate but do not have any kind of probability statement attached that might indicate the accuracy of the estimate. Confidence intervals are interval estimates that are based on probability distributions. These intervals have a designated confidence level (or degree of confidence) and are denoted $(1 - \alpha)100\%$ confidence intervals on the parameter of interest. Some texts express the degree of confidence as a decimal (i.e., 0.95), whereas others express the confidence level as a percent (95%). Commonly used confidence levels are 90%, 95%, and 99%.

The confidence level gives rise to the interpretation of the confidence interval. Assume 100 random samples of a given size n are selected from a population and that a 95% confidence interval is calculated on the parameter for each sample. We would expect 95 of these intervals to contain the true parameter value and 5 of them not to contain that value. As sampling is repeated over and over, 95% of the intervals would contain the value of the parameter, and 5% would not. In the real world, when only one sample is drawn at random, we are 95% confident that the single interval we calculate is one of the 95% that contain the true value rather than the one of the 5% that do not.

The general form of many of the confidence intervals used to estimate population parameters is $(1 - \alpha)100\%$ confidence interval = the value of the point estimate $\pm$ (the critical value)(the standard error of the estimate). The critical value is a value from the sampling distribution of the point estimate that divides that distribution into likely and unlikely values. Critical values are found by using the appropriate probability distribution table. The standard error of the estimate is the standard deviation of the sampling distribution. The product of the critical value and the standard error is called the margin of error (also called the bound of error or error of estimation).

The margin of error is denoted E and is the largest distance between the point estimate and the parameter that is likely for the designated confidence level. The endpoints of the confidence interval are called the confidence limits. The point estimate minus the margin of error gives the lower confidence limit (LCL), whereas the point estimate plus the margin of error gives the upper confidence limit (UCL). The interval is usually written as (LCL, UCL).

Note that all the confidence intervals in this chapter are two-sided confidence intervals; both a lower and an upper confidence limit are calculated. One-sided confidence intervals are beyond the scope of most introductory statistics courses. It should also be mentioned that confidence intervals can be calculated on many other parameters, such as the population variance, are not covered in this unit.

Structure of confidence interval using general form

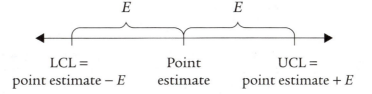

$$
\begin{array}{ccc}
 & E & \quad E \\
\text{LCL} = & \text{Point} & \text{UCL} = \\
\text{point estimate} - E & \text{estimate} & \text{point estimate} + E
\end{array}
$$

 FLASH REVIEW

Determine whether each of the following is a point estimate or interval estimate, and state the parameter of interest.

1. A researcher estimates that the average age of college students in the United States is between 22 and 26 years.

2. The researcher also estimates that the standard deviation of the age of college students in the United States is 5.2 years.

CHAPTER 7—One Population

Section 7.1—Population Mean

FLASH SUMMARY

The mean of a population is one of the most frequently estimated parameters. The point estimator of the population mean μ is the sample mean $\overline{X}$. The sample mean is used because it is an unbiased estimator. An unbiased estimator has the property that its expected value is equal to the value of the parameter: $E(\overline{X}) = \mu$. Recall that the mean of the sampling distribution of the sample mean is $\mu_{\overline{X}} = \mu$, and the expected value is equal to the mean of the distribution. In other words, an unbiased estimator is one that neither underestimates nor overestimates the parameter systematically.

Problems requesting a point estimate for μ may be stated in the following ways: "Estimate the mean," "Calculate an estimate of the mean," or "Find the point estimate of the mean." For example, suppose Professor Rice wants to estimate the average GPA of her statistics students. She takes a random sample of five students and finds the GPAs of the students to be 3.1, 2.8, 3.7, 3.2, and 2.6. Her estimate of the average GPA of her statistics students would be:

$$\overline{x} = \frac{\sum x}{n} = \frac{15.4}{5} = 3.08 \text{ points.}$$

Confidence intervals on the population mean follow the general form given in Chapter 6:

$(1 - \alpha)100\%$ confidence interval = the value of the point estimate
$\pm$ (the critical value)(the standard error of the estimate). Thus, confidence intervals on the population mean have the form

$(1 - \alpha)100\%$ confidence interval on $\mu = \overline{X} \pm$ (the critical value)(the standard error of the estimate). The critical value and the standard error of the estimate depend on what assumptions can be met. For the confidence intervals in this section, it will be assumed that samples are random, the data are measured at the interval or ratio level, and the random variable X has a normal distribution. The other assumptions for these intervals relate to the population standard deviation and the sample size. The table at the end of the Flash Summary section can be helpful in identifying which confidence interval formula is appropriate for a given situation.

The first confidence interval considered assumes that the value of the population standard deviation is known. The interval is then constructed based on the knowledge that the distribution of $\overline{X}$ is normal with $\mu_{\overline{X}} = \mu$ and $\sigma_{\overline{X}} = \frac{\sigma}{\sqrt{n}}$. For a $(1 - \alpha)100\%$ confidence interval on μ,

$$P\left(-z_{\frac{\alpha}{2}} < Z < z_{\frac{\alpha}{2}}\right) = P\left(-z_{\frac{\alpha}{2}} < \frac{\overline{X} - \mu_{\overline{X}}}{\sigma_{\overline{X}}} < z_{\frac{\alpha}{2}}\right) = 1 - \alpha$$

where $z_{\frac{\alpha}{2}}$ is the critical value from the normal standard distribution. Some texts use the notation z_c or z_α for the critical value. The likely values for $\overline{X}$ are close to the mean and fall in the area between $-z_{\frac{\alpha}{2}}$ and $z_{\frac{\alpha}{2}}$, whereas unlikely values fall outside this area.

The confidence interval formula is derived from this probability by algebraically manipulating the quantity $\left(-z_{\frac{\alpha}{2}} < \frac{\overline{X} - \mu_{\overline{X}}}{\sigma_{\overline{X}}} < z_{\frac{\alpha}{2}}\right)$ and substituting μ for $\mu_{\overline{X}}$.

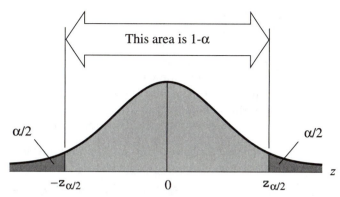

This yields the formula $(1 - \alpha)100\%$ confidence interval on $\mu = \overline{X} \pm z_{\frac{\alpha}{2}} \cdot \sigma_{\overline{X}}$. where $\sigma_{\overline{X}} = \dfrac{\sigma}{\sqrt{n}}$.

Because the interval is constructed based on the sampling distribution of the sample mean, the interpretation of the resulting interval is based on that probability, and NOT on the probability that the value of the population mean is between two specific values. Keep in mind that μ is not a random variable; it has a single value that is unknown because the entire population was not measured. The probability that μ lies between the lower confidence limit and the upper confidence limit is zero if μ is outside the limits and one if μ is inside the limits. The confidence level refers to the probability that the single interval that was calculated from the sample that was actually taken is one of the $(1 - \alpha)100\%$ confidence intervals that would contain the actual value of μ if repeated samples were taken. A common interpretation reads as follows: "We are $[(1 - \alpha)100]\%$ confident that the true average [context] is between [LCL] and [UCL] [units]." The information inside the square brackets is taken from the statement of the problem and the calculation of the confidence interval. For example, "We are 95% confident that the true average cost of a new car is between \$15,000 and \$20,000."

Problems requesting a confidence interval estimate of μ are often stated: "Estimate the population mean with 90% confidence," "Construct a 99% confidence interval for the population average," or "Find a 95% interval estimate for the population mean." Note that a confidence level must be given.

Consider the previous example in which Professor Rice is estimating the average GPA. She assumes that GPAs are normally distributed and that the standard deviation of the population of GPAs is 0.5 points. She now wants to estimate the average GPA of her statistics students with 90% confidence. Because the population standard deviation is known, the formula for the interval would be:

$$(1 - \alpha)100\% \text{ confidence interval on } \mu = \overline{X} \pm z_{\frac{\alpha}{2}} \cdot \sigma_{\overline{X}}.$$

The critical value (from the standard normal probability table) and the standard error of the estimate are:

$$z_{\frac{\alpha}{2}} = z_{0.05} = 1.645 \text{ and}$$

$$\sigma_{\overline{X}} = \dfrac{\sigma}{\sqrt{n}} = \dfrac{0.5}{\sqrt{5}} = 0.224$$

to three decimal places (0.223606797 to nine decimal places). Note that some instructors discourage rounding values until the final answer is reached so that rounding error is not accumulated when a rounded calculation is used to calculate another value. Then the

$$90\% \text{ confidence interval on } \mu = \overline{X} \pm z_{\frac{\alpha}{2}} \cdot \sigma_{\overline{X}} = 3.08 \pm (1.645)(0.223606797)$$

$$= (2.712, 3.448)$$

to three decimal places. The margin of error is $E = (1.645)(0.223606797) = 0.367833182$. Hence, the confidence limits are LCL $= 3.08 - 0.367833182 = 2.712$ and UCL $= 3.08 + 0.367833182 = 3.448$ (each to three decimal places).

The interpretation of the interval would be: "We are 90% confident that the true average GPA of Professor Rice's statistics students is between 2.712 and 3.448 points."

The first confidence interval assumes that the value of the population standard deviation for the random variable X is known. However, in practice, it is unlikely that the value of σ is known if the value of μ is unknown. The second confidence interval assumes that the value of σ is unknown but that the sample size is large. For large samples, the sample standard deviation, s, is a good estimator of the population standard deviation, σ. Because the distribution of $\overline{X}$ is approximately normal with $\mu_{\overline{X}} = \mu$ and $\sigma_{\overline{X}} = \dfrac{\sigma}{\sqrt{n}}$ for large n, and s is a good estimate of σ, it is still reasonable to use the standard normal distribution for the quantity $\dfrac{\overline{X} - \mu_{\overline{X}}}{s_{\overline{X}}}$. Substituting s for σ, the formula for the confidence interval is:

$$(1 - \alpha)100\% \text{ confidence interval on } \mu = \overline{X} \pm z_{\frac{\alpha}{2}} \cdot s_{\overline{X}} \text{ where } s_{\overline{X}} = \frac{s}{\sqrt{n}}.$$

Suppose Professor Westfall is interested in estimating the average GPA of his statistics students with 95% confidence. He assumes that the population of GPAs are normally distributed and takes a random sample of 50 students. He finds the average GPA of the sample to be 2.83 points with a standard deviation of 0.72 points. Then:

$$z_{\frac{\alpha}{2}} = z_{0.025} = 1.96,$$

$$s_{\overline{X}} = \frac{s}{\sqrt{n}} = \frac{0.72}{\sqrt{50}} = 0.101823376, \text{ and the}$$

$$95\% \text{ confidence interval on } \mu = \overline{X} \pm z_{\frac{\alpha}{2}} \cdot s_{\overline{X}} = 2.83 \pm (1.96)(0.101823376)$$

$$\doteq (2.630, 3.030).$$

The interpretation of this interval would read, "We are 95% confident that the true average GPA of Professor Westfall's statistics students is between 2.63 and 3.03 points."

If the value of the population standard deviation is unknown and the sample size is small, the quantity $\dfrac{\overline{X} - \mu_{\overline{X}}}{s_{\overline{X}}}$ is best described by a t distribution rather than by a standard normal distribution. Recall from Unit 2 that t distributions are bell-shaped, symmetric about the mean of zero, and approach the standard normal distribution as n gets very large. In fact, the previous confidence interval can be thought of as estimating the confidence interval used when σ is unknown and n is small. A t distribution has one parameter, called degrees of freedom (df), where $df = n - 1$. This is the only parameter needed to identify which t distribution is appropriate because $\mu = 0$ for all t distributions, and the standard deviation is a function of the degrees of freedom. The critical values for these confidence intervals are found on the t distribution probability table and are commonly denoted $t_{\frac{\alpha}{2}, df}$, $t_{c, df}$, or $t_{\frac{\alpha}{2}}(df)$. Be sure to read the instructions in your text for using the table. Using a t critical value rather than a z critical value, the formula for the confidence interval is:

$$(1 - \alpha)100\% \text{ confidence interval on } \mu = \overline{X} \pm t_{\frac{\alpha}{2}, df} \cdot s_{\overline{X}} \text{ where } s_{\overline{X}} = \frac{s}{\sqrt{n}}.$$

Suppose Professor Lucas is interested in estimating the average GPA of his statistics students with 99% confidence. He assumes that the population of GPAs are normally distributed and takes a random sample of 10 students. He finds the average GPA of the sample to be 2.68 points with a standard deviation of 1.02 points. Then:

$$t_{\frac{\alpha}{2}, df} = t_{0.005, 9} = 3.250,$$

$$s_{\overline{X}} = \frac{s}{\sqrt{n}} = \frac{1.02}{\sqrt{10}} = 0.322552321, \text{ and the}$$

$$99\% \text{ confidence interval on } \mu = \overline{X} \pm t_{\frac{\alpha}{2}, df} \cdot s_{\overline{X}} = 2.68 \pm (3.25)(0.322552321)$$

$$= (1.632, 3.728).$$

The interpretation of this interval would read, "We are 95% confident that the true average GPA of Professor Lucas's statistics students is between 1.632 and 3.728 points."

Note that higher confidence levels have larger critical values and, therefore, wider intervals. In addition, larger samples yield smaller standard errors and lead to narrower confidence intervals.

Some textbook exercises provide information about the confidence interval and ask that the student find such values as the point estimate, the width of the interval, the margin of error, and the standard error of the estimate. If the confidence limits are given, the point estimate can be found by averaging the endpoints because the point estimate is at the center of the interval. The width can be found by finding the distance between the confidence limits, and the margin of error can be found by dividing the width by two because E is the distance between the point estimate (the center) and each endpoint. If the confidence level is given in addition to the confidence limits, the standard error of the estimate can be calculated by dividing the margin of error by the critical value. The standard deviation can only be found if the sample size is given.

The three preceding confidence interval examples ask for the construction of a confidence interval after a random sample has been taken and the mean and standard deviation of the sample have been calculated. However, a researcher may want to know what size sample should be selected for a given confidence level and given margin of error. Assuming the value of the population standard deviation is known, the margin of error is:

$$E = z_{\frac{\alpha}{2}} \cdot \sigma_{\overline{X}} = z_{\frac{\alpha}{2}} \cdot \frac{\sigma}{\sqrt{n}} \quad \text{and}$$

$$n = \frac{z_{\frac{\alpha}{2}}^2 \cdot \sigma}{E^2}$$

This is the smallest sample size necessary for the given confidence level with the given margin of error, thus the answer should be rounded UP to the nearest whole number. If the value of σ is unknown, the value of s cannot be used for an estimate because the sample has not yet been selected. Common methods of estimating the population standard deviation to estimate the sample size include using a sample standard deviation from a previous study, conducting a small pilot study to obtain a value for s, and using $\hat{\sigma} = \dfrac{Range}{4}$ where $\hat{\sigma}$ (pronounced "sigma-hat") is the estimated standard deviation and *Range* is the range of the data in the population.

Suppose Professor Rice wanted to determine the sample size needed to be 95% confident that her estimate of the average GPA of her statistics students is within 0.5 points of the population mean. It was stated previously that the population standard deviation of GPAs is 0.5. The word "within" indicates the margin of error. Then:

$$n = \frac{z_{\frac{\alpha}{2}}^2 \cdot \sigma^2}{E^2} = \frac{1.96^2 \cdot 0.5^2}{0.25^2} = 15.3664.$$

Selecting the appropriate estimator for the population mean

Q: Point estimate or interval estimate?	Point	$\overline{X}$				
	Interval	Q: Is the value of σ known?	Yes	$\overline{X} \pm z_{\frac{\alpha}{2}} \cdot \sigma_{\overline{X}}$		
			No	Q: Is $n \geq 30$	Yes	$\overline{X} \pm z_{\frac{\alpha}{2}} \cdot s_{\overline{X}}$
					No	$\overline{X} \pm t_{\frac{\alpha}{2}, df} \cdot s_{\overline{X}}$ where $df = n - 1$

Rounding up to the nearest whole number, Professor Rice should take a random sample of 16 students for a 95% confidence interval with a margin of error of 0.5.

FLASH REVIEW

1. A statistics instructor wants to estimate the average number of hours her students spend studying for the first exam, assuming study time is normally distributed. She takes a random sample of 10 students and records the number of hours they report having studied the week prior to the first exam: 2.1, 3.5, 4.4, 5.3, 6.0, 6.5, 6.5, 6.8, 7.4, 8.2.

   a. Estimate the average study time for the instructor's statistics students.

   b. Estimate the average study time for the instructor's statistics students with 95% confidence.

   c. Interpret the interval you calculated in part b.

2. A prospective home buyer wants to estimate the average cost of a three bedroom home in Cole County. He takes a random sample of 50 three bedroom homes and finds the mean be $51,000 with a standard deviation of $9,500. Estimate the average cost of a three bedroom home in Cole County with 99% confidence.

3. IQ scores as measured on the Wechsler Adult Intelligence Scale are normally distributed with a standard deviation of 15 points. An instructor wants to estimate the average IQ of students enrolled at Connor College. A random sample of 25 students has a mean IQ score of 117 with a standard deviation of 12. Estimate the average IQ score of Connor College students with 90% confidence.

4. Suppose the instructor in Problem 3 wanted to estimate the average IQ score of students enrolled at Connor College to within 5 points with 99% confidence. How large a sample should be selected?

Section 7.2—Population Proportion

FLASH SUMMARY

Another commonly estimated parameter is the population proportion. Proportions arise in the context of binomial experiments. A characteristic of interest is defined, and each experimental unit in the population either has the characteristic (success) or does not have the characteristic (failure). The population proportion, denoted in most texts as p or π, is defined to be the ratio between the number of experimental units in the population with the characteristic of interest to the total number of experimental units:

$$p = \frac{\text{the number of successes in the population}}{N}.$$

This is consistent with the parameter p for the binomial distribution as it was discussed in Unit 2.

The sample proportion, denoted $\hat{p}$, is used for the point estimator of the population proportion. The sample proportion is the ratio of the number of experimental units with the characteristic of interest in the sample to the total sample size:

$$\hat{p} = \frac{\text{the number of successes in the sample}}{n}.$$

Note that the value of both p and $\hat{p}$ must be between zero and one inclusive.

As stated in Section 7.1, the confidence intervals in this chapter assume at least interval level measurement of the data. It would seem that this type of confidence interval could not be constructed for the population proportion because it is based on nominal level data. However, the normal distribution can be used to approximate the binomial distribution if $np \geq 5$ and $n(1 - p) \geq 5$. Therefore, this approximation can generally be used for large samples. Confidence interval estimates on the population proportion when these assumptions are not met are beyond the scope of most introductory statistics courses. Using the normal approximation to the binomial, a

$$(1 - \alpha)100\% \text{ confidence interval on } p = \hat{p} \pm z_{\frac{\alpha}{2}} \cdot s_{\hat{p}} \text{ where } s_{\hat{p}} = \sqrt{\frac{\hat{p}(1 - \hat{p})}{n}}.$$

Note that $1 - \hat{p}$ is the probability of a failure and is denoted by $\hat{q}$ in many texts.

The interpretation of this confidence interval is very similar to the interpretation for confidence intervals on the population mean. A general statement might read, "We are $[(1 - \alpha)100]\%$ confident that the true proportion [context] is between [LCL] and [UCL]." The information inside the brackets is taken from the statement of the problem and the calculation of the confidence interval. Note that there are no units for proportions.

Suppose a researcher wants to estimate the proportion of NRA members who are male. A random sample of 100 members is selected, and it is determined that 83 of the members sampled are male. The point estimate of p would be

$$\hat{p} = \frac{83}{100} = 0.83.$$

If the researcher wanted to estimate the percentage of NRA members who are male, the proportion can be converted to a percentage: $(0.83)100\% = 83\%$. A 95% confidence interval for the proportion of NRA members who are male would be calculated with

$$z_{\frac{\alpha}{2}} = z_{0.025} = 1.96 \text{ and}$$

$$s_{\hat{p}} = \sqrt{\frac{\hat{p}(1 - \hat{p})}{n}} = \sqrt{\frac{(0.83)(0.27)}{100}} = 0.047339201.$$

Then the

$$95\% \text{ confidence interval on } p = \hat{p} \pm z_{\frac{\alpha}{2}} \cdot s_{\hat{p}} = 0.83 \pm (1.96)(0.047339201)$$

$$= (0.737, 0.923).$$

The interpretation of this interval would be, "We are 95% confident that the true proportion of NRA members who are male is between 0.737 and 0.923." A confidence interval for the percentage of NRA members who are male must be calculated using the sample proportion and then converting the confidence limits to percentages.

The sample size necessary to estimate the population proportion for a given confidence level and given margin of error can be calculated using

$$n = \frac{z_{\frac{\alpha}{2}}^2 \cdot p(1 - p)}{E^2}.$$

However, p is unknown and $\hat{p}$ cannot be used as an estimator because the sample has not yet been selected. Estimates of p may be obtained from previous studies or pilot studies. An alternative estimate is to use $\hat{p} = 0.5$ because this gives a more conservative sample size. In this context, conservative means large; using $\hat{p} = 0.5$ generates the largest possible sample size for the given confidence level and margin of error. Hence, the formula to calculate the sample size would be:

$$n = \frac{z_{\frac{\alpha}{2}}^2 \cdot \hat{p}(1 - \hat{p})}{E^2}.$$

Suppose the researcher in the previous examples wants to determine the sample size necessary to estimate the proportion of male NRA members to within 0.1 with 90% confidence. Because an estimate for p was not given in the statement of the problem, $\hat{p} = 0.5$ is used and:

$$n = \frac{z_{\frac{\alpha}{2}}^2 \cdot \hat{p}(1 - \hat{p})}{E^2} = \frac{1.645^2 \cdot (0.5)(0.5)}{0.1^2} = 67.650625$$

This value is rounded up to the next whole number, thus the necessary sample size is $n = 68$.

Selecting the appropriate estimator for the population proportion

Q: Point estimate or interval estimate?	Point	$\hat{p}$		
	Interval	Q: Is $n \geq 30$?	Yes	$\hat{p} \pm z_{\frac{\alpha}{2}} \cdot s_{\hat{p}}$
			No	beyond the scope of the course

FLASH REVIEW

1. A researcher is interested in the proportion of left-handed students at Connor College. She takes a random sample of 200 students and finds that 24 of these students are left-handed.

   a. Estimate the proportion of left-handed students at Connor College.

   b. If there are 6,425 students enrolled at Connor College, estimate the number of those students who are left-handed.

   c. Estimate the proportion of left-handed students at Connor College with 90% confidence.

2. A campaign manager for a mayoral candidate is going to conduct an exit poll at noon on election day to estimate the proportion of people voting for the manager's candidate. He wants to estimate the proportion to within 3% with 95% confidence.

   a. Determine the sample size necessary if no previous estimate for the proportion is available.

   b. Determine the sample size necessary if the campaign manager uses the estimate $\hat{p} = 0.72$ from a poll conducted a month prior to the election.

Section 7.3—Linear Relationships Between Two Variables

FLASH SUMMARY

Often, a researcher will want to describe the relationship between variables measured on the same experimental unit. For example, one might suspect that there is a relationship between an individual's height and weight. Frequently, researchers will explore the linear relationship between an explanatory variable (X) and a response variable (Y). Recall that the scatterplots discussed in Unit 1 presented pictures of the linear relationships between two variables. Statistical methods are available that quantify these relationships and allow for prediction of the response variable based on the linear relationship between X and Y. In other words, if there is a linear relationship between X and Y, then knowing the value of X gives some indication of the value of Y.

A correlation coefficient allows us to calculate a number that describes the strength and direction of the linear relationship between the explanatory variable and the response variable. The assumptions made for parametric correlation coefficients are: (1) the data consists of two measurements on the same experimental unit, often written in the form (x, y); (2) at least interval-level measurement is used; and (3) both X and Y are normally distributed. The population correlation coefficient, denoted ρ, is a measure of the ratio of how X and Y vary together (called the covariance of X and Y) to how X and Y vary separately. The formula is:

$$\rho = \frac{Cov\,(X, Y)}{\sqrt{\sigma_X^2 \cdot \sigma_Y^2}} = \frac{\dfrac{\sum(x - \mu_X)(y - \mu_Y)}{N}}{\sqrt{\left(\dfrac{\sum(x - \mu_X)^2}{N}\right)\left(\dfrac{\sum(y - \mu_Y)^2}{N}\right)}} = \frac{\sum(x - \mu_X)(y - \mu_Y)}{\sqrt{\sum(x - \mu_X)^2 \cdot \sum(y - \mu_Y)^2}}$$

where N is the number of pairs of data in the population.

Note that $-1 \le \rho \le 1$. The sign on the correlation coefficient indicates the direction of the linear relationship, and the absolute value of the correlation coefficient (called the magnitude) indicates the strength. Two variables for which $\rho = 1$ are said to have a perfect positive linear relationship while $\rho = -1$ describes a perfect negative (or inverse) relationship. A value of zero for the population correlation coefficient means there is not a linear relationship between the two variables.

As with the population mean and the population proportion, the population correlation coefficient is rarely calculated because the entire population is rarely measured. The statistic from a random sample used to estimate ρ, denoted r, is called the Pearson product moment correlation coefficient, or Pearson's r for short. The ratio for r is constructed as follows:

$$r = \frac{\left(\dfrac{\sum(x - \bar{x})(y - \bar{y})}{n}\right)}{\sqrt{\left(\dfrac{\sum(x - \bar{x})^2}{n}\right)\left(\dfrac{\sum(y - \bar{y})^2}{n}\right)}} = \frac{\sum(x - \bar{x})(y - \bar{y})}{\sqrt{\sum(x - \bar{x})^2 \cdot \sum(y - \bar{y})^2}}$$

where n is the number of data pairs in the sample. Recall from the calculation formula presented in Unit 1 that:

$$\sum(x - \bar{x})^2 = \sum x^2 - \frac{(\sum x)^2}{n}.$$

This quantity is called the sum of squares for X and is denoted SS_X. Then:

$$SS_Y = \sum y^2 - \frac{(\sum y)^2}{n}, \quad \text{and}$$

$$SS_{XY} = \sum xy - \frac{(\sum x)(\sum y)}{n}.$$

The quantity $\sum xy$ is called the sum of the cross-products. The calculation formula for the point estimate of the population correlation coefficient is:

$$r = \frac{SS_{XY}}{\sqrt{SS_X \cdot SS_Y}}.$$

Both SS_X and SS_Y must be non-negative; however, SS_{XY} may be negative, and thus r may be negative.

Values of r must be between -1 and 1 inclusive. Values close to -1 indicate a strong inverse linear relationship between X and Y, values close to zero indicate a weak linear relationship, and values close to $+1$ indicate a strong positive linear relationship. Note that r describes only **linear** relationships. X and Y could have a very strong curvilinear relationship and generate an r value close to zero. A general interpretation of r might be, "There appears to be a [strength], [direction] linear relationship between [X] and [Y]." The information in the brackets is taken from the statement of the problem and the calculation of r.

The following information is used for examples throughout the rest of this section. A personnel director of a very large company is interested in a possible linear relationship between the number of years of formal education an employee has completed (X) and the employee's annual salary (Y). Assume that in this company, years of education and annual salary are normally distributed. The personnel director takes a random sample of 15 employees; education (in years) and annual salary (in thousands of dollars) are recorded in the following table.

Employee	1	2	3	4	5	6	7	8	9	10	11	12	13	14	15
Education	8	10	12	12	12	13	13	14	15	16	16	16	18	20	22
Salary	12	16	22	20	25	24	26	25	31	30	35	42	49	47	53

Summary values are calculated:
$$\sum x = 217, \quad \sum x^2 = 3{,}331, \quad \sum y = 457, \quad \sum y^2 = 16{,}055, \quad \sum xy = 7{,}225.$$
The summary values are used to calculated the following quantities:
$$SS_X = \sum x^2 - \frac{(\sum x)^2}{n} = 3{,}331 - \frac{217^2}{15} = 191.7\overline{3},$$
$$SS_Y = \sum y^2 - \frac{(\sum y)^2}{n} = 16{,}055 - \frac{457^2}{15} = 2131.7\overline{3}, \text{ and}$$
$$SS_{XY} = \sum xy - \frac{(\sum x)(\sum y)}{n} = 7{,}225 - \frac{(217)(457)}{15} = 613.7\overline{3}.$$
The point estimate of the correlation coefficient for this data is:
$$r = \frac{SS_{XY}}{SS_X \cdot SS_Y} = \frac{613.7\overline{3}}{\sqrt{(191.7\overline{3})(2131.7\overline{3})}} = 0.959985033.$$

Because 0.960 (rounded to three decimal places) is close to $+1$, the interpretation would be, "There appears to be a strong, positive linear relationship between years of education and annual salary for employees of this large company."

The correlation coefficient r is strongly influenced by outliers and by the use of averages instead of raw data. The interpretation deals with **association** (the linear relationship) of the two variables, not with **causation.**

It is not necessary to designate which variable is the explanatory variable and which is the response variable in correlation. This designation is often made, however, because a moderate to strong linear relationship often leads the researcher to construct a regression equation to predict the value of the response variable based on the value of the explanatory variable. A regression equation is a mathematical description of the relationship between X and Y. If there is no relationship ($r = 0$), the mean of the y values is the best predicted value for y at any given value of $X = x$.

Simple linear regression deals with one response variable and one explanatory variable, whereas multiple linear regression deals with more than one explanatory variable. Only simple linear regression is discussed in this resource. The assumptions that must be met are: (1) the data consist of two measurements on the same experimental unit, often written in the form (x, y); (2) at least interval-level measurement is used; and (3) the distribution of Y is normal at each value of X.

Recall from algebra the equation of a line: $y = mx + b$ where m is the slope of the line and b is the y-intercept. In statistics, this equation for the line in the population is usually expressed as:
$$y = \beta_0 + \beta_1 x$$

where β_0 is the y-intercept and β_1 is the slope. Again, we will estimate the population parameters with statistics obtained from random samples. Symbols for the statistics vary from text to text. Common notations for the y-intercept include a, b_0, and $\hat{\beta}$; common notations for the slope include b, b_1, and $\hat{\beta}_1$. Because they are frequently used on calculators, the symbols a and b are used here to denote the y-intercept and the slope, respectively.

When a sample is taken and the pairs of data plotted, there are many different lines that could be drawn through the data points. The point estimates for the y-intercept and the slope are derived using the method of least squares. This method minimizes the distance between the data points and the line. A data point is designated by a pair of values (x, y); the value of y produced by the regression equation is denoted $\hat{y}$ or y'. The residual is the distance between y and $\hat{y}$. The method of least squares minimizes the sum of the squared residuals:

$$\sum(y - \hat{y})^2.$$

This method produces a line that passes through the mean of the distribution of possible Y values at each possible X value so the predicted values are averages. The estimated regression equation, also called the predication equation or prediction line, is $\hat{y} = a + bx$ where a is the point estimate of the y-intercept and b is the point estimates of the slope. The line will always pass through the point $(\bar{x}, \bar{y})$.

The formula for the point estimate of the slope is:

$$b = \frac{SS_{XY}}{SS_X}.$$

Note that b is a function of r where: $b = r\sqrt{\dfrac{SS_Y}{SS_X}}.$

Both the slope of the line and the correlation coefficient yield information about the linear relationship between X and Y. The slope of a line is defined as the ratio of the change in Y to the change in X; the interpretation of the point estimate of the slope of the regression line is based on this definition. Because the regression line is drawn through the mean of the y values at each x value, a common interpretation states, "For each additional [unit increase in X], [Y] [changes] by an average of [b] [units]." The [changes] bracket is filled in with either "increases" if the slope is positive or "decreases" if the slope is negative.

Consider the personnel director example. The point estimate of the slope of the regression line would be:

$$b = \frac{SS_{XY}}{SS_X} = \frac{613.7\overline{3}}{191.7\overline{3}} = 3.200973575.$$

The interpretation would read, "For each additional year of education, annual income increases by an average of \$3,200.97." An alternative statement would be, "For each additional year of education, we expect an employee's annual salary to increase by \$3,200.97."

The formula for the point estimate of the y-intercept is $a = \bar{y} - b\bar{x}$. The y-intercept is the y value from the regression equation where $x = 0$ (when $x = 0$, $y = a$). The interpretation is, "For no [units of X], we expect the value of [Y] to be [a]." However, one would interpret the y-intercept only when appropriate. Criteria for this interpretation are:

1) $x = 0$ makes sense, and

2) $x = 0$ is a value in the range of the sample data.

For the example:

$$a = \bar{y} - b\bar{x} = 30.4\overline{6} - (3.200973575)(14.4\overline{6}) = -15.84075106.$$

The value of the point estimate of the y-intercept would not be interpreted in this situation. The statement, "For no years of education, we expect an employee's annual salary to be −\$15,840.75," makes no sense. In addition, the value $x = 0$ was not included in the range of the sample data.

Confidence interval estimates may also be found for the slope and the y-intercept of the regression equation. Both of the these confidence intervals have a critical value from the t distribution with $df = n - 2$. The standard error of the estimated regression equation, s_e, is used to find the standard error of the point estimate of the y-intercept and the standard error of the point estimate of the slope. The calculation formula for the standard error of the estimate of the regression equation is:

$$s_e = \sqrt{\frac{SS_Y - bSS_{XY}}{n - 2}}.$$

The standard error of a and standard error of b, respectively, are:

$$s_a = s_e \sqrt{\frac{1}{n} + \frac{\bar{x}^2}{SS_X}}, \text{ and}$$

$$s_b = \frac{s_e}{\sqrt{SS_X}}.$$

The confidence interval formulas follow the general form:

$(1 - \alpha)100\%$ confidence interval on $\beta_0 = a \pm t_{\frac{\alpha}{2}, df} \cdot s_a$ and

$(1 - \alpha)100\%$ confidence interval on $\beta_1 = b \pm t_{\frac{\alpha}{2}, df} \cdot s_b$.

The interpretation of these intervals follows the same general form as for the confidence intervals on the mean and proportion.

Suppose the personnel director in the example wished to estimate the y-intercept and the slope of the regression line with 95% confidence. The critical value and the standard error of the estimated regression equation would be:

$$t_{\frac{\alpha}{2}, df} = t_{0.025, 13} = 2.160, \text{ and}$$

$$s_e = \sqrt{\frac{SS_Y - bSS_{XY}}{n - 2}} = \sqrt{\frac{2131.7\overline{3} - (3.200973575)(613.7\overline{3})}{13}} = 3.586182361.$$

Then:

$$s_a = s_e \sqrt{\frac{1}{n} + \frac{\bar{x}^2}{SS_X}} = (3.586182361) \sqrt{\frac{1}{15} + \frac{14.4\overline{6}^2}{191.7\overline{3}}} = 3.859448458, \text{ and the}$$

95% confidence interval on $\beta_0 = a \pm t_{\frac{\alpha}{2}, df} \cdot s_a = -15.84075106 \pm (2.16)(3.859448458)$

$$= (-24.177, -7.504).$$

The interpretation would be, "We are 95% confident that the true y-intercept of the regression equation is between -24.177 and -7.504." For the slope:

$$s_b = \frac{s_e}{\sqrt{SS_X}} = \frac{3.586182361}{\sqrt{191.7\overline{3}}} = 0.258990335, \text{ and the}$$

95% confidence interval $\beta_1 = b \pm t_{\frac{\alpha}{2}, df} \cdot s_b = 3.200973575 \pm (2.16)(0.258990335)$

$$= (2.642, 3.760).$$

This interval would be interpreted, "We are 95% confident that the true slope of the regression equation is between 2.642 and 3.76."

The estimated regression equation is of the form $\hat{y} = a + bx$. Any value of x between the smallest and largest values of x obtained in the sample data may be substituted into the equation to obtain a predicted value for y. Prediction for values less than the smallest value or greater than the largest value of x in the sample data is discouraged because the estimated regression equation is constructed using data within this interval. For the personnel manager example, the estimated regression line is

$$\hat{y} = 15.841 + 3.201x$$

(rounded to three decimal places), and predicted values of y may be obtained for values of $8 \leq x \leq 22$. The predicted value of y, $\hat{y}$, is a point estimate for the given x value; in fact, it is the mean of the distribution of possible Y values for that level of x. The interpretation of the point estimate of y is, "[Experimental units] with [units of X] will have an average of [units of Y]."

Suppose the personnel manager in the example wishes to estimate the annual salary of employees with 17 years of education. Substituting $x = 17$ into the regression equation:

$$\hat{y} = -15.841 + 3.201x = -15.841 + 3.201(17) = 38.576.$$

The personnel manager can state, "Employees with 17 years of education will have an average annual salary of \$38,576." Now consider estimating the annual salary for $x = 14$. The predicted value for y is:

$$\hat{y} = -15.841 + 3.201x = -15.841 + 3.201(14) = 28.973.$$

Thus, the predicted value of the annual salary is not equal to the value of 25 found in the sample. Also note that calculated answers for predicted values may vary slightly due to rounding error based on whether the full or rounded values of the estimates of the slope and y-intercept are used.

Confidence intervals on the value of y are called prediction intervals. These intervals must be calculated at a given value of x, often denoted x_0. The intervals follow the general form, have critical values from the t distribution with $df = n - 2$, and use the standard error of the estimated regression line to calculate the standard error of the predicted value:

$$s_{\hat{y}} = s_e \sqrt{1 + \frac{1}{n} + \frac{(x_0 - \bar{x})^2}{SS_X}}.$$

The formula for a

$$(1 - \alpha)100\% \text{ confidence interval on } y = \hat{y} \pm t_{\frac{\alpha}{2}, df} \cdot s_{\hat{y}}.$$

Suppose the personnel manager in the example wants to estimate the annual salary for employees with 17 years of education with 90% confidence. The critical value and standard error terms are:

$$t_{\frac{\alpha}{2}, df} = t_{0.05, 13} = 1.771, \text{ and}$$

$$s_{\hat{y}} = s_e \sqrt{1 + \frac{1}{n} + \frac{(x_0 - \bar{x})^2}{SS_X}} = (3.586182361)\sqrt{1 + \frac{1}{15} + \frac{(17 - 14.4\overline{6})^2}{191.7\overline{3}}}$$

$$= 3.761457565.$$

Then the 90% confidence interval on $y = \hat{y} \pm t_{\frac{\alpha}{2}, df} \cdot s_{\hat{y}} = 38.576 \pm (1.771)(3.761457565)$

$$= (31.9\overline{14}, 45.238),$$

and would be interpreted, "We are 90% confident that the true average salary of employees with 17 years of education is between \$31,589 and \$45,563."

The coefficient of determination is a statistic that helps to quantify how well the estimated regression equation predicts values of y. The total variation between the actual values of y and the predicted values can be divided into the variation that is accounted for by the linear relationship between X and Y and the variation that is not accounted for by this relationship. The unexplained variation can be due to random variation and/or variation that could be accounted for by linear relationships between the response variable and other explanatory variables. The coefficient of determination, r^2, is the proportion of the total variation that is accounted for by the linear relationship between the explanatory variable and the response variable considered in the regression equation. As implied by the notation r^2, the coefficient of determination is calculated by squaring the value of the correlation coefficient. Possible values for r^2 are between zero and one inclusive and are most often expressed as a percentage. The correlation coefficient for the personnel manager example was found to be $r = 0.960$; then $r^2 = 0.9216$, and approximately 92% of the variation in annual salaries can be accounted for by the linear relationship between annual salaries and years of education.

Parameter (Symbol)	Point Estimate	Confidence Interval
Correlation coefficient (ρ)	$r = \dfrac{SS_{XY}}{\sqrt{SS_X \cdot SS_Y}}$	
y-intercept (β_0)	$a = \bar{y} - b\bar{x}$	$a \pm t_{\frac{\alpha}{2}, df} \cdot s_a$ where $s_a = s_e \sqrt{\dfrac{1}{n} + \dfrac{\bar{x}^2}{SS_X}}$ and $df = n - 2$
Slope (β_1)	$b = \dfrac{SS_{XY}}{SS_X}$	$b \pm t_{\frac{\alpha}{2}, df} \cdot s_b$ where $s_b = \dfrac{s_e}{\sqrt{SS_X}}$ and $df = n - 2$

FLASH REVIEW

Daci did a project for an education class in which she explored a linear relationship between the number of hours that students study for the final exam in statistics (X) and the students' final exam grades (Y). She took a random sample of 10 statistics students and recorded the number of study hours and their final exam grade for each.

Student	1	2	3	4	5	6	7	8	9	10
Hours	0	7.1	3.5	2.6	5.4	6.0	1.7	5.8	4.2	6.5
Grade	43	89	74	68	86	92	55	85	80	97

1. Calculate the correlation coefficient for study time and exam grade. Interpret this value in the context of the problem.

2. Find the point estimates for the y-intercept and the slope, and use these values to write the estimated regression equation.

3. Interpret the values of the point estimates of the y-intercept and slope.

4. Estimate the values of the y-intercept and slope with 95% confidence.

5. Predict the final exam grade for students who study five hours.

6. Predict the final exam grade for students who study for five hours with 90% confidence.

CHAPTER 8—TWO POPULATIONS

Section 8.1—Difference Between Two Population Means

FLASH SUMMARY

In Chapter 7, point and interval estimates on the parameter μ are discussed. For instance, an instructor might want to estimate the average score on the first exam for students in a class. This chapter considers situations in which the parameter to be estimated is the difference between two population means, denoted $\mu_1 - \mu_2$.

In this case, X_1 is the random variable for the first population, and is the random variable for the second population. The following assumptions are made:

1. samples are random;

2. X_1 and X_2 are measured at the interval or ratio level; and

3. X_1 is normally distributed with a mean of μ_1 and a standard deviation of σ_1, and X_2 is normally distributed with a mean of μ_2 and a standard deviation of σ_2.

Then $\overline{X}_1$ is normally distributed with a mean of μ_1 and a standard error of $\sigma_{\overline{X}_1} = \dfrac{\sigma_1}{\sqrt{n_1}}$,

and $\overline{X}_2$ is normally distributed with a mean of μ_2 and a standard error of $\sigma_{\overline{X}_2} = \dfrac{\sigma_2}{\sqrt{n_2}}$.

One random sample is taken from each of the populations under consideration. The relationship between the samples determines the method by which the estimate of $\mu_1 - \mu_2$ is calculated. Dependent samples consist of paired or matched data in which there is a reason for a particular observation in the sample from the first population to be paired with a particular observation in the sample from the second population. A common example of dependent samples is a study in which two measurements are taken on the same experimental unit, one prior to treatment and one following treatment. Unless there is an obvious reason for matching data from the two samples, the samples are considered to be independent.

Suppose an instructor wants to estimate the average difference in scores between the first exam and the second exam for students in a class. If the instructor takes a random sample of 10 first-exam scores then takes a random sample of 10 second-exam scores, the samples are independent because there is no reason to match a particular observation from the first sample with a particular observation from the second sample. However, if the instructor takes a random sample of 10 students and records both the first- and second-exam scores for each student, the samples are dependent. The first-exam score for Student 1 would be paired with the second-exam score for Student 1.

If samples are dependent, the parameter of interest, $\mu_1 - \mu_2$, is often denoted μ_D. Both point and interval estimates of μ_D are very similar to the estimates for one population mean as the differences between the two sample values are utilized. The difference for each pair is found, then the mean ($\overline{X}_D$) and standard deviation (S_D) of the differences are calculated. The point estimator for μ_D is $\overline{X}_D$ and a

$$(1 - \alpha)100\% \text{ confidence interval on } \mu_D = \overline{X}_D \pm t_{\frac{\alpha}{2}, df_D} \cdot s_{\overline{X}_D}$$

where the standard error of $\overline{X}_D$ is $s_{\overline{X}_D} = \dfrac{s_D}{\sqrt{n_D}}$,

n_D is the number of data pairs, and $df_D = n_D - 1$.

Consider the example of estimating the average difference between scores on Exam 1 and Exam 2 in which a random sample of 10 students is selected.

Student	1	2	3	4	5	6	7	8	9	10
Exam 1	56	71	76	68	76	85	83	81	90	98
Exam 2	54	65	78	71	75	79	86	88	86	95

The first step is to calculate the difference between the score on Exam 1 and Exam 2 for each student. The order of subtraction does not matter as long as the order remains the same for each student, although in some situations the subtraction makes more sense in one direction than in the other. The differences produced by taking Exam 1 − Exam 2 are:

Student	1	2	3	4	5	6	7	8	9	10
Difference	2	6	−2	−3	1	6	−3	−7	4	3

The statistics are calculated using this set of differences—the original scores are ignored—so the estimation problem now looks just like a one population situation. The mean and standard deviation of the set of sample differences are:

$$\overline{X}_D = 0.7 \text{ and}$$
$$s_D = 4.321779469.$$

The point estimate of μ_D is:

$$\overline{X}_D = 0.7$$

The critical value needed to estimate the average difference in the population means with 95% confidence is:

$$t_{\frac{\alpha}{2}, df_D} = t_{0.0.25, 9} = 2.262,$$

and the standard error terms is:

$$s_{\overline{X}_D} = \frac{s_D}{\sqrt{n_D}} = \frac{4.321779469}{\sqrt{10}} = 1.3\overline{6}.$$

Then the 95% confidence interval on $\mu_D = \overline{X}_D \pm t_{\frac{\alpha}{2}, df_D} \cdot s_{\overline{X}_D} = 0.7 \pm (2.262)(1.3\overline{6})$
$$= (-2.391, 3.791).$$

We are 95% confident that the true average difference in scores between Exam 1 and Exam 2 is between −2.391 and 3.791 points. Note that the LCL is negative, whereas the UCL is positive. This indicates that some students score better on the first exam, whereas others score better on the second exam.

If the samples are independent, a random sample of size n_1 is taken from the first population, and a separate random sample of size n_2 is selected from the second population. The point estimate of $\mu_1 - \mu_2$ is $\overline{X}_1 - \overline{X}_2$. The quantity $\overline{X}_1 - \overline{X}_2$ is normally distributed with a mean of $\mu_1 - \mu_2$ and standard error of:

$$\sigma_{\overline{X}_1 - \overline{X}_2} = \sqrt{\frac{\sigma_1^2}{n_1} + \frac{\sigma_2^2}{n_2}}.$$

As in the previous chapter, the critical value and standard error term depend on the assumptions made about the values of the population standard deviations and the sample sizes. If the values of both population standard deviations are known, the critical value comes from the distribution of Z, and the standard error term uses the known values for the standard deviation. The formula for a

$$(1 - \alpha)100\% \text{ confidence interval on } \mu_1 - \mu_2 = (\overline{X}_1 - \overline{X}_2) \pm z_{\frac{\alpha}{2}} \cdot \sigma_{\overline{X}_1 - \overline{X}_2}.$$

However, in practical situations, it is extremely rare that both the values of σ_1 and σ_2 will be known if the values of the population means are unknown.

If the values of one or both of the population standard deviations are unknown, but both samples are large ($n_1 \geq 30$ **and** $n_2 \geq 30$), the values of the sample standard deviations can be substituted into the formula for calculating the standard error of $\overline{X}_1 - \overline{X}_2$ to find the estimated standard error term

$$s_{\overline{X}_1 - \overline{X}_2} = \sqrt{\frac{s_1^2}{n_1} + \frac{s_2^2}{n_2}}.$$

Then a $(1 - \alpha)100\%$ confidence interval on $\mu_1 - \mu_2 = (\overline{X}_1 - \overline{X}_2) \pm z_{\frac{\alpha}{2}} \cdot s_{\overline{X}_1 - \overline{X}_2}$.

Consider the previous example of estimating the average difference in scores between Exam 1 and Exam 2. Now assume that a random sample of 50 Exam 1 scores and a random sample of 50 Exam 2 scores were selected. The average score from the Exam 1 sample was 75.2 with a standard deviation of 11.3; the average score from the Exam 2 sample was 70.4 with a standard deviation of 13.6. The point estimate of the average difference in exam scores is $\overline{X}_1 - \overline{X}_2 = 75.2 - 70.4 = 4.8$.

Suppose an estimate of $\mu_1 - \mu_2$ with 90% confidence is desired. The critical value and the standard error of the point estimate are:

$$z_{\frac{\alpha}{2}} = z_{0.05} = 1.645 \text{ and}$$

$$s_{\overline{X}_1 - \overline{X}_2} = \sqrt{\frac{s_1^2}{n_1} + \frac{s_2^2}{n_2}} = \sqrt{\frac{11.3^2}{50} + \frac{13.6^2}{50}} = 2.500599928.$$

Then the

$$90\% \text{ confidence interval on } \mu_1 - \mu_2 = (\overline{X}_1 - \overline{X}_2) \pm z_{\frac{\alpha}{2}} \cdot s_{\overline{X}_1 - \overline{X}_2}$$
$$= 4.8 \pm (1.645)(2.500599928)$$
$$= (0.687, 8.913).$$

We are 90% confident that the true average difference in scores between Exam 1 and Exam 2 is between 0.687 and 8.913 points. Although equal sample sizes are used in this example, $n_1 = n_2$ is **not** an assumption that is made when using this confidence interval.

If the values of σ_1 and/or σ_2 are unknown, and one or both of the samples are small, more information about the relative sizes of the sample variances is needed. The critical value and standard error of $\overline{X}_1 - \overline{X}_2$ depend on whether $\sigma_1^2 = \sigma_2^2$ or $\sigma_1^2 \neq \sigma_2^2$. Because the values of σ_1 and/or σ_2 are unknown (hence the values of the population variances are also unknown), the determination of the equality or nonequality of the two population variances requires a hypothesis test. Because hypothesis testing is covered in the next unit, equality or nonequality of the two population variances is stated as an assumption for the remainder of this unit.

If $\sigma_1^2 \neq \sigma_2^2$, then s_1^2 is needed to estimate σ_1^2 and s_2^2 is needed to estimate σ_2^2. Then the standard error of $\overline{X}_1 - \overline{X}_2$ is:

$$s_{\overline{X}_1 - \overline{X}_2} = \sqrt{\frac{s_1^2}{n_1} + \frac{s_2^2}{n_2}}$$

just as it was in the previous interval. However, if $\sigma_1^2 = \sigma_2^2$, the quantities s_1^2 and s_2^2 can be combined to estimate a single value. The pooled variance estimate (s_{pooled}^2) is a weighted average of the sample variances, and the calculation formula is:

$$s_{pooled}^2 = \frac{(n_1 - 1)s_1^2 + (n_2 - 1)s_2^2}{n_1 + n_2 - 2}.$$

The pooled estimate is substituted for both s_1^2 and s_2^2 to calculate the standard error term:

$$\sqrt{\frac{s_1^2}{n_1} + \frac{s_2^2}{n_2}} = \sqrt{\frac{s_{pooled}^2}{n_1} + \frac{s_{pooled}^2}{n_2}} = s_{pooled}\sqrt{\frac{1}{n_1} + \frac{1}{n_2}}.$$

When the sample sizes are equal, the standard error term is the same whether or not the pooled variance estimate is used.

When the pooled variance estimate is used, the degrees of freedom associated with the standard error term can also be pooled, thus:

$$df = n_1 - 1 + n_2 - 1 = n_1 + n_2 - 2.$$

Note that this is the quantity in the denominator of the pooled variance estimate. If $\sigma_1^2 \neq \sigma_2^2$ the degrees of freedom are estimated. Let $df_1 = n_1 - 1$ for the first sample and $df_2 = n_2 - 1$ for the second sample. Some texts advise using the smaller of df_1 and df_2 as the estimate for the degrees of freedom associated with the confidence interval on $\mu_1 - \mu_2$. A better approximation is called the Satterthwaite approximation, denoted df'. The approximation is calculated:

$$df' = \frac{(n_1 - 1)(n_2 - 1)\left(\dfrac{s_1^2}{n_1} + \dfrac{s_2^2}{n_2}\right)^2}{(n_2 - 1)\left(\dfrac{s_1^2}{n_1}\right)^2 + (n_1 - 1)\left(\dfrac{s_2^2}{n_2}\right)^2}.$$

This value is rounded **down** to the nearest whole number.

The confidence interval formulas follow the general form. If $\sigma_1^2 = \sigma_2^2$, a

$$(1 - \alpha)100\% \text{ confidence interval on } \mu_1 - \mu_2 = (\overline{X}_1 - \overline{X}_2) \pm t_{\frac{\alpha}{2}, df'} \cdot s_{pooled}\sqrt{\frac{1}{n_1} + \frac{1}{n_2}}.$$

If $\sigma_1^2 \neq \sigma_2^2$, a

$$(1 - \alpha)100\% \text{ confidence interval on } \mu_1 - \mu_2 = (\overline{X}_1 - \overline{X}_2) \pm t_{\frac{\alpha}{2}, df'} \cdot s_{\overline{X}_1 - \overline{X}_2}.$$

Consider once again the previous example of estimating the average difference in scores between Exam 1 and Exam 2. Suppose that a random sample of 12 Exam 1 scores are selected and have a mean and standard deviation of 75 and 11, respectively. A random sample of 15 Exam 2 scores are selected and yield a mean and standard deviation of 70 and 13, respectively. We want to estimate the difference in the averages of exam scores with 90% confidence. In practice, it must be assumed either that $\sigma_1^2 = \sigma_2^2$ or that $\sigma_1^2 \neq \sigma_2^2$, not both. However, for the sake of comparison, the confidence interval for this example will be calculated both ways.

First assume that $\sigma_1^2 = \sigma_2^2$. Then:

$$df = n_1 + n_2 - 2 = 12 + 15 - 2 = 25,$$

$$t_{\frac{\alpha}{2}, df} = t_{0.05, 25} = 1.708,$$

$$s_{pooled}^2 = \frac{(n_1 - 1)s_1^2 + (n_2 - 1)s_2^2}{n_1 + n_2 - 2} = \frac{(11)(11^2) + (14)(13^2)}{25} = 147.88,$$

$$s_{pooled}\sqrt{\frac{1}{n_1} + \frac{1}{n_2}} = \sqrt{147.88} \cdot \sqrt{\frac{1}{12} + \frac{1}{15}} = 4.709777065, \text{ and the}$$

$$(1 - \alpha)100\% \text{ confidence interval on } \mu_1 - \mu_2 = (\overline{X}_1 - \overline{X}_2) \pm t_{\frac{\alpha}{2}, df} \cdot s_{pooled}\sqrt{\frac{1}{n_1} + \frac{1}{n_2}}$$

$$= 5 \pm (1.708)(4.709777065)$$
$$= (-3.044, 13.044).$$

Now assume that $\sigma_1^2 \neq \sigma_2^2$. Then:

$$df' = \frac{(n_1 - 1)(n_2 - 1)\left(\dfrac{s_1^2}{n_1} + \dfrac{s_2^2}{n_2}\right)^2}{(n_2 - 1)\left(\dfrac{s_1^2}{n_1}\right)^2 + (n_1 - 1)\left(\dfrac{s_2^2}{n_2}\right)^2} = \frac{(11)(14)\left(\dfrac{11^2}{12} + \dfrac{13^2}{15}\right)^2}{(14)\left(\dfrac{11^2}{12}\right)^2 + (11)\left(\dfrac{13^2}{15}\right)^2} = 24,$$

$$t_{\frac{\alpha}{2}, df} = t_{0.05, 24} = 1.711, s_{\overline{X}_1 - \overline{X}_2} = \sqrt{\frac{s_1^2}{n_1} + \frac{s_2^2}{n_2}} = \sqrt{\frac{11^2}{12} + \frac{13^2}{15}} = 4.620606021, \text{ and the}$$

$$(1 - \alpha)100\% \text{ confidence interval on } \mu_1 - \mu_2 = (\overline{X}_1 - \overline{X}_2) \pm t_{\frac{\alpha}{2}, df'} \cdot s_{\overline{X}_1 - \overline{X}_2}$$
$$= 5 \pm (1.711)(4.620606021)$$
$$= (-2.906, 12.906).$$

In this example, the number of degrees of freedom associated with the pooled variance estimate is larger than the estimated degrees of freedom when sample variances are not pooled. In fact, in all cases, $df' \leq n_1 + n_2 - 2$.

The standard error term with the pooled variance estimate is slightly larger than the standard error term calculated without pooling the sample variance. The greater the disparity in the sample variance values, the greater the difference in the standard error estimates.

Selecting the appropriate estimator for the difference between two population means

Part 1

Q: Point estimate or interval estimate ?	Point	Q: Are samples dependent ?	Yes	$\overline{X}_D$		
			No	$\overline{X}_1 - \overline{X}_2$		
	Interval	Q: Are samples dependent ?	Yes	$\overline{X}_D \pm t_{\frac{\alpha}{2}, df_D} \cdot s_{\overline{X}_D}$ where $df_D = n_D - 1$		
			No	Q: Are the values of σ_1 and σ_2 known?	Yes	$(\overline{X}_1 - \overline{X}_2) \pm z_{\frac{\alpha}{2}} \cdot \sigma_{\overline{X}_1 - \overline{X}_2}$
					No	See *Part 2*

Part 2

Q: Is $n_1 \geq 30$ **and** $n_2 \geq 30$?	Yes	$(\overline{X}_1 - \overline{X}_2) \pm z_{\frac{\alpha}{2}} \cdot \sigma_{\overline{X}_1 - \overline{X}_2}$		
	No	Q: Does $\sigma_1^2 = \sigma_2^2$? (Note: The method used to answer this question is discussed in Unit 4)	Yes	$(\overline{X}_1 - \overline{X}_2) \pm t_{\frac{\alpha}{2}, df} \cdot s_{pooled}\sqrt{\frac{1}{n_1} + \frac{1}{n_2}}$ where $df = n_1 + n_2 - 2$
			No	$(\overline{X}_1 - \overline{X}_2) \pm t_{\frac{\alpha}{2}, df'} \cdot s_{\overline{X}_1 - \overline{X}_2}$ where $df' = \dfrac{(n_1 - 1)(n_2 - 1)\left(\dfrac{s_1^2}{n_1} + \dfrac{s_2^2}{n_2}\right)^2}{(n_2 - 1)\left(\dfrac{s_1^2}{n_1}\right)^2 + (n_1 - 1)\left(\dfrac{s_2^2}{n_2}\right)^2}$

 FLASH REVIEW

1. A researcher wants to estimate the difference in the average of amount of time males and females spend watching television during a week. A random sample of 14 males had a mean watching time of 22.3 hours with a standard deviation of 6.7 hours. A

random sample of 16 females had a mean watching time of 16.7 hours with a standard deviation of 6.5 hours. Assume that the population variances are equal.

    a. Estimate the difference in average television-watching time of males and females.

    b. Estimate the difference in average television-watching time of males and females with 90% confidence.

2. A golf pro wants to estimate the average difference in golf scores for players before and after a golfing workshop. He randomly selected eight golfers, recorded the score of a round they shot the day before the workshop, then recorded the score of a round they shot the day after the workshop was completed. The results are in the following table:

Player	1	2	3	4	5	6	7	8
Before	68	72	79	80	83	89	91	93
After	70	71	73	82	76	81	85	90

Estimate the average difference in scores before and after the workshop with 99% confidence.

3. A clothing store owner wants to estimate the difference in the average amount spent per month on clothing between individuals who are 20 to 35 years of age and individuals who are 50 to 65 years of age. A random sample of 15 persons ages 20 to 35 spent an average of $165 per month on clothing with a standard deviation of $35. A random sample of 15 persons ages 50 to 65 years of age spent an average of $97 per month on clothing with a standard deviation of $12. Assuming the population variances are not equal, estimate the average difference in amount spent on clothing during one month with 95% confidence.

Section 8.2—Difference Between Two Population Proportions

FLASH SUMMARY

Another parameter of interest in estimation is the difference between two population proportions, $p_1 - p_2$. The point estimator is the difference of the sample proportions, $\hat{p}_1 - \hat{p}_2$. If both sample sizes are large, the normal approximation to the binomial can be used when constructing the confidence interval. The standard error of $\hat{p}_1 - \hat{p}_2$ is :

$$s_{\hat{p}_1 - \hat{p}_2} = \sqrt{\frac{\hat{p}_1(1 - \hat{p}_1)}{n_1} + \frac{\hat{p}_2(1 - \hat{p}_2)}{n_2}}.$$

Then the formula for a

$$(1 - \alpha)100\% \text{ on } p_1 - p_2 = (\hat{p}_1 - \hat{p}_2) \pm z_{\frac{\alpha}{2}} \cdot s_{\hat{p}_1 - \hat{p}_2}.$$

Assume a researcher wants to estimate with 90% confidence the difference in the proportions of males and females who are left-handed. Forty males were found to be left-handed in a random sample of 250 males, and there were 17 left-handed females in a random sample of 250 females. Then:

$$\hat{p}_1 = \frac{40}{250} = 0.16,$$

$$\hat{p}_2 = \frac{17}{250} = 0.068,$$

and the point estimate of $p_1 - p_2$ is $\hat{p}_1 - \hat{p}_2 = 0.16 - 0.068 = 0.092.$
The critical value and the standard error of $\hat{p}_1 - \hat{p}_2$ are

$$z_{\frac{\alpha}{2}} = z_{0.05} = 1.645 \text{ and}$$

$$s_{\hat{p}_1 - \hat{p}_2} = \sqrt{\frac{\hat{p}_1(1 - \hat{p}_1)}{n_1} + \frac{\hat{p}_2(1 - \hat{p}_2)}{n_2}} = \sqrt{\frac{(0.16)(0.84)}{250} + \frac{(0.068)(0.932)}{250}} = 0.028126571.$$

Then the 90% confidence interval on $p_1 - p_2 = (\hat{p}_1 - \hat{p}_2) \pm z_{\frac{\alpha}{2}} \cdot s_{\hat{p}_1 - \hat{p}_2}$

$$= 0.092 \pm (1.645)(0.028126571)$$

$$= (0.046, 0.138).$$

We are 90% confident that the true difference in the proportion of left-handers between males and females is between 0.046 and 0.138.

Selecting the appropriate estimator for the difference between two population proportions

Q: Point estimate or interval estimate?	Point	$\hat{p}_1 - \hat{p}_2$		
	Interval	Q: Is $n_1 \geq 30$ **and** $n_2 \geq 30$?	Yes	$(\hat{p}_1 - \hat{p}_2) \pm z_{\frac{\alpha}{2}} \cdot s_{\hat{p}_1 - \hat{p}_2}$
			No	beyond the scope of the course

 FLASH REVIEW

An instructor wants to estimate the difference in the proportions of juniors and seniors who had completed a course in statistics. Of 100 juniors selected randomly, 15 had completed a statistics course, whereas 25 of a random sample of 100 seniors had completed a course in statistics.

1. Estimate the difference in the proportions of juniors and seniors who have completed a statistics course.

2. Estimate the difference in the proportions of juniors and seniors who have completed a statistics course with 95% confidence.

Solutions to Flash Review Problems in Unit 3

Chapter 6—Fundamentals of Estimation

1. interval, μ

2. point, σ

Chapter 7—Section 7.1, Population Mean

1. **a.** the point estimate of μ is $\bar{x} = 5.67$

    b. the value of σ is not given, the sample is small,

    $$t_{0.025,9} = 2.262,$$
    $$s = 1.866696428,$$
    $$s_{\bar{X}} = \frac{s}{\sqrt{n}} = \frac{1.866696428}{\sqrt{10}} = 0.590301241,$$

    95% confidence interval on $\mu = \bar{X} \pm t_{\frac{\alpha}{2},df} \cdot s_{\bar{X}} = 5.67 \pm (2.262)(0.590301241)$
    $$= (4.335, 7.005)$$

    c. We are 95% confident that the true average study time for the statistics instructor's students is between 4.335 and 7.005 hours.

2. the value of σ is not given, the sample is large,

    $$z_{0.005} = 2.575,$$
    $$s_{\bar{X}} = \frac{s}{\sqrt{n}} = \frac{9500}{\sqrt{50}} = 1343.502884,$$

    99% confidence interval on $\mu = \bar{X} \pm z_{\frac{\alpha}{2}} \cdot s_{\bar{X}} = 51000 \pm (2.575)(1343.502884)$
    $$= (47540.48, 54459.52)$$

3. $z_{0.05} = 1.645,$

    $$\sigma = 15 \text{ so } \sigma_{\bar{X}} = \frac{\sigma}{\sqrt{n}} = \frac{15}{\sqrt{25}} = 3,$$

    90% confidence interval on $\mu = \bar{X} \pm z_{\frac{\alpha}{2}} \cdot \sigma_{\bar{X}} = 117 \pm (1.645)(3)$
    $$= (112.065, 121.935)$$

4. $n = \dfrac{z_{\frac{\alpha}{2}}^2 \cdot \sigma^2}{E^2} = \dfrac{2.575^2 \cdot 15^2}{5^2} = 59,675625$, thus a sample of $n = 60$ should be taken

Chapter 7—Section 7.2, Population Proportion

1. **a.** $\hat{p} = \dfrac{24}{200} = 0.12$

    b. the estimated number would be found by multiplying the estimated proportion by the size of the population, thus $\hat{p} \cdot N = (0.12)(6425) = 771$

    c. $z_{0.05} = 1.645,$

    $$s_{\hat{p}} = \sqrt{\frac{\hat{p}(1-\hat{p})}{n}} = \sqrt{\frac{(0.12)(0.88)}{200}} = 0.02297825,$$

    90% confidence interval on $p = \hat{p} \pm z_{\frac{\alpha}{2}} \cdot s_{\hat{p}} = 0.12 \pm (1.645)(0.02297825),$
    $$= (0.082, 0.158)$$

2. a. $n = \dfrac{z_{\frac{\alpha}{2}}^2 \cdot \hat{p}(1-\hat{p})}{E^2} = \dfrac{1.96^2 \cdot (0.5)(0.5)}{0.03^2} = 1067.\overline{1}$, thus $n = 1068$

b. $n = \dfrac{z_{\frac{\alpha}{2}}^2 \cdot \hat{p}(1-\hat{p})}{E^2} = \dfrac{1.96^2 \cdot (0.72)(0.28)}{0.03^2} = 860.5184$, thus $n = 861$

Chapter 7—Section 7.3, Linear Relationships Between Two Variables

$\sum x = 42.8,\quad \sum x^2 = 231,\quad \sum y = 769,\quad \sum y^2 = 61{,}789,\quad \sum xy = 3{,}637.1;$

$SS_X = \sum x^2 - \dfrac{(\sum x)^2}{n} = 231 - \dfrac{42.8^2}{10} = 47.816,$

$SS_Y = \sum y^2 - \dfrac{(\sum y)^2}{n} = 61{,}789 - \dfrac{769^2}{10} = 2{,}652.9,$

$SS_{XY} = \sum xy - \dfrac{(\sum x)(\sum y)}{n} = 3637.1 - \dfrac{(42.8)(769)}{10} = 345.78$

1. $r = \dfrac{SS_{XY}}{\sqrt{SS_X \cdot SS_Y}} = \dfrac{345.78}{\sqrt{(47.816)(2652.9)}} = 0.970851506$

There appears to be a strong positive linear relationship between study time and final exam score.

2. $b = \dfrac{SS_{XY}}{SS_X} = \dfrac{345.78}{47.816} = 7.231470637,$

$a = \bar{y} - b\bar{x} = 76.9 - (7.231470637)(4.28) = 45.94930567,$

$\hat{y} = a + bx = 45.949 + 7.231x$

3. Interpretation for a: For students who do not study, we expect the final exam score to be 45.949 points.

Interpretation for b: For each additional hour studied, final exam score increases by an average of 7.23 points

4. $t_{0.025,8} = 2.306,$

$s_e = \sqrt{\dfrac{SS_Y - bSS_{XY}}{n-2}} = \sqrt{\dfrac{2{,}652.9 - (7.231470637)(345.78)}{8}} = 4.364660398,$

$s_a = s_e\sqrt{\dfrac{1}{n} + \dfrac{\bar{x}^2}{SS_X}} = (4.364660398)\sqrt{\dfrac{1}{10} + \dfrac{4.28^2}{47.816}} = 3.033680407,$

$s_b = \dfrac{s_e}{\sqrt{SS_X}} = \dfrac{4.364660398}{\sqrt{47.816}} = 0.631195416,$

95% confidence interval on $\beta_0 = a \pm t_{\frac{\alpha}{2},df} \cdot s_a$

$\qquad\qquad = 45.94930567 \pm (2.306)(3.033680407)$

$\qquad\qquad = (38.945, 52.945),$

95% confidence interval on $\beta_1 = b \pm t_{\frac{\alpha}{2},df} \cdot s_b$

$\qquad\qquad = 7.231470637 \pm (2.306)(0.631195416)$

$\qquad\qquad = (5.776, 8.687)$

5. $\hat{y} = 45.949 + 7.231x = 45.949 + (7.231)(5) = 82.104$

6. $s_{\hat{y}} = s_e\sqrt{1 + \dfrac{1}{n} + \dfrac{(x_0 - \bar{x})^2}{SS_X}} = (4.364660398)\sqrt{1 + \dfrac{1}{10} + \dfrac{(5 - 4.28)^2}{47.816}}$

$\qquad = 4.600197926,$

$t_{0.05,8} = 1.860,$

90% confidence interval on $y = \hat{y} \pm t_{\frac{\alpha}{2},df} \cdot s_{\hat{y}}$

$$= 82.104 \pm (1.86)(4.600197926)$$
$$= (73.548, 90.660)$$

Chapter 8—Section 8.1, Difference Between Two Population Means

1. **a.** samples are independent, thus $\overline{X}_1 - \overline{X}_2 = 22.3 - 16.7 = 5.6$

   b. population variances values are unknown but equal, small samples,

   $df = n_1 + n_2 - 2 = 14 + 16 - 2 = 28$,

   $t_{0.05,28} = 1.701$,

   $s^2_{pooled} = \dfrac{(n_1 - 1)s_1^2 + (n_2 - 1)s_2^2}{n_1 + n_2 - 2} = \dfrac{(13)(6.7^2) + (15)(6.5^2)}{28} = 43.47571429$,

   90% confidence interval on $\mu_1 - \mu_2 = (\overline{X}_1 - \overline{X}_2) \pm t_{\frac{\alpha}{2},df} \cdot s_{pooled} \sqrt{\dfrac{1}{n_1} + \dfrac{1}{n_2}}$

   $$= 5.6 \pm (1.701)\left(\sqrt{43.47571429}\right)\left(\sqrt{\dfrac{1}{14} + \dfrac{1}{16}}\right)$$

   $$= (1.495, 9.705)$$

2. dependent samples; differences (before − after): $-2, 1, 6, -2, 7, 8, 6, 3$;

   $\overline{X}_D = 3.375$,

   $S_D = 3.997767234$,

   $df = n_D - 1 = 7$,

   $t_{0.005,7} = 3.500$,

   $s_{\overline{X}_D} = \dfrac{s_D}{\sqrt{n_D}} = \dfrac{3.997767234}{\sqrt{8}} = 1.41342416$,

   95% confidence interval on $\mu_D = \overline{X}_D \pm t_{\frac{\alpha}{2},df_D} \cdot s_{\overline{X}_D} = 3.375 \pm (3.5)(1.41342416)$

   $$= (-1.572, 8.322)$$

3. population variances values are unknown and not equal, small samples,

   $$df' = \dfrac{(n_1 - 1)(n_2 - 1)\left(\dfrac{s_1^2}{n_1} + \dfrac{s_2^2}{n_2}\right)^2}{(n_2 - 1)\left(\dfrac{s_1^2}{n_1}\right)^2 + (n_1 - 1)\left(\dfrac{s_2^2}{n_2}\right)^2} = \dfrac{(14)(14)\left(\dfrac{35^2}{15} + \dfrac{12^2}{15}\right)^2}{(14)\left(\dfrac{35^2}{15}\right)^2 + (14)\left(\dfrac{12^2}{15}\right)^2} = 17,$$

   $t_{0.025,17} = 2.110$, $s_{\overline{X}_1 - \overline{X}_2} = \sqrt{\dfrac{s_1^2}{n_1} + \dfrac{s_2^2}{n_2}} = \sqrt{\dfrac{35^2}{15} + \dfrac{12^2}{15}} = 9.553358921$,

   $\overline{X}_1 - \overline{X}_2 = 165 - 97 = 68$,

   95% confidence interval on $\mu_1 - \mu_2 = (\overline{X}_1 - \overline{X}_2) \pm t_{\frac{\alpha}{2},df'} \cdot s_{\overline{X}_1 - \overline{X}_2}$

   $$= 68 \pm (2.11)(9.553358921)$$

   $$= (47.842, 88.158)$$

Chapter 8—Section 8.2, Difference Between Two Population Proportions

1. $\hat{p}_1 = \dfrac{15}{100} = 0.15$,

   $\hat{p}_1 = \dfrac{25}{100} = 0.25$,

   $\hat{p}_1 - \hat{p}_2 = 0.15 - 0.25 = -0.1$

2. $z_{0.25} = 1.96$,

$$s_{\hat{p}_1 - \hat{p}_2} = \sqrt{\frac{\hat{p}_1(1-\hat{p}_1)}{n_1} + \frac{\hat{p}_2(1-\hat{p}_2)}{n_2}} = \sqrt{\frac{(0.15)(0.85)}{100} + \frac{(0.25)(0.75)}{100}} = 0.05612486,$$

95% confidence interval on $p_1 - p_2 = (\hat{p}_1 - \hat{p}_2) \pm z_{\frac{\alpha}{2}} \cdot s_{\hat{p}_1 - \hat{p}_2}$

$$= -0.1 \pm (1.96)(0.05612486)$$
$$= (-0.21, 0.01)$$

FLASH TEST

The following pages contain a practice test so that you may assess your understanding of the material presented in Unit 3. Answers and explanations follow the exam. For any questions you miss, be sure to review the explanation carefully and reread the appropriate portion of the section to which the question applies. If you still do not understand the correct answer, review the concept in your text and/or ask your instructor for assistance.

FLASH TEST FOR UNIT 3

TRUE/FALSE (3 points each)

_____ **1.** The critical value for a confidence interval based on a t distribution depends on the sample size.

_____ **2.** The value of the standard error of the predicted value, $s_{\hat{y}}$, is equal for all possible values of the explanatory variable.

_____ **3.** When calculating a confidence interval on μ_D, a sample of size 20 will produce a wider interval than a sample of size 10.

_____ **4.** A school superintendent wants to estimate the average difference in national rankings between two schools in his district. Random samples of size 50 are taken from each school. An appropriate estimate of the difference would be a 95% confidence interval on $\mu_1 - \mu_2 = (\overline{X}_1 - \overline{X}_2) \pm z_{\frac{\alpha}{2}} \cdot s_{\overline{X}_1 - \overline{X}_2}$.

_____ **5.** A 90% confidence interval on p is found to be (0.26, 0.48). The value of $\hat{p}$ from the sample is 0.37.

MULTIPLE CHOICE (3 points each)

_____ **6.** Which of the following is an appropriate interpretation for $b = -0.5$?

A. For each additional unit of X, Y increases by an average of 0.5 units.

B. For each additional unit of X, Y decreases by an average of 0.5 units.

C. For $X = 0$, the average value of Y is -0.5.

D. Twenty-five percent of the variation in Y can be accounted for by the linear relationship between X and Y.

_____ **7.** Which of the following is the appropriate standard error term calculation for a confidence interval on $\mu_1 - \mu_2$?

A. $\sqrt{\dfrac{s_1^2}{n_1} + \dfrac{s_2^2}{n_2}}$

B. $\sqrt{\dfrac{\sigma_1^2}{n_1} + \dfrac{\sigma_2^2}{n_2}}$

C. $s_{pooled}\sqrt{\dfrac{1}{n_1} + \dfrac{1}{n_2}}$

D. cannot determine from the information given

_____ **8.** A researcher wants to calculate a confidence interval estimate of the difference in averages between populations with two independent samples where $n_1 = n_2 = 20$. He does not know the values of the population standard deviations but is assuming that the population variances are unequal. The $(1 - \alpha)100\%$ confidence interval on $\mu_1 - \mu_2 = $

A. $\overline{X}_D \pm t_{\frac{\alpha}{2}, df_D} \cdot s_{\overline{X}}$

B. $(\overline{X}_1 - \overline{X}_2) \pm z_{\frac{\alpha}{2}} \cdot s_{\overline{X}_1 - \overline{X}_2}$

C. $(\overline{X}_1 - \overline{X}_2) \pm t_{\frac{\alpha}{2}, df'} \cdot s_{\overline{X}_1 - \overline{X}_2}$

D. $(\overline{X}_1 - \overline{X}_2) \pm t_{\frac{\alpha}{2}, df} \cdot s_{pooled}\sqrt{\dfrac{1}{n_1} + \dfrac{1}{n_2}}$

9. If the value of sample correlation coefficient is -0.742, the value of the coefficient of determination is:

A. 0.551

C. 0.742

B. -0.551

D. cannot determine from the information given

10. A researcher wants to estimate the difference in the proportions of Republicans and Democrats who are members of the NRA. Which of the following is the appropriate estimator?

A. $\hat{p}$

C. $\hat{p} \pm z_{\frac{\alpha}{2}} \cdot s_{\hat{p}}$

B. $\hat{p}_1 - p_2$

D. $(\hat{p}_1 - \hat{p}_2) \pm z_{\frac{\alpha}{2}} \cdot s_{\hat{p}_1 - \hat{p}_2}$

11. Which of the following sample correlation coefficients indicates the strongest linear relationship between X and Y?

A. 0.83

B. -0.87

C. 0.24

D. -0.17

12. Estimation of which of the following parameters does **not** use paired data?

A. ρ

B. μ_D

C. β_1

D. $p_1 - p_2$

13. Which of the following degrees of freedom calculations is appropriate for a prediction interval?

A. $n - 1$

C. $n - 2$

B. $n_D - 1$

D. $n_1 + n_2 - 2$

14. If the sample correlation coefficient indicates an inverse linear relationship between X and Y, the slope of the estimated regression line

A. is negative

C. can be negative or positive

B. is positive

D. can be equal to zero

15. A 95% confidence interval on μ calculated from a large sample where the population variance is unknown is (20, 40). The value of the standard error of $\overline{X}$ is equal to:

A. 1.96

B. 5.1

C. 10

D. 30

SHORT ANSWER (3 points each)

16. Which is wider: a 90% confidence interval or a 95% confidence interval? Justify your answer.

17. The school nurse at Connor College wants to estimate the average weight (in pounds) of male students with 95% confidence. The interval (152.8, 187.6) was calculated from a random sample. Interpret the interval.

18. The correlation coefficient between two random variables was estimated to be $r = 0.87$. Would it be appropriate to calculate an estimated regression equation? Justify your answer.

19. A consumer wants to estimate the average difference in prices between items at Discount Drug and Drugs for Less. He randomly selects eight items from a list. He purchases the eight items at Discount Drug and purchases the same eight items at Drugs for Less. He records the price of each item at each store. Are the samples independent or dependent? Justify your answer.

20. Stacey is getting ready to move to Tulsa, OK, and wants to estimate the difference of the average monthly housing rental cost between the suburbs of Broken Arrow and Jenks with 90% confidence. She takes a random sample of 40 rental units in each suburb. State the appropriate confidence interval formula for this estimate. Justify your answer by stating the questions you would ask (in order) and the answers to those questions.

CALCULATIONS (5 points each)

Use the following information for problems 21 through 24. Eric wants to explore the linear relationship between the age of students at Connor College and the amount of time students spend socializing during finals week. He takes a random sample of 10 students and records their ages and socialization time.

Student	1	2	3	4	5	6	7	8	9	10
Age	19	20	20	21	23	25	26	29	32	40
Social time	15.2	8.3	11.7	12.2	8.2	7.5	5.4	7.6	2.3	1.5

21. Calculate the estimated correlation coefficient.

22. Find the estimated regression equation.

23. Estimate the slope with 95% confidence.

24. Predict the socialization time for a 30-year-old student.

25. A Republican candidate wants to estimate the difference in the proportions of registered Republicans in two small towns. He takes a random sample of 200 registered voters in each town and finds the proportions of Republicans to be 0.37 and 0.28 in Town 1 and Town 2, respectively. Estimate the difference in the proportions with 90% confidence.

26. A recruiter at Connor College wants to estimate the average distance (in miles) that commuter students drive to campus with 99% confidence. The mean distance for a random sample of 100 students is 30 miles with a standard deviation of 5 miles. Calculate the confidence interval.

27. A confidence interval on $\mu_1 - \mu_2$ is to be calculated. The values of the population standard deviations are unknown, and it is assumed that the population variances are not equal. Calculate the appropriate degrees of freedom if $n_1 = 10, s_1 = 5, n_2 = 15$, and $s_2 = 12$.

28. A statistics instructor wants to estimate the difference in average final exam scores between fall and spring semesters. The values of σ_1 and σ_2 are unknown, and it is assumed that $\sigma_1^2 = \sigma_2^2$. A random sample of 13 fall semester students had an average final exam score of 76 points with a standard deviation of 10 points. A random sample of 15 spring semester students had a mean final exam score of 68 points with a standard deviation of 9 points. Estimate the difference in average final exam scores between the two semesters with 95% confidence.

Answers to the practice test begin on the next page.

SOLUTIONS TO FLASH TEST FOR UNIT 3

TRUE/FALSE

1. T; the value of the critical value depends on $df = n - 1$

2. F; $s_{\hat{y}} = s_e \sqrt{1 + \dfrac{1}{n} + \dfrac{(x_0 - \bar{x})^2}{SSx}}$ depends on x_0 (a specific value)

3. F; the sample size affects both the critical value and the standard error of the point estimate: (1) the smaller the value of n, the larger the critical value; and (2) the smaller the value of n, the larger the value of the standard error which generates a larger margin of error.

4. F; this interval requires at least interval level data, but ranks are ordinal

5. T; the point estimate is at the center of the interval, thus $\hat{p} = \dfrac{0.26 + 0.48}{2} = 0.37$

MULTIPLE CHOICE

6. B; the slope is the average change in Y for one unit change in X, the negative sign indicates the Y decreases as X increases

7. D; more information is needed: whether the values of σ_1 and σ_2 are known, the sizes of the samples, and if population variances are equal

8. C; this interval is for independent samples, values of σ_1 and σ_2 unknown, small samples and unequal population variances

9. A; the coefficient of determination is $r^2 = (-0.742)^2 = 0.551$

10. B; A and C are for one population, D would require that a confidence level be given

11. B; the magnitude indicates the strength, thus -0.87 is the strongest even though it is negative

12. D; ρ is the correlation coefficient, μ_D is the difference of the population means for matched pairs, β_1 is the slope of the regression line

13. C; A is for one population mean, B is for the difference of the population means for dependent samples, D is for the difference of the population means for independent samples

14. A; the sign on r and b is the same

15. B; A is the critical value, C is the margin of error, D is the sample mean

SHORT ANSWER

16. A 95% confidence interval will be wider than a 90% confidence interval. The critical value will be larger, thus the margin of error will be greater.

17. We are 95% confident that the true average weight of male students at Connor College is between 152.8 and 187.6 pounds.

18. Yes, constructing an estimated regression equation would be appropriate because there appears to be a strong positive linear relationship between the two variables. Also, $r^2 = 0.757$; hence, approximately 75.7% of the variation in the response variable is accounted for by the linear relationship between the explanatory variable and the response variable.

19. The samples are dependent because the exact same items are purchased. The consumer would pair the prices for each item, find the difference in the prices, and use the differences to calculate the estimate.

20. The appropriate confidence interval formula is: 90% confidence interval on

$$\mu_1 - \mu_2 = (\overline{X}_1 - \overline{X}_2) \pm z_{\frac{\alpha}{2}} \cdot s_{\overline{X}_1 - \overline{X}_2}.$$

Q1: Are the samples dependent?	A1: No
Q2: Are the values of σ_1 and σ_2 known?	A2: No
Q3: Is $n_1 \geq 30$ and $n_2 \geq 30$?	A3: Yes

CALCULATIONS

The following information applies to the answers to problems 21 through 24:

$$\sum x = 255, \quad \sum x^2 = 6{,}897, \quad \sum y = 79.9, \quad \sum y^2 = 803.61, \quad \sum xy = 1{,}815.5,$$

$$n = 10, \ \overline{x} = 25.5, \quad \overline{y} = 7.99,$$

$$SS_X = \sum x^2 - \frac{(\sum x)^2}{n} = 6{,}897 - \frac{255^2}{10} = 394.5,$$

$$SS_Y = \sum y^2 - \frac{(\sum y)^2}{n} = 803.61 - \frac{79.9^2}{10} = 165.209,$$

$$SS_{XY} = \sum xy - \frac{(\sum x)(\sum y)}{n} = 1{,}815.5 - \frac{(255)(79.9)}{10} = -221.95$$

21. $r = \dfrac{SS_{XY}}{\sqrt{SS_X \cdot SS_Y}} = \dfrac{-221.95}{\sqrt{(394.5)(165.209)}} = -0.869390308$

22. $b = \dfrac{SS_{XY}}{SS_X} = \dfrac{-221.95}{394.5} = -0.562610899,$

$a = \overline{y} - b\overline{x} = 7.99 - (-0.562610899)(25.5) = 22.33657792,$

$\hat{y} = a + bx = 22.37 - 0.563x$

23. $t_{0.025,8} = 2.306,$

$$S_e = \sqrt{\frac{SS_Y - bSS_{XY}}{n-2}} = \sqrt{\frac{165.209 - (-0.562610899)(-221.95)}{8}} = 2.245481879,$$

$$S_b = \frac{S_e}{\sqrt{SS_X}} = \frac{2.245481879}{\sqrt{394.5}} = 0.11305403,$$

95% confidence interval on $\beta_1 = b \pm t_{\frac{\alpha}{2},df} \cdot S_b$

$$= -0.562610899 \pm (2.306)(0.11305403)$$
$$= (-0.823, -0.302)$$

24. $\hat{y} = 22.337 - 0.562x = 22.337 - (0.563)(30) = 5.447$

25. $\hat{p}_1 - \hat{p}_2 = 0.37 - 0.28 = 0.09,$

$z_{0.05} = 1.645,$

$$s_{\hat{p}_1 - \hat{p}_2} = \sqrt{\frac{\hat{p}_1(1-\hat{p}_1)}{n_1} + \frac{\hat{p}_2(1-\hat{p}_2)}{n_2}} = \sqrt{\frac{(0.37)(0.63)}{200} + \frac{(0.28)(0.72)}{200}} = 0.04662081,$$

90% confidence interval on $p_1 - p_2 = (\hat{p}_1 - \hat{p}_2) \pm z_{\frac{\alpha}{2}} \cdot s_{\hat{p}_1 - \hat{p}_2}$

$$= 0.09 \pm (1.645)(0.04662081)$$
$$= (0.013, 0.167)$$

26. $z_{0.005} = 2.575,$

$$s_{\bar{X}} = \frac{s}{\sqrt{n}} = \frac{5}{\sqrt{100}} = 0.5,$$

99% confidence interval on $\mu = \bar{X} \pm t_{\frac{\alpha}{2}, df} \cdot s_{\bar{X}} = 30 \pm (2.575)(0.5)$

$$= (28.713, 31.288)$$

27. $df' = \dfrac{(n_1 - 1)(n_2 - 1)\left(\dfrac{s_1^2}{n_1} + \dfrac{s_2^2}{n_2}\right)^2}{(n_2 - 1)\left(\dfrac{s_1^2}{n_1}\right)^2 + (n_1 - 1)\left(\dfrac{s_2^2}{n_2}\right)^2} = \dfrac{(9)(14)\left(\dfrac{5^2}{10} + \dfrac{12^2}{15}\right)^2}{(14)\left(\dfrac{5^2}{10}\right)^2 + (9)\left(\dfrac{12^2}{15}\right)^2} = 20,$ (rounded down

to the nearest whole number)

28. $\bar{X}_1 - \bar{X}_2 = 76 - 68 = 8,$

$df = n_1 + n_2 - 2 = 13 + 15 - 2 = 26,$

$t_{0.025, 26} = 2.056,$

$$s_{pooled}^2 = \frac{(n_1 - 1)s_1^2 + (n_2 - 1)s_2^2}{n_1 + n_2 - 2} = \frac{(12)(10^2) + (14)(9^2)}{26} = 89.76923077,$$

90% confidence interval on $\mu_1 - \mu_2 = (\bar{X}_1 - \bar{X}_2) \pm t_{\frac{\alpha}{2}, df} \cdot s_{pooled} \sqrt{\frac{1}{n_1} + \frac{1}{n_2}}$

$$= 8 \pm (2.056)(\sqrt{89.76923077})\left(\sqrt{\frac{1}{13} + \frac{1}{15}}\right)$$

$$= (0.618, 15.382)$$

FLASH FOCUS

After completing this chapter, you will be able to:

✓ Understand the basic terms associated with hypothesis testing

✓ Understand the method of hypothesis testing

✓ Determine the appropriate hypothesis test for a given parameter

✓ Conduct hypothesis tests on a variety of parameters

✓ Calculate *p*-values for selected hypothesis tests

The following table lists the core concepts in this unit, along with definitions and/or explanations. Space is provided to add concepts discussed by your instructor.

Core Concepts in Unit 4

Chapter 9—Fundamentals of Hypothesis Testing	
Concept	**Definition and/or Explanation**
Hypothesis	a statement about a characteristic of a population (in this unit, a statement about a parameter)
Hypothesized value	a specific value for a population parameter
Null hypothesis	a statement of no difference between the population parameter and the hypothesized value
Alternative hypothesis	the logical alternative to the null hypothesis
Test statistic	a quantity with a known or approximated distribution that is compared with the critical value to make a decision about the null hypothesis (in this unit, a quantity that measures the distance between the point estimate and the hypothesized value of the parameter)
Critical value	a value from the distribution of the test statistic that separates the distribution into likely and unlikely values of the statistic
Significance level	determines the critical value; the size of the area in the tail of the distribution of the test statistic associated with unlikely values of the statistic
Rejection region	the area defined by the significance level
Decision rule	a mathematical expression that describes the values of the test statistic that are unlikely if the null hypothesis is true—rule for determining whether to reject or fail to reject the null hypothesis
Type I error	rejecting a null hypothesis when it is true

(continued)

(*continued*)

Type II error	failing to reject a null hypothesis when it is false
p-value	the probability of getting a value of the test statistic at least as extreme as the one from the sample assuming the null hypothesis is true

Chapter 10—One Population and Chapter 11—Two Populations

Hypothesis sets	the possible null hypothesis and corresponding alternative hypothesis for each parameter of interest
Test statistic tables	tables to determine the appropriate test statistic for given information are presented in cases when there is more than one possible statistic for the parameter of interest
Decision rule tables	tables to determine the appropriate decision rule for the hypothesis test

Chapter 12—More Than Two Populations

Analysis of variance	method of hypothesis testing for differences among more than two population means that uses ratios of variances
Factor	the independent variable that separates groups into categories
Levels	the categories of the factor
Mean square	an estimate of a variance component calculated by finding the ratio of the sum of squares to the degrees of freedom
Multiple comparisons	tests for determining which pairs of population means are significantly different
Main effect	the effect of one factor averaged over the other factor
Interaction	the effect of both factors together

FLASH LINK

The following table lists Web sites that may be helpful in studying the material in Unit 4. Space is provided to add other web sites suggested in your text or by your instructor or those you find on your own. Key to resource type: D, definitions; E, examples; X, exercises; C, calculation; M, demonstration; HT, hypothesis testing.

Chapter	Resource Type	URL
9	D (basics of HT)	http://stat.tamu.edu/stat30x/notes/node108.html (also node109, node111, node114, node115, node116)
9	D, E, X (basics of HT)	http://davidmlane.com/hyperstat/logic_hypothesis.html
9	D, E, X (errors)	http://www.bmj.com/collections/statsbk/5.shtml
10	D, E (μ)	http://www.psychstat.smsu.edu/introbook/SBK20.htm
10	M	http://www.math.csusb.edu/faculty/stanton/m262/proportions/proportions.html
10–11	D, E, X (μ, $\mu_1 - \mu_2$, p, $p_1 - p_2$)	http://www.stat.berkeley.edu/users/stark/SticiGui/Text/ch22.htm
10–11	D, E, X (μ, $\mu_1 - \mu_2$, p, $p_1 - p_2$)	http://davidmlane.com/hyperstat/hypothesis_testing_se.html
10–11	D, E, X (μ, $\mu_1 - \mu_2$, p, $p_1 - p_2$, β_1)	http://www.anu.edu.au/nceph/surfstat/surfstat-home
10–12	X	http://occ.awlonline.com/bookbind/pubbooks/triola_awl/chapter7/deluxe.html (also chapter8, chapter9, chapter11)
10–12	X	http://occ.awlonline.com/bookbind/pubbooks/weiss2_awl/chapter9/deluxe.html (also chapter12, chapter15, chapter16)
11	D, E ($\mu_1 - \mu_2$)	http://trochim.human.cornell.edu/kb/stat_t.htm
11	D, E, X ($\mu_1 - \mu_2$, $p_1 - p_2$, ρ)	http://www.bmj.com/collections/statsbk/6.shtml (also 7, 11)
11	C	http://faculty.vassar.edu/~lowry/t_ind_stats.html (also t_corr_stats)
12	D (one-way ANOVA)	http://stat.tamu.edu/stat30x/notes/node126.html (also node129)

(continued)

12	D (one- and two-way ANOVA)	http://www2.chass.ncsu.edu/garson/pa765/anova.htm
12	D, E (one-way ANOVA)	http://www.psychstat.smsu.edu/introbook/SBK27.htm
12	D, E (two-way ANOVA)	http://trochim.human.cornell.edu/kb/EXPFACT.htm
12	D, E, M (one- and two-way ANOVA)	http://www.ruf.rice.edu/~lane/stat_sim/one_way (also two_way)
12	D, E, X (one- and two-way ANOVA)	http://davidmlane.com/hyperstat/intro_ANOVA.html (also factorial_ANOVA)

CHAPTER 9—Fundamentals of Hypothesis Testing

FLASH SUMMARY

A hypothesis is a statement about a characteristic of a population. The characteristic may be a parameter, a distribution, or a relationship between variables. In Unit 3, various methods of estimation were utilized to attempt to answer questions about possible reasonable values for population values using sample statistics. In this unit, methods are discussed that attempt to answer more specific questions about values for population parameters. In other words, given a particular value of the population parameter, how can one determine if that value is reasonable from the information provided by the sample? This particular value is called the hypothesized value of the parameter. Unit 5 presents hypothesis tests for answering questions about distributions of populations and relationships between variables.

In this chapter, the Greek letter theta, θ, is used to represent a general population parameter, and θ_0 is used to denote the hypothesized value. Hypothesis tests on the specific parameters discussed in Unit 3 (μ, $\mu_1 - \mu_2$, p, $p_1 - p_2$, ρ, β_0, and β_1) are addressed in Chapters 10 and 11, as is testing the equality of population variances. It is important to note that the assumptions made for using the confidence intervals in Unit 3 hold for the analogous hypothesis tests in this unit.

The simplest form of the question underlying hypothesis testing on a population parameter is, "If $\theta = \theta_0$, how much distance can there be between the point estimate and the hypothesized value of the parameter before the researcher believes that that $\theta \neq \theta_0$?" To answer this question, a hypothesis test is conducted in which a test statistic is constructed and compared to a critical value. A test statistic is a quantity that measures the distance between the point estimate and the hypothesized value of the parameter (usually in standard error units) for which the probability distribution is known or can be approximated. The critical value is a value from the distribution of the test statistic that separates the distribution into likely and unlikely values of the test statistic given that $\theta = \theta_0$. Based on the comparison between the test statistic and the critical value, a decision is made whether to believe that θ_0 is a reasonable value for the population parameter.

The number of steps in hypothesis testing, as well as the information supplied in each, varies from text to text. However, the necessary components of those steps are:

1. *Stating the hypotheses*

   A hypothesis test requires the statement of two hypotheses that are mutually exclusive and exhaustive. All possible values for the population parameter must fall within one and only one of the hypothesis statements. The null hypothesis, denoted H_0, is defined as a statement of no difference between the population parameter and its hypothesized value. Then the general null hypothesis would be of the form $H_0 : \theta = \theta_0$.

   This is the statement that is actually tested when the test statistic and critical value are compared. However, this definition can be generalized so that the researcher is not limited only to the case of equality versus nonequality. Other possible null hypotheses include:

   $$H_0 : \theta \leq \theta_0 \quad \text{and} \quad H_0 : \theta \geq \theta_0.$$

   The equality must always be included in the null hypothesis.

   The alternative hypothesis, denoted H_1 or H_a, is the mathematical alternative to the null. This is similar to the concept of the complement of an event. Because the hypotheses must be mutually exclusive and exhaustive, all possible values for the parameter that are not included in the null must be considered in the alternative. Then the possible set of null and alternative hypotheses are:

   $$H_0 : \theta = \theta_0 \text{ v. } H_1 : \theta \neq \theta_0,$$
   $$H_0 : \theta \leq \theta_0 \text{ v. } H_1 : \theta > \theta_0, \text{ and}$$
   $$H_0 : \theta \geq \theta_0 \text{ v. } H_1 : \theta < \theta_0.$$

   The alternative hypothesis is often called the research hypothesis because it is often the situation that the researcher really believes is true. It is extremely important to understand that hypothesis testing **does not** allow the user to **prove** a claim is true. Hypothesis testing simply allows the user to decide whether the null hypothesis or alternative hypothesis is more reasonable based on the both the information from the data and the probability distribution of the test statistic. Keep in mind that if the test leads to a conclusion that $\theta \neq \theta_0$, either: 1) this conclusion is true, or 2) $\theta = \theta_0$, but the sample produced an unlikely but possible value of the test statistic.

   Many textbook problems for hypothesis testing contain phrases such as "Determine if . . .," "Test the claim that . . .," or "Is the parameter . . . ." The problem will indicate the parameter of interest and the hypothesized value of the parameter and states a claim that frequently indicates the mathematical sign for the alternative hypothesis (although the claim can be phrased in terms of the null hypothesis).

2. *Determining the appropriate test statistic and calculating the value*

   The formula for the test statistic is based on a quantity with a known or approximated distribution. Remember that the test statistics in this unit require at least interval level data and normal (or approximately normal) distribution of the random variable(s). The test statistics discussed will follow Z, t, or F, distributions. Let $\hat{\theta}$ represent the point estimate of the population parameter θ. Then, the general form of a z or t test statistic is:

   $$\frac{\hat{\theta} - \theta_0}{\text{Standard error of } \hat{\theta}}.$$

   F test statistics are constructed as the ratio of two variances.

   Selecting the test statistic for a given situation is based on the same type of information as selecting the confidence interval: the parameter of interest, whether population standard deviations are known, sample sizes, and equality of population variances. Tables to assist in this selection when there is more than one option are displayed at the end of the Flash Summary sections.

3. *Determining the decision rule*

The decision rule is a mathematical expression that describes the values of the test statistic that are unlikely if the null hypothesis is true. The decision rule compares the test statistic to a critical value; the decision is phrased in terms of the null hypothesis. If the decision rule is true for the sample data, the decision is "reject H_0." If the decision rule is false, the decision is "fail to reject H_0."

The criteria for determining the appropriate decision rule include the test statistic, the level of significance, the direction of the sign in the alternative hypothesis, and the critical value. The level of significance, denoted α, indicates the size of the area under the probability distribution associated with unlikely values of the test statistic. This area is called the rejection region and is actually a picture of the comparison in the decision rule. The critical value separates the area under the probability curve of the test statistic into the rejection region and the remainder of the area $(1 - \alpha)$. The sign in the alternative hypothesis determines which tail(s) contains the rejection region. Hypothesis tests with alternative hypotheses of $H_1: \theta > \theta_0$ and $H_1: \theta < \theta_0$ are called one-tailed tests, whereas a hypothesis test with $H_1: \theta \neq \theta_0$ is called a two-tailed test. If $H_1: \theta > \theta_0$, the rejection region is in the right tail; if $H_1: \theta < \theta_0$, the rejection region is in the left tail. If $H_1: \theta \neq \theta_0$, α is split between the two tails so there are two rejection regions of size $\dfrac{\alpha}{2}$. For example, for a hypothesis test of $H_0: \mu = \mu_0$ v. $H_1: \mu \neq \mu_0$ where $n \geq 30$,

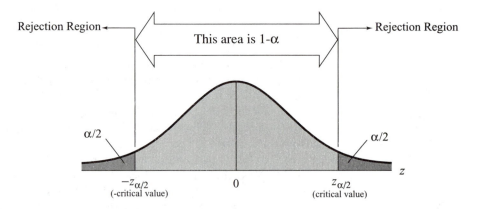

If the value of the test statistic falls in the rejection region, the null hypothesis is rejected because it is an unlikely value for the statistic if the null hypothesis is true.

The decision rules are phrased: "Reject H_0 if the calculated value of the test statistic is more extreme than the critical value." The definition of "more extreme" is expressed in the decision rule and depends on the level of significance, the distribution of the test statistic, and the sign in the alternative hypothesis. Specific rules are given in the following chapters for each of the parameters of interest.

An alternative method of making the decision is to compare the level of significance to the *p*-value. The *p*-value is the probability of getting a value of the test statistic at least as extreme as the one from the sample data, assuming the H_0 is true. Note that α is the area in the tail(s) of the distribution associated with the critical value. The *p*-value is the area in the tail(s) of the distribution associated with the calculated value of the test statistic. Therefore, one may compare either the values or the areas. When comparing the *p*-value to α, the null hypothesis is rejected if *p*-value $< \alpha$. In many cases, the decision is made based on the comparison of the test statistic to the critical value, and the *p*-value is also reported. The *p*-value of a hypothesis test is:

p-value $= P(\text{test statistic} > \text{calculated value})$, if $H_1: \theta > \theta_0$;

p-value $= P(\text{test statistic} < \text{calculated value})$, if $H_1: \theta < \theta_0$; and

p-value $= (2)P(\text{test statistic} > \text{calculated value})$, if $H_0: \theta \leq \theta_0$.

Following is a picture of the *p*-value for a right-tailed test:

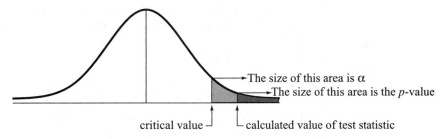

The size of this area is α
The size of this area is the *p*-value
critical value
calculated value of test statistic

4. *Making the decision*

    Once the decision rule has been determined and the value of the test statistic calculated, the decision to reject or fail to reject the null hypothesis can be made. Recall that the decision made is based on sample information and a probability distribution so that the decision can be correct or incorrect. Correct decisions are: (1) H_0 is false and is rejected, and (2) H_0 is true and is not rejected. If the null hypothesis is in reality true but is rejected, a Type I error is made. The level of significance, α, is the probability of making a Type I error. If the null hypothesis is false, but the researcher fails to reject it, a Type II error is made. The probability of a Type II error is β.

Reality

Decision	H_0 is true	H_0 is false
Reject H_0	Type I Error	No Error
Fail to reject H_0	No Error	Type II Error

When a hypothesis test is conducted, the level of either α or β can be controlled, but not both simultaneously. For a sample of size *n*, as α increases, the value of β decreases. In the traditional method of hypothesis testing, a Type I error is usually less desirable than a Type II error, thus the level of significance is set as high as can be tolerated, and the value of β can be calculated (although this calculation is beyond the scope of most introductory statistics courses). Common values for the significance level are 0.001, 0.01, 0.05, and 0.10.

5. *Stating the conclusion*

    While the decision is made in terms of the null hypothesis, the conclusion is generally stated in terms of the alternative hypothesis. The conclusion needs to be worded in the context of the problem, indicating the parameter of interest and describing the population.

    A general form of the conclusion might be: There [is/is not] sufficient evidence to conclude that the [parameter] [variable] of [population from context] is significantly [different/less/greater] than [the hypothesized value] [units] for [α = level of significance]." "Is" is used in the first bracket when the null hypothesis is rejected, and "is not" is used when the decision is to fail to reject the null. The choice of different/less/greater is based on the sign in the alternative hypothesis. In this context, the word "significantly" indicates that a hypothesis test was conducted, not that the result is important. For example, if a hypothesis test on the average exam score of an instructor's statistics students is conducted with $H_0: \mu \geq 75$ v. $H_1: \mu < 75$, and the null hypothesis is rejected for $\alpha = 0.01$, the conclusion would read, "There is sufficient evidence to conclude that the average exam score of the instructor's statistics students is significantly less than 75 points for $\alpha = 0.01$."

FLASH REVIEW

For each problem below, determine the parameter of interest, whether the problem calls for a confidence interval or a hypothesis test, and give the sign $(<, >, \neq)$ in the alternative hypothesis for hypothesis test problems.

1. A researcher wants to determine if the proportion of nontraditional students currently at Connor College is significantly higher than the proportion from 10 years ago at $\alpha = 0.05$.

2. A researcher wants to estimate the strength and direction of the linear relationship between a student's annual income and amount of financial aid received at Connor College with 90% confidence.

3. A college recruiter claims that there is a significant difference in the average GPA of students at United University and the average GPA of students at Connor College. Test the claim at the 0.01 level of significance.

CHAPTER 10—One Population

Section 10.1—Population Mean

FLASH SUMMARY

The information in the previous chapter can now be used to test hypotheses about one population mean. Recall that the assumptions that applied to constructing confidence intervals for one population mean also hold for the complementary hypothesis tests. The possible sets of null and alternative hypotheses for these hypothesis tests are:

$$H_0: \mu = \mu_0 \text{ v. } H_1: \mu \neq \mu_0,$$
$$H_0: \mu \leq \mu_0 \text{ v. } H_1: \mu > \mu_0, \text{ and}$$
$$H_0: \mu \geq \mu_0 \text{ v. } H_1: \mu < \mu_0,$$

where μ_0 is the hypothesized value.

If the value of the population standard deviation is known, the quantity $\dfrac{\overline{X} - \mu_0}{\sigma_{\overline{X}}}$ has a standard normal distribution. Then the test statistic is:

$$z_{calc} = \frac{\overline{X} - \mu_0}{\sigma_{\overline{X}}} \text{ where } \sigma_{\overline{X}} = \frac{\sigma}{\sqrt{n}}.$$

The *calc* subscript indicates that this is a value calculated from the sample data. The value of the calculated test statistic is usually rounded to the same number of decimal places as the critical value.

The critical value will also come from the standard normal distribution and will depend on the sign in the alternative hypothesis. For a right-tailed test, the critical value is z_α, whereas the critical value for a left-tailed test $-z_\alpha$. The negative sign indicates a value in the left tail of the distribution. When conducting a two-tailed test, there is a rejection region in each tail. Then, a value separating likely from unlikely values of the distribution is needed for each tail. These values are $-z_{\frac{\alpha}{2}}$ and $z_{\frac{\alpha}{2}}$. However, because the distribution is symmetric, the decision rule is constructed using only the positive value. The decision rules are displayed in the following table:

If H_1:	Reject H_0 if
$\mu \neq \mu_0$	$\left| z_{calc} \right| > z_{\frac{\alpha}{2}}$
$\mu > \mu_0$	$z_{calc} > z_\alpha$
$\mu < \mu_0$	$z_{calc} < -z_\alpha$

Suppose Professor Rice claims that the average GPA of her students is higher than the average GPA for all Connor College students. The GPA of all students at the college is normally distributed with a mean of 2.5 and standard deviation of 0.5. The mean GPA of a random sample of five of Professor Rice's students is 3.08 with a standard deviation of 0.421. She wants to test her claim at the 0.01 level of significance.

The hypothesized value for the population mean is $\mu_0 = 2.5$, and the sign in the alternative hypothesis would be $>$ because she is claiming a higher average. The value of the population standard deviation is known to be $\sigma = 0.5$, thus

$$\sigma_{\overline{X}} = \frac{\sigma}{\sqrt{n}} = \frac{0.5}{\sqrt{5}} = 0.223606797.$$

Note that the sample standard deviation is given but not needed. The hypothesis test would proceed as follows:

Hypotheses: $H_0: \mu \leq 2.5$ v. $H_1: \mu > 2.5$

Test statistic: $z_{calc} = \dfrac{\overline{X} - \mu_0}{\sigma_{\overline{X}}} = \dfrac{3.08 - 2.5}{0.233606797} = 2.59$

Critical value: $z_\alpha = z_{0.01} = 2.33$

Decision rule: Reject H_0 if $z_{calc} > 2.33$

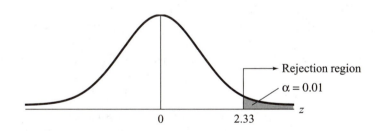

Decision: Reject H_0 because $2.59 > 2.33$

Conclusion: There is sufficient evidence to conclude that the average GPA of Professor Rice's students is significantly greater than 2.5 points for $\alpha = 0.01$.

The p-value for this test can be calculated by finding the area in the tail to the right of the calculated test statistic:

p-value $= P(Z > 2.59) = 0.0048.$

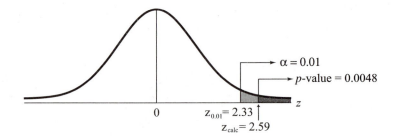

As with confidence intervals, if the value of the population variance is unknown, and the sample size is large, the sample standard deviation provides a good estimate of the population standard deviation. It is then appropriate to use:

$$z_{calc} = \frac{\overline{X} - \mu_0}{s_{\overline{X}}} \text{ where } s_{\overline{X}} = \frac{s}{\sqrt{n}}.$$

The critical values and decision rules are the same as in the previous test.

Professor Westfall wants to test his belief that the average GPA of his students is different from the average GPA of 2.6 for all college students in the state at $\alpha = 0.05$. He takes a random sample of 50 of his students and finds the mean GPA to be 2.83 points with a standard deviation of 0.72. Then, $\mu_0 = 2.6$ and $s_{\overline{X}} = 0.101823376$. Testing Professor Westfall's belief:

Hypotheses: $H_0: \mu = 2.6$ v. $H_1: \mu \neq 2.6$

Test statistic: $z_{calc} = \dfrac{\overline{X} - \mu_0}{s_{\overline{X}}} = \dfrac{2.83 - 2.6}{0.101823376} = 2.26$

Critical value: $\pm z_{\frac{\alpha}{2}} = \pm z_{0.025} = \pm 1.96$

Decision rule: Reject H_0 if $|z_{calc}| > 1.96$

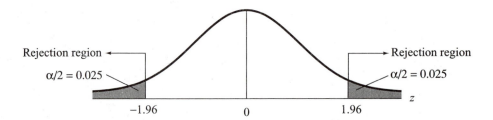

Decision: Reject H_0 because $2.26 > 1.96$

Conclusion: There is sufficient evidence to conclude that the average GPA of Professor Westfall's students is significantly different than 2.6 points for $\alpha = 0.05$.

Recall from Unit 3 the question asked for a confidence interval: "What is a reasonable value for μ?" For Professor Westfall's students, the two-sided 95% confidence interval from the same sample data was (2.63, 3.03). The question asked in the hypothesis test was, "Is 2.6 a reasonable value for μ?" Because the confidence interval and hypothesis test are both two-tailed with $\alpha = 0.05$, the interval can be used to answer the hypothesis test question. According to the confidence interval, reasonable values for μ are between 2.63 and 3.03. Because 2.6 does not fall between these values, it would not be considered a reasonable value for μ, and the null hypothesis would be rejected. This relationship holds for all two-sided confidence intervals and two-tailed hypothesis tests with the same α level.

The p-value for this test can be calculated by finding the area in the tail to the right of the calculated test statistic and doubling that area because it is a two-tailed test:

p-value $= (2)P(Z > 2.26) = (2)(0.0119) = 0.0238$.

If the value of the population standard deviation is unknown, and the sample size is small, the quantity $\dfrac{\overline{X} - \mu_0}{s_{\overline{X}}}$ has the t distribution with $df = n - 1$. Then the test statistic is:

$$t_{calc} = \frac{\overline{X} - \mu_0}{s_{\overline{X}}} \text{ where } s_{\overline{X}} = \frac{s}{\sqrt{n}}.$$

The critical value will be a value from the t distribution with $df = n - 1$ and will depend on the sign in the alternative hypothesis. The critical values are $t_{\alpha, df}$ for a right-tailed test, $-t_{\alpha, df}$ for a left-tailed test, and $\pm t_{\frac{\alpha}{2}, df}$ for a two-tailed test. The decision rules are displayed in the following table:

If H_1:	Reject H_0 if
$\mu \neq \mu_0$	$\left| t_{calc} \right| > t_{\frac{\alpha}{2}, df}$ where $df = n - 1$
$\mu > \mu_0$	$t_{calc} > t_{\alpha, df}$ where $df = n - 1$
$\mu < \mu_0$	$t_{calc} < -t_{\alpha, df}$ where $df = n - 1$

Professor Lucas wants to know if the average GPA of his students has decreased. The average GPA of students taking his courses for the past 20 years is 3.25. He takes a random sample of 10 of his current students and finds the average GPA of the sample to be 2.68 with a standard deviation of 1.02.

To determine if the average GPA has decreased at the 0.05 level of significance, he conducts the following hypothesis test:

Hypotheses: $\quad H_0: \mu \geq 3.25$ v. $H_1: \mu < 3.25$

Test statistic: $\quad t_{calc} = \dfrac{\overline{X} - \mu_0}{s_{\overline{X}}} = \dfrac{2.68 - 3.25}{0.322552321} = -1.767$

Critical value: $\quad -t_{\alpha, df} = -t_{0.05, 9} = -1.833$

Decision rule: $\quad$ Reject H_0 if $t_{calc} < -1.833$

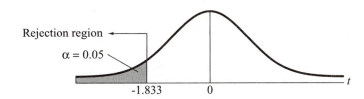

Decision: $\qquad$ Fail to reject H_0 because $-1.767 > -1.833$

Conclusion: $\qquad$ There is not sufficient evidence to conclude that the average GPA of Professor Lucas' students is significantly less than 3.25 points for $\alpha = 0.05$.

In the previous examples, a single value was calculated for the p-value due to the nature of the standard normal table. Exact p-values for t distributions can be found with computer programs. However, the tables for t distributions are not as complete as the Z table; in fact, there are usually only six or seven values of t for each value of df. Therefore, using the table only provides enough information to build an interval around the p-value. This method requires that the closest tabled value smaller than the calculated test statistic and the closest tabled value greater than the calculated test statistic be found. The area values in the tail associated with these two tabled values are also found. If the calculated value is negative, look for the absolute value in the table because t distributions are symmetric. In the preceding example, $df = 9$, thus the closest value smaller than $|-1.761| = 1.761$ is 1.383, and the closest value larger than 1.761 is 1.833. The probability associated with 1.383 is 0.10, and the probability associated with 1.833 is 0.05. Because $-1.833 < -1.761 < -1.383$ (an interval around the calculated test statistic), $0.05 < $ p-value < 0.10 (an interval around the p-value).

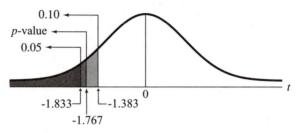

Selecting the test statistic for the population mean

Q: Is the value of σ known?	Yes	$z_{calc} = \dfrac{\bar{X} - \mu_0}{\sigma_{\bar{X}}}$		
	No	Q: Is $n \geq 30$?	Yes	$z_{calc} = \dfrac{\bar{X} - \mu_0}{s_{\bar{X}}}$
			No	$t_{calc} = \dfrac{\bar{X} - \mu_0}{s_{\bar{X}}}$ where $df = n - 1$

 FLASH REVIEW

1. A statistics instructor claims that the average number of hours her students spend studying for the final exam is significantly greater than the average study time of four hours reported for all students at Connor College. She takes a random sample of 10 of her students and records the number of hours they report having studied the week prior to the first exam: 2.1, 3.5, 4.4, 5.3, 6.0, 6.5, 6.5, 6.8, 7.4, 8.2.

   a. Test the instructors claims at the 0.01 level of significance.

   b. Find the p-value for the test.

2. A prospective home buyer believes the average cost of a three bedroom home in Cole County is significantly lower than the average of $53,000 in neighboring Carol County. He takes a random sample of 50 three bedroom homes in Cole County and finds the mean to be $51,000 with a standard deviation of $9,500.

   a. Determine if the average cost of a three bedroom home in Cole County is lower than $53,000 at $\alpha = 0.05$.

   b. Find the p-value for the test.

3. IQ scores as measured on the Wechsler Adult Intelligence Scale (WAIS) are normally distributed with a mean of 100 and a standard deviation of 15 points. An instructor claims that the average IQ of students enrolled at Connor College is significantly different than the mean of the WAIS. A random sample of 25 students has a mean IQ score of 117 with a standard deviation of 12.

   a. Test the instructor's claim at the 0.10 level of significance.

b. The same sample data yielded a 90% confidence interval on $\mu = (112.065, 121.935)$. Does this confidence interval lead you to the same conclusion as the hypothesis test? Justify your answer.

Section 10.2—Population Proportion

FLASH SUMMARY

Hypothesis tests may also be performed on one population proportion. The same assumptions required for confidence intervals on the population proportion are also required for the hypothesis tests. The possible sets of null and alternatives hypotheses for tests on one population proportion are:

$$H_0: p = p_0 \text{ v. } H_1: p \neq p_0,$$
$$H_0: p \leq p_0 \text{ v. } H_1: p > p_0, \text{ and}$$
$$H_0: p \geq p_0 \text{ v. } H_1: p < p_0,$$

where p_0 is the hypothesized value.

For large samples, the normal approximation to the binomial may be used. Then the test statistic is:

$$z_{calc} = \frac{\hat{p} - p_0}{\sigma_{p_0}} \text{ where } \sigma_{p_0} = \sqrt{\frac{p_0(1 - p_0)}{n}}.$$

Note that the standard error of p_0 is used rather than the standard error of $\hat{p}$ (as in the confidence intervals).

The critical values come from the standard normal distribution, and the decision rules are in the following table:

If H_1:	Reject H_0 if
$p \neq p_0$	$\left| z_{calc} \right| > z_{\frac{\alpha}{2}}$
$p > p_0$	$z_{calc} > z_\alpha$
$p < p_0$	$z_{calc} < -z_\alpha$

Pictures of the rejection region are similar to those for z tests on the population mean.

Problems for hypothesis tests on one population proportion are often stated in terms of a percentage rather than a proportion. The percentage is converted to a proportion for the test, then converted back to a percentage in the conclusion.

Suppose a researcher wants to determine if the percent of NRA members who are male is decreasing. In the past, 89% of NRA members have been male. A random sample of 100 members is selected, and it is determined that 83 of the members sampled are male. Then $p_0 = 0.89$, $\hat{p} = 0.83$ and:

$$\sigma_{p_0} = \sqrt{\frac{p_0(1 - p_0)}{n}} = \sqrt{\frac{(0.89)(0.11)}{100}} = 0.031288975.$$

The hypothesis test to determine if there is a significant decrease in male membership at the 0.05 level of significance is as follows:

Hypotheses: $H_0: p \geq 0.89 \text{ v. } H_1: p < 0.89$

Test statistic: $z_{calc} = \dfrac{\hat{p} - p_0}{\sigma_{p_0}} = \dfrac{0.83 - 0.89}{0.031288975} = -1.918$

Critical value: $-z_\alpha = -z_{0.05} = -1.645$

Decision rule: Reject H_0 if $z_{calc} < -1.645$

Decision: Reject H_0 because $-1.918 < -1.645$

Conclusion: There is sufficient evidence to conclude that the percentage of NRA members who are male is significantly less than 89% for $\alpha = 0.05$.

The p-value for this test can be calculated by finding the area in the tail to the left of the calculated test statistic (rounded to two decimal places to match the standard normal table):

$$p\text{-value} = P(Z < -1.92) = 0.0274.$$

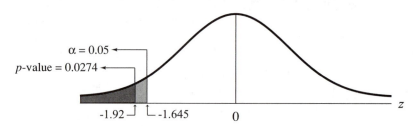

Comparison of two-sided confidence interval and two-tailed hypothesis test on p

	Point Estimate	Standard Error	Critical Value	Formula
Confidence interval	$\hat{p}$	$s_{\hat{p}} = \sqrt{\dfrac{\hat{p}(1 - \hat{p})}{n}}$	$z_{\frac{\alpha}{2}}$	$(1 - \alpha)100\%$ confidence interval on $p = \hat{p} \pm z_{\frac{\alpha}{2}} \cdot s_{\hat{p}}$
Hypothesis test	$\hat{p}$	$\sigma_{p_0} = \sqrt{\dfrac{p_0(1 - p_0)}{n}}$	$z_{\frac{\alpha}{2}}$	$z_{calc} = \dfrac{\hat{p} - p_0}{\sigma_{p_0}}$

FLASH REVIEW

1. A researcher believes the proportion of left-handed students at Connor College is significantly greater than the proportion of 0.10 left-handers in the nation. She takes a random sample of 200 students and finds that 24 of these students are left-handed.

   a. Determine if the proportion of left-handed students at Connor College is significantly greater than the national proportion at the 0.10 level of significance.

   b. Find the p-value for the test.

2. A campaign manager for a mayoral candidate believes that the proportion of people voting for his candidate in a poll one month prior to election day is significantly different from the proportion of 0.68 who voted for the candidate in a previous poll. In a random sample of 1,000 people who participated in the poll one month prior to election day, 720 voted for the manager's candidate.

   a. Test the campaign manager's belief at $\alpha = 0.01$.

   b. Find the p-value for the test.

FLASH SUMMARY

Hypothesis testing may be done on the parameters associated with correlation and regression. Tests on the population correlation coefficient and the slope of the population regression line both consider the linear relationship between the explanatory variable and the response variable. Although the hypothesized value in these tests can be any appropriate value (recall that the value for the correlation coefficient must be between -1 and $+1$ inclusive), most frequently these tests are done with a hypothesized value of 0. Then the test answers the question, "Is there a significant linear relationship between the explanatory variable and the response variable?" The direction of the relationship may also be explored by utilizing the appropriate sign in the alternative hypothesis.

Hypothesis tests may be done on the y-intercept of the regression line but often are not considered because deleting the y-intercept from the equation forces the regression line through the point $(0, 0)$. Tests on the y-intercept will not be considered in the section.

Hypothesis tests on the population correlation coefficient, ρ, and the slope of the population regression equation, β_1, not only answer the same question but produce the same value for each of calculated test statistics. Which parameter is tested depends on the phrasing of the problem and the information given.

The set of possible null and alternative hypotheses for the population correlation coefficient are:

$$H_0: \rho = 0 \text{ v. } H_1: \rho \neq 0,$$

$$H_0: \rho \leq 0 \text{ v. } H_1: \rho > 0, \text{ and}$$

$$H_0: \rho \geq 0 \text{ v. } H_1: \rho < 0,$$

where $p_0 = 0$ is assumed to be the hypothesized value. Only tests with a hypothesized value of 0 will be considered in this section. The first set of hypotheses is used when determining if there is a linear relationship between X and Y, the second when determining if the there is a positive relationship, and the third when determining if there is a negative or inverse relationship. The analogous sets of hypotheses for the slope of the population regression line are:

$$H_0: \beta_1 = 0 \text{ v. } H_1: \beta_1 \neq 0,$$

$$H_0: \beta_1 \leq 0 \text{ v. } H_1: \beta_1 > 0, \text{ and}$$

$$H_0: \beta_1 \geq 0 \text{ v. } H_1: \beta_1 < 0.$$

The quantities $\dfrac{r}{s_r}$ and $\dfrac{b}{s_b}$ both follow t distributions with $df = n - 2$. Then, the test statistics for tests on ρ and β_1, respectively, are:

$$t_{calc} = \frac{r}{s_r} \text{ where } s_r = \sqrt{\frac{1 - r^2}{n - 2}}, \text{ and}$$

$$t_{calc} = \frac{b}{s_b} \text{ where } s_b = \frac{s_e}{\sqrt{SS_X}} \text{ and } s_e = \sqrt{\frac{SS_Y - bSS_{XY}}{n - 2}}.$$

The critical values come from the t distribution with $df = n - 2$, and the decision rules are displayed in the following table:

ρ	β_1	
If H_1:	If H_1:	Reject H_0 if
$\rho \neq 0$	$\beta_1 \neq 0$	$\left| t_{calc} \right| > t_{\frac{\alpha}{2}, df}$ where $df = n - 2$
$\rho > 0$	$\beta_1 > 0$	$t_{calc} > t_{\alpha, df}$ where $df = n - 2$
$\rho < 0$	$\beta_1 < 0$	$t_{calc} < -t_{\alpha, df}$ where $df = n - 2$

Consider the example from Unit 3 in which a personnel director of a very large company was interested in a possible linear relationship between the number of years of formal education an employee had completed (X) and the employee's annual salary (Y). The calculated point estimate of ρ was $r = 0.959985033$, whereas the point estimate of β_1 was $b = 3.200973575$ with a standard error of $s_b = 0.258990335$. The standard error of r is calculated to be:

$$s_r = \sqrt{\frac{1 - r^2}{n - 2}} = \sqrt{\frac{1 - (0.959985033)^2}{13}} = 0.077672258.$$

To determine if there is a significant linear relationship between years of education and annual salary at the 0.05 level of significance, either of the following hypothesis tests can be conducted:

Hypothesis Test 1

Hypotheses: $H_0: \rho = 0$ v. $H_1: \rho \neq 0$

Test statistic: $t_{calc} = \dfrac{r}{s_r} = \dfrac{0.959985033}{0.077672258} = 12.359$

Critical value: $\pm t_{\frac{\alpha}{2}, df} = \pm t_{0.025, 13} = 2.160$

Decision rule: Reject H_0 if $\left| t_{calc} \right| > 2.160$

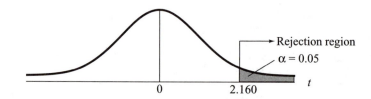

Decision: Reject H_0 because $12.359 > 2.160$

Conclusion: There is sufficient evidence to conclude that the there is a significant linear relationship between years of education and annual salary at $\alpha = 0.05$.

Hypothesis Test 2

Hypotheses: $H_0: \beta_1 = 0$ v. $H_1: \beta_1 \neq 0$

Test statistic: $t_{calc} = \dfrac{b}{s_b} = \dfrac{3.200973575}{0.258990335} = 12.359$

Critical value: $\pm t_{\frac{\alpha}{2}, df} = \pm t_{0.025, 13} = 2.160$

Decision rule: Reject H_0 if $\left| t_{calc} \right| > 2.160$

Decision: Reject H_0 because $12.359 > 2.160$

Conclusion: There is sufficient evidence to conclude that the there is a significant linear relationship between years of education and annual salary at $\alpha = 0.05$.

Note that the only differences between Hypothesis Test 1 and Hypothesis Test 2 are the statement of the hypotheses and the way the test statistic is calculated.

Suppose Eric claims that there is an inverse linear relationship between the age of students at Connor College and the amount of time students spend socializing during finals week. From a random sample of 10 students, he finds $r = -0.869390308$. Then:

$$s_r = \sqrt{\frac{1 - r^2}{n - 2}} = \sqrt{\frac{1 - (-0.869390308)^2}{8}} = 0.176499918.$$

The hypothesis test of his claim at the 0.01 level of significance is:

Hypotheses: $H_0: \rho \geq 0$ v. $H_1: \rho < 0$

Test statistic: $t_{calc} = \dfrac{r}{s_r} = \dfrac{-0.869390308}{0.174699918} = -4.976$

Critical value: $-t_{\alpha,df} = -t_{0.01,8} = -2.896$

Decision rule: Reject H_0 if $t_{calc} < -2.896$

Decision: Reject H_0 because $-4.976 < -2.896$

Conclusion: There is sufficient evidence to conclude that there is a significant inverse linear relationship between the age of students at Connor College and the amount of time students spend socializing during finals week at $\alpha = 0.01$.

For this example, a similar test on β_1 would have been equally appropriate. If the example had stated that Eric claims the population regression equation has a negative slope, the hypothesis test on β_1 would have been conducted.

Parameter (Symbol)	Test Statistic	Standard Error
Correlation coefficient (ρ)	$t_{calc} = \dfrac{r}{s_r}$	$s_r = \sqrt{\dfrac{1 - r^2}{n - 2}}$
Slope (β_1)	$t_{calc} = \dfrac{b}{s_b}$	$s_b = \dfrac{s_e}{\sqrt{SS_X}}$ where $s_e = \sqrt{\dfrac{SS_Y - bSS_{XY}}{n - 2}}$

FLASH REVIEW

1. Daci did a project for an education class in which she explored a linear relationship between the number of hours that students study for the final exam in statistics (X) and the students' final exam grades (Y). She took a random sample of 10 statistics students and found the point estimate of the correlation coefficient to be $r = 0.970851506$. Determine if there is a significant linear relationship between the two variables at $\alpha = 0.05$.

2. A researcher believes that the slope of a regression line between students' ACT scores (X) and their GPAs at the end of their freshman year (Y) has a positive slope. He takes a random sample of 15 students and finds the estimated regression equation to be $\hat{y} = 0.523 + 0.105x$. If $s_b = 0.055$, test the researcher's belief at the 0.01 level of significance.

CHAPTER 11—Two Populations

Section 11.1—Difference Between Two Population Variances

 FLASH SUMMARY

In Section 8.1, the selection of the appropriate confidence interval on $\mu_1 - \mu_2$ for small independent samples and unknown population standard deviations depended on whether the population variances could be assumed to be equal or unequal. A similar determination is necessary in hypothesis testing on $\mu_1 - \mu_2$. A hypothesis test is used to make this determination, and the null and alternative hypotheses are:

$$H_0: \sigma_1^2 = \sigma_2^2 \text{ v. } H_1: \sigma_1^2 \neq \sigma_2^2.$$

These are equivalent to the statements:

$$H_0: \sigma_1^2 - \sigma_2^2 = 0 \text{ and } H_1: \sigma_1^2 - \sigma_2^2 \neq 0.$$

Note that testing the claim that one variance is larger than the other is possible. Also note that tests about the relative sizes of the variances in which the hypothesized value is a quantity other than zero is also possible. However, one-tailed tests and tests for hypothesized values other than zero are not covered here.

If the values of the population variances are equal, then the ratio of the variances will be equal to one:

$$\frac{\sigma_1^2}{\sigma_2^2} = 1.$$

Because the values of the population variances are unknown, the ratio of the sample variances are used to test the equality of the population variances. The quantity $\frac{s_N^2}{s_D^2}$ has an F distribution where $df_N = n_N - 1$ is the degrees of freedom associated with the sample variance in the numerator, and $df_D = n_D - 1$ is the degrees of freedom associated with the sample variance in the denominator. F distributions are right-skewed and, values of F cannot be negative. Because it does not matter which sample variance is placed in the numerator and which in the denominator, the test statistic is set up so that the calculated value is always at least one. This means that although a two-tailed test is being conducted, only a critical value and a decision rule for the right tail are needed. Hence, s_N^2 is the larger of s_1^2 and s_2^2, and s_D^2 is the smaller of the two sample values. Then the test statistic is:

$$F_{calc} = \frac{s_N^2}{s_D^2} \text{ with } df_N = n_N - 1 \text{ and } df_D = n_D - 1.$$

The critical value for the test is $F_{\frac{\alpha}{2}, df_N, df_D}$ and is found on the F tables in your text. Be careful to keep the two degrees of freedom terms in the correct order when looking up values in the table because, in general, $F_{\frac{\alpha}{2}, df_N, df_D} \neq F_{\frac{\alpha}{2}, df_D, df_N}$. When using the F table, the exact values for one or other of the degrees of freedom may not be available. Either the next lower value or the closest value may be used. In this unit, the next lower value is used. The decision rule is:

Reject H_0 if $F_{calc} > F_{\frac{\alpha}{2}, df_N, df_D}$.

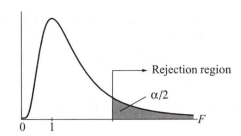

The results of this test allow for the selection of the appropriate confidence interval or hypothesis test for the parameter $\mu_1 - \mu_2$ by providing an answer to the question, "Does $\sigma_1^2 = \sigma_2^2$?"

Consider the example in Unit 3 in which the confidence interval was calculated first assuming that σ_1^2 and σ_2^2 and then assuming that $\sigma_1^2 \neq \sigma_2^2$: "Suppose that a random sample of 12 Exam 1 scores are selected and have a mean and standard deviation of 75 and 11, respectively. A random sample of 15 Exam 2 scores are selected and yield a mean and standard deviation of 70 and 13, respectively. We want to estimate the difference in the averages of exam scores with 90% confidence." A hypothesis test can be conducted at $\alpha = 0.10$ to determine which confidence interval was appropriate. The second sample has the larger standard deviation, thus:

$$s_N^2 = 13^2 = 169 \text{ with } df_N = n_N - 1 = 15 - 1 = 14, \text{ and}$$

$$s_D^2 = 11^2 = 121 \text{ with } df_D = n_D - 1 = 12 - 1 = 11.$$

The hypothesis test is conducted:

Hypotheses: $H_0 : \sigma_1^2 = \sigma_2^2$ v. $H_1 : \sigma_1^2 \neq \sigma_2^2$

Test statistic : $F_{calc} = \dfrac{s_N^2}{s_D^2} = \dfrac{169}{121} = 1.3967$

Critical value: $F_{\frac{\alpha}{2}, df_N, df_D} = F_{0.05,14,10} \approx F_{0.05,12,10} = 2.9130$

Decision rule: Reject H_0 if $F_{calc} > 2.9130$

Decision: Fail to reject H_0 because $1.3967 < 2.9130$

Conclusion: There is not sufficient evidence to conclude that the variance of Exam 1 scores is significantly different than the variance of Exam 2 scores at $\alpha = 0.10$.

This means that the appropriate confidence interval for the example was the interval that assumed $\sigma_1^2 = \sigma_2^2$ and used the pooled variance estimate.

FLASH REVIEW

1. A researcher wants to estimate the difference in the average amount of time males and females spend watching television during a week. A random sample of 14 males had a mean watching time of 22.3 hours with a standard deviation of 6.7 hours. A random sample of 16 females had a mean watching time of 16.7 hours with a standard deviation of 6.5 hours. Determine if the population variances are equal at the 0.10 level of significance.

2. A clothing store owner claims that individuals who are 20 to 35 years of age spend more on clothing in a month than individuals who are 50 to 65 years of age. A random sample of 15 persons ages 20 to 35 spent an average of $165 per month on clothing with a standard deviation of $35. A random sample of 15 persons ages 50

to 65 years of age spent an average of $97 per month on clothing with a standard deviation of $12. Test for equality of the population variances at the 0.05 level of significance.

Section 11.2—Difference Between Two Population Means

FLASH SUMMARY

As with confidence intervals, hypothesis tests on the difference between two population means consider the issues of independence of samples, known values of population standard deviations, sample sizes, and equality of population variances. The hypothesized difference is denoted D_0, and very frequently $D_0 = 0$. Although the formulas in this section are given in the more general form in which the hypothesized value is not required to equal zero, all examples will assume $D_0 = 0$. Assumptions for confidence intervals on $\mu_1 - \mu_2$ apply to the complementary hypothesis tests.

When the question asks if there is a difference in the population means, the alternative hypothesis will be $H_1: \mu_1 - \mu_2 \neq 0$ because $\mu_1 \neq \mu_2$ implies $\mu_1 - \mu_2 \neq 0$. If the claim is that $\mu_1 > \mu_2$, the alternative hypothesis is $H_1: \mu_1 - \mu_2 > 0$; the alternative hypothesis for a statement of $\mu_1 < \mu_2$ is $H_1: \mu_1 - \mu_2 < 0$.

If samples are dependent, the test is based on the sample differences. The possible sets of null and alternative hypotheses for these hypothesis tests are:

$$H_0: \mu_D = D_0 \text{ v. } H_1: \mu_D \neq D_0,$$
$$H_0: \mu_D \leq D_0 \text{ v. } H_1: \mu_D > D_0, \text{ and}$$
$$H_0: \mu_D \geq D_0 \text{ v. } H_1: \mu_D < D_0.$$

The test statistic is:

$$t_{calc} = \frac{\overline{X}_D - D_0}{s_{\overline{X}_D}} \text{ where } s_{\overline{X}_D} = \frac{s_D}{\sqrt{n_D}} \text{ and } df_D = n_D - 1.$$

Note that when $D_0 = 0$, the test statistic simplifies to $t_{calc} = \dfrac{\overline{X}_D}{s_{\overline{X}_D}}$. The critical value will also come from the t distribution with $df_D = n_D - 1$. The decision rules are displayed in the following table:

If H_1:	Reject H_0 if
$\mu_D \neq D_0$	$|t_{calc}| > t_{\frac{\alpha}{2}, df_D}$ where $df_D = n_D - 1$
$\mu_D > D_0$	$t_{calc} > t_{\alpha, df_D}$ where $df_D = n_D - 1$
$\mu_D < D_0$	$t_{calc} = t_{a, df_p}$ where $df_D = n_D - 1$

Consider the example from Unit 3 in which the average scores on Exam 1 and Exam 2 were being compared for a random sample of 10 students. Suppose the instructor wants to test her belief that the average score on the second exam is lower than the average score on the first exam at the 0.01 level of significance. Notice that the order of subtraction for the differences will determine the sign in the alternative hypothesis for one-tailed tests. If the differences are calculated Exam 1 − Exam 2, then $\mu_D = \mu_1 - \mu_2 > D_0$. However, if the differences are calculated Exam 2 − Exam 1, then $\mu_D = \mu_1 - \mu_2 < D_0$. The instructor did not quantify the size of the difference, thus $D_0 = 0$. In this example, the order of subtraction was Exam 1 − Exam 2, and the summary statistics on the differences were $\overline{X}_D = 0.7$ and $s_D = 4.321779469$; hence, $s_{\overline{X}_D} = 1.3\overline{6}$. Then the hypothesis test of the instructor's claim is as follows:

Hypotheses: $H_0: \mu_D \le 0$ v. $H_1: \mu_D > 0$

Test statistic: $t_{calc} = \dfrac{\overline{X}_D - D_0}{s_{\overline{X}_D}} = \dfrac{0.7}{1.3\overline{6}} = 0.512$

Critical value: $t_{\alpha, df_D} = t_{0.01, 9} = 2.821$

Decision rule: Reject H_0 if $t_{calc} > 2.821$

Decision: Fail to reject H_0 because $0.512 < 2.821$

Conclusion: There is not sufficient evidence to conclude that the average score on Exam 1 is significantly higher than the average score on Exam 2 for $\alpha = 0.01$.

If the samples are independent, the possible sets of null and alternative hypotheses are:

$$H_0: \mu_1 - \mu_2 = D_0 \text{ v. } H_1: \mu_1 - \mu_2 \ne D_0,$$
$$H_0: \mu_1 - \mu_2 \le D_0 \text{ v. } H_1: \mu_1 - \mu_2 > D_0, \text{ and}$$
$$H_0: \mu_1 - \mu_2 \ge D_0 \text{ v. } H_1: \mu_1 - \mu_2 < D_0.$$

If the values of the population standard deviations are known, the test statistic is:

$$z_{calc} = \frac{(\overline{X}_1 - \overline{X}_2) - D_0}{\sigma_{\overline{X}_1 - \overline{X}_2}} \text{ where } \sigma_{\overline{X}_1 - \overline{X}_2} = \sqrt{\frac{\sigma_1^2}{n_1} + \frac{\sigma_2^2}{n_2}}.$$

The critical value comes from the standard normal distribution, and the decision rules are as follows:

If H_1:	Reject H_0 if
$\mu_1 - \mu_2 \ne D_0$	$\left\| z_{calc} \right\| > z_{\frac{\alpha}{2}}$
$\mu_1 - \mu_2 > D_0$	$z_{calc} > z_{\alpha}$
$\mu_1 - \mu_2 < D_0$	$z_{calc} < -z_{\alpha}$

Because it is highly unlikely that the population variances will be known when the population means are not, this test is used infrequently.

When samples are independent, but the values of the population standard deviations are unknown, the test statistic, critical value, and decision rules depend on the sample size. For large samples, the test statistic is:

$$z_{calc} = \frac{(\overline{X}_1 - \overline{X}_2) - D_0}{s_{\overline{X}_1 - \overline{X}_2}} \text{ where } s_{\overline{X}_1 - \overline{X}_2} = \sqrt{\frac{s_1^2}{n_1} + \frac{s_2^2}{n_2}},$$

and the critical value is from the standard normal distribution. The decision rules for this case are the same as for the previous hypothesis test.

Suppose an instructor wanted to determine if there is a difference in the average scores between Exam 1 and Exam 2. Assume that a random sample of 50 Exam 1 scores and a random sample of 50 Exam 2 scores were selected. The average score from the Exam 1 sample was 75.2 with a standard deviation of 11.3; the average score from the Exam 2 sample was 70.4 with a standard deviation of 13.6. The point estimate of the average difference in exam scores is $\overline{X}_1 - \overline{X}_2 = 4.8$, and the standard error of the point estimate is $s_{\overline{X}_1 - \overline{X}_2} = 2.500599928$. The instructor would set up the following hypothesis test to determine if there is a difference in average scores between Exam 1 and Exam 2 at the 0.05 level of significance:

Hypotheses: $H_0: \mu_1 - \mu_2 = 0$ v. $H_1: \mu_1 - \mu_2 \ne 0$

$$\text{Test statistic:} \quad Z_{calc} = \frac{(\overline{X}_1 - \overline{X}_2) - D_0}{s_{\overline{X}_1 - \overline{X}_2}} = \frac{4.8}{2.500599928} = 1.92$$

$$\text{Critical value:} \quad \pm z_{\frac{\alpha}{2}} = \pm z_{0.025} = \pm 1.96$$

Decision rule: Reject H_0 if $\left| z_{calc} \right| > 1.96$

Decision: Fail to reject H_0 because $1.92 < 1.96$

Conclusion: There is not sufficient evidence to conclude that the average score on Exam 1 is significantly different than the average score on Exam 2 for $\alpha = 0.05$.

A reminder of the idea behind hypothesis testing is in order at this point. Some would say that there is obviously a difference between the means because 75.2 is not equal to 70.4. Keep in mind, however, that these are the **sample** means. The hypothesis test helps to answer a question about the difference between the **population** means. In addition, the hypothesis test does not **prove** that a difference does or does not exist. It simply draws a conclusion about a hypothesized difference between the population means from information obtained in the samples for a specific level of significance. Note that the p-value for the preceding example is:

$$p\text{-value} = (2)\text{P}(Z > 1.92) = (2)(0.0274) = 0.0548.$$

If the significance level of the test had been 0.10, the null hypothesis would have been rejected because $0.0548 < 0.10$. A different set of samples might also have yielded a different conclusion.

For the case of independent samples when the values of the population standard deviations are unknown and the sample sizes are small, the standard error term and degrees of freedom depend on whether the population variances are assumed to be equal or unequal. The hypothesis test discussed in Section 11.1 can be used to make the determination about equality of variances. If it is assumed that $\sigma_1^2 = \sigma_2^2$, the test statistic is:

$$t_{calc} = \frac{(\overline{X}_1 - \overline{X}_2) - D_0}{\left(s_{pooled} \sqrt{\frac{1}{n_1} + \frac{1}{n_2}} \right)} \quad \text{where}$$

$$s_{pooled}^2 = \frac{(n_1 - 1)s_1^2 + (n_2 - 1)s_2^2}{n_1 + n_2 - 2} \quad \text{and}$$

$$df = n_1 = n_2 - 2.$$

The critical value is from a t-distribution with $df = n_1 + n_2 - 2$, and the decision rules are displayed in the following table:

If H_1:	Reject H_0 if
$\mu_1 - \mu_2 \neq D_0$	$\left\| t_{calc} \right\| > t_{\frac{\alpha}{2}, df}$ where $df = n_1 + n_2 - 2$
$\mu_1 - \mu_2 > D_0$	$t_{calc} > t_{\alpha, df}$ where $df = n_1 + n_2 - 2$
$\mu_1 - \mu_2 < D_0$	$t_{calc}, t_{\alpha, df}$ where $df = n_1 + n_2 - 2$

If it is assumed that $\sigma_1^2 \neq \sigma_2^2$, the test statistic is:

$$t_{calc} = \frac{(\overline{X}_1 - \overline{X}_2) - D_0}{s_{\overline{X}_1 - \overline{X}_2}} \quad \text{where} \quad s_{\overline{X}_1 - \overline{X}_2} = \sqrt{\frac{s_1^2}{n_1} + \frac{s_2^2}{n_2}}$$

and degrees of freedom are found with the Satterthwaite approximation:

$$df' = \frac{(n_1 - 1)(n_2 - 1)\left(\frac{s_1^2}{n_1} + \frac{s_2^2}{n_2}\right)^2}{(n_2 - 1)\left(\frac{s_1^2}{n_1}\right)^2 + (n_1 - 1)\left(\frac{s_2^2}{n_2}\right)^2}.$$

The decision rules are the same as for the test when the pooled variance estimator is used with df' substituted for df.

Suppose a student claims that Professor Riley's first exam is much easier than Professor Wayne's first exam. To test the claim, the average first exam score from the two professors could be compared. A random sample of 10 students' first exam scores from Professor Riley's class yielded a mean of 78.5 points with a standard deviation of 6.2 points. The mean of a sample of 16 students' first exam scores from Professor Wayne's class was 69.4 with a standard deviation of 14.3.

Because the population standard deviations are not given, and the sample sizes are small, it must first be determined if the population variances will be assumed to be equal or unequal. A hypothesis test, assuming $\alpha = 0.05$, is conducted to make this determination:

Hypotheses: $H_0 : \sigma_1^2 = \sigma_2^2$ v. $H_1 : \sigma_1^2 \neq \sigma_2^2$

Test statistic: $F_{calc} = \dfrac{s_N^2}{s_D^2} = \dfrac{14.3^2}{6.2^2} = 5.3197$

Critical value: $F_{\frac{\alpha}{2}, df_N, df_D} = F_{0.025, 15, 9} = 3.7694$

Decision rule: Reject H_0 if $F_{calc} > 3.7694$

Decision: Reject H_0 because $5.3197 > 3.7694$

Conclusion: There is sufficient evidence to conclude that the variance of first exam scores in Professor Riley's class is significantly different than the variance of first exam scores in Professor Wayne's class at $\alpha = 0.05$.

For the hypothesis test on the difference between the population means, it will be assumed that $\sigma_1^2 \neq \sigma_2^2$. If first exam scores of students in Professor Riley's class are labeled Population 1, then the statement that Professor Riley's exam is easier implies $\mu_1 > \mu_2$. Calculations for the standard error term and the degrees of freedom are:

$$s_{\overline{X}_1 - \overline{X}_2} = \sqrt{\frac{s_1^2}{n_1} + \frac{s_2^2}{n_2}} = \sqrt{\frac{6.2^2}{10} + \frac{14.3^2}{16}} = 4.077330622, \text{ and}$$

$$df' = \frac{(n_1 - 1)(n_2 - 1)\left(\frac{s_1^2}{n_1} + \frac{s_2^2}{n_2}\right)^2}{(n_2 - 1)\left(\frac{s_1^2}{n_1}\right)^2 + (n_1 - 1)\left(\frac{s_2^2}{n_2}\right)^2} = \frac{(9)(15)\left(\frac{6.2^2}{10} + \frac{14.3^2}{16}\right)^2}{(15)\left(\frac{6.2^2}{10}\right)^2 + (9)\left(\frac{14.3^2}{16}\right)^2} = 22.$$

Then the hypothesis test on the difference of the means at the 0.05 level of significance can be conducted:

Hypotheses: $H_0 : \mu_1 - \mu_2 \leq 0$ v. $H_1 : \mu_1 - \mu_2 > 0$

Test statistic: $t_{calc} = \dfrac{(\overline{X}_1 - \overline{X}_2) - D_0}{s_{\overline{X}_1 - \overline{X}_2}} = \dfrac{(78.5 - 69.4) - 0}{4.077330622} = 2.232$

Critical value: $t_{\alpha, df'} = t_{0.05, 22} = 1.717$

Decision rule: Reject H_0 if $t_{calc} > 1.717$

Decision: Reject H_0 because $2.232 > 1.717$

Conclusion: There is sufficient evidence to conclude that the average first exam score in Professor Riley's class is significantly higher than the average first exam score in Professor Wayne's class for $\alpha = 0.05$.

Selecting the appropriate test statistic for the difference of two population means

Part 1

Q: Are samples dependent?	Yes	$t_{calc} = \dfrac{\bar{X}_D - D_0}{s_{\bar{X}_D}}$ where $df_D = n_D - 1$			
	No	Q: Are the values of σ_1 and σ_2 known?		Yes	$z_{calc} = \dfrac{(\bar{X}_1 - \bar{X}_2) - D_0}{\sigma_{\bar{X}_1 - \bar{X}_2}}$
				No	See **Part 2**

Part 2

Q: Is $n_1 \geq 30$ **and** $n_2 \geq 30$?	Yes	$z_{calc} = \dfrac{(\bar{X}_1 - \bar{X}_2) - D_0}{s_{\bar{X}_1 - \bar{X}_2}}$			
	No	Q: Does $\sigma_1^2 = \sigma_2^2$?		Yes	$t_{calc} = \dfrac{(\bar{X}_1 - \bar{X}_2) - D_0}{\left(s_{pooled}\sqrt{\dfrac{1}{n_1} + \dfrac{1}{n_2}}\right)}$ where $df = n_1 + n_2 - 2$
				No	$t_{calc} = \dfrac{(\bar{X}_1 - \bar{X}_2) - D_0}{s_{\bar{X}_1 - \bar{X}_2}}$ where $df' = \dfrac{(n_1 - 1)(n_2 - 1)\left(\dfrac{s_1^2}{n_1} + \dfrac{s_2^2}{n_2}\right)^2}{(n_2 - 1)\left(\dfrac{s_1^2}{n_1}\right)^2 + (n_1 - 1)\left(\dfrac{s_2^2}{n_2}\right)^2}$

FLASH REVIEW

When the problem requires determining if population variances are equal, use $\alpha = 0.10$ for the hypothesis test for equality of population variances. Use the level of significance in the problem for the hypothesis test on $\mu_1 - \mu_2$.

1. A statistics instructor claims that the average final exam scores between fall and spring semesters are significantly different. A random sample of 13 fall semester students had an average final exam score of 76 points with a standard deviation of 10 points. A random sample of 15 spring semester students had a mean final exam score of 68 points with a standard deviation of 9 points. Test the instructor's claim at the 0.05 level of significance.

2. A golf pro claims that average score for players after attending a golf workshop are significantly better than average scores before (in golf, lower scores are better). He randomly selected eight golfers, recorded the score of a round they shot the day before the workshop, then recorded the score of a round they shot the day after the workshop was completed. The results are in the following table:

Player	1	2	3	4	5	6	7	8
Before	68	72	79	80	83	89	91	93
After	70	71	73	82	76	81	85	90

Test the pro's claim at the 0.05 level of significance.

Section 11.3—Difference Between Two Population Proportions

FLASH SUMMARY

Testing claims about the difference between two population proportions involves the same assumptions as were made with confidence intervals on $p_1 - p_2$ and the use of the normal approximation to the binomial for large samples. The possible sets of null and alternative hypotheses are:

$$H_0: p_1 - p_2 = D_0 \text{ v. } H_1: p_1 - p_2 \neq D_0,$$
$$H_0: p_1 - p_2 \leq D_0 \text{ v. } H_1: p_1 - p_2 > D_0, \text{ and}$$
$$H_0: p_1 - p_2 \geq D_0 \text{ v. } H_1: p_1 - p_2 < D_0.$$

While D_0 can be any value between zero and one inclusive, the examples in this section are restricted to the case where $D_0 = 0$.

The test statistic is:

$$z_{calc} = \frac{(\hat{p}_1 - \hat{p}_2) - D_0}{s_{\hat{p}_1 - \hat{p}_2}} \text{ where } s_{\hat{p}_1 - \hat{p}_2} = \sqrt{\frac{\hat{p}_1(1 - \hat{p}_1)}{n_1} + \frac{\hat{p}_2(1 - \hat{p}_2)}{n_2}}$$

The critical value comes from the standard normal distribution, and the decision rules are in the following table:

If H_1:	Reject H_0 if
$p_1 - p_2 \neq D_0$	$\left\lvert z_{calc} \right\rvert > z_{\frac{\alpha}{2}}$
$p_1 - p_2 > D_0$	$z_{calc} > z_{\alpha}$
$p_1 - p_2 < D_0$	$z_{calc} < -z_{\alpha}$

Assume that a researcher wants to determine if there is a significant difference in the proportions of males and females who are left-handed at the 0.01 level of significance. Forty males were found to be left-handed in a random sample of 250 males, and there were 17 left-handed females in a random sample of 250 females. Then $\hat{p}_1 = 0.16$, $\hat{p}_2 = 0.068$, $\hat{p}_1 - \hat{p}_2 = 0.092$, and $s_{\hat{p}_1 - \hat{p}_2} = 0.028126571$. The hypothesis test on $p_1 - p_2$ would be constructed as follows:

Hypotheses: $H_0: p_1 - p_2 = 0 \text{ v. } H_1: p_1 - p_2 \neq 0$

Test statistic: $z_{calc} = \dfrac{(\hat{p}_1 - \hat{p}_2) - D_0}{s_{\hat{p}_1 - \hat{p}_2}} = \dfrac{0.092}{0.028126571} = 3.271$

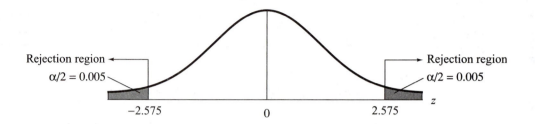

Critical value: $\pm z_{\frac{\alpha}{2}} = \pm z_{0.005} = \pm 2.575$

Decision rule: Reject H_0 if $|z_{calc}| > 2.575$

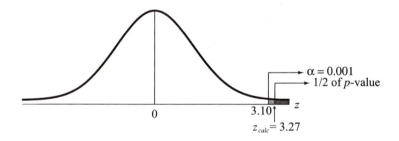

Rejection region ←
α/2 = 0.005

Rejection region →
α/2 = 0.005

−2.575   0   2.575   z

Decision: Reject H_0 because $3.271 > 2.575$

Conclusion: There is sufficient evidence to conclude that the proportion of
                 males who are left-handed is significantly different than the pro-
                 portion of females who are left-handed at $\alpha = 0.01$.

Even though a z test statistic was used in the example for the difference of two
population proportions, an exact value for the p-value cannot be obtained from the
standard normal table due to the magnitude of z_{calc}. Many standard normal tables only
include values up to 3.09 and suggest using 0.0001 to estimate the probability in the
tail area for values of 3.10 and up. Then the p-value for the example may be estimated
p-value $= (2)P(Z > 3.27) \approx (2)(0.0001) = 0.0002$.

α = 0.001
1/2 of p-value

0   3.10↑   z
                        $z_{calc} = 3.27$

Because significance levels less than 0.001 are rarely used, this p-value is frequently
stated as p-value < 0.001.

FLASH REVIEW

An instructor claims that the proportion of seniors who have completed a course in
statistics is significantly higher than the proportion of juniors. Of 100 seniors selected
randomly, 25 had completed a statistics course, whereas 15 of a random sample of 100
juniors had completed a course in statistics.

1. At the 0.01 level of significance, test the instructor's claim.

2. Find the p-value for the test.

CHAPTER 12—More than Two Populations

Section 12.1—One-Way Analysis of Variance

FLASH SUMMARY

In the previous chapter, hypothesis testing on the difference between two population means was discussed. In many cases, researchers may want to extend the hypothesis test to more than two populations. One method of doing this might be to conduct a series of hypothesis tests between all possible pairs of the population means. Unfortunately, although each test would have a significance level of α, the probability of making a Type I error accumulates across the series of tests. A method of testing for differences among more than two populations means for which the overall level of significance remains at α is needed.

The method used for this hypothesis test is called analysis of variance (ANOVA). The test statistic for ANOVA is F, which is a ratio of two variances (as in the hypothesis test for the equality of two population variances). The F test in analysis of variance compares the variance among samples, called groups, and the variance within groups to determine if the population means are different.

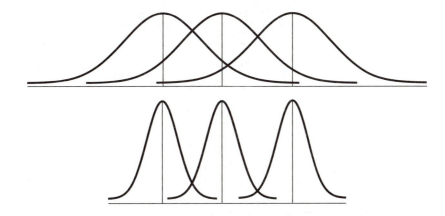

In the first illustration, the variance among groups is small compared the variance within groups thus the ANOVA is not likely to find a significant difference among the population means. In the second illustration, the variance among groups is large compared with the variance within groups, thus the ANOVA is more likely to find a significant difference among the population means, even though the mean for each of the groups is the same as in the first illustration.

This section deals with one-way analysis of variance in which groups are categorized on one criterion (one independent variable), whereas the following section discusses two-way ANOVA in which there are two independent variables. The independent variables are called factors or treatments, and the categories of the factors are called levels. The assumptions for one-way analysis of variance are:

1. the response variable is measured at the interval or ratio level;

2. independent random samples are taken from each population;

3. the response variable is normally distributed in each population; and

4. the population variances are equal.

Some statisticians claim that analysis of variance works fairly well even if the normality and equal variance assumptions are violated, as long as the departure from the assumptions is not too extreme. This issue is still being debated.

The hypotheses used in one-way ANOVA are:

$H_0: \mu_1 = \mu_2 = \cdots = \mu_k$ v. H_1: at least one pair of population means is not equal where k is the number of groups and $k \geq 3$. Analysis of variance can actually be used with two groups because $F = t^2$, but the computations from the previous chapter are less complex. Other ways of wording the alternative hypothesis include H_1: Not H_0 or $H_1: H_0$ is false. It is **not** appropriate to state $H_1: \mu_1 \neq \mu_2 \neq \cdots \neq \mu_k$ because this implies that **all** pairs of population means are not equal. It is important to understand that the F test simply determines if differences among means exist; it does not indicate which pairs of population means differ.

The definition and calculation of several quantities are necessary to construct and calculate the F test statistic for a one-way ANOVA. Notation for these quantities varies widely from text to text. Following is the notation used in the discussion in this chapter:

x_{ij}	the jth observation in the ith sample
n	the total sample size
$\bar{x}$	the mean of all observations (sometimes called the grand mean or mean total)
s^2	the variance of all observations
n_i	the size of sample i
$\bar{x}_i$	the mean of sample i
s_i^2	the variance of sample i
SS_{Tot}	the sum of squares of all observations
SS_B	the sum of squares between groups
SS_W	the sum of squares within groups
MS_B	the mean square between groups
MS_W	the mean square within groups

where $i = 1, \ldots, k$ and $j = 1, \ldots, n_i$.

Recall that the sum of squares is the squared deviation of the observations in a data set from the mean of the data set. SS_{Tot} is this quantity for all the observations and can be separated into the sum of squares between groups and the sum of squares within groups, thus:

$$SS_{Tot} = \sum_{i=1}^{k} \sum_{j=1}^{n_i} (x_{ij} - \bar{x})^2 = \sum_{i=1}^{k} n_i(\bar{x}_i - \bar{x})^2 + \sum_{i=1}^{k} \sum_{j=1}^{n_i} (x_{ij} - \bar{x}_i)^2 = SS_B + SS_W.$$

While the preceding formula defines the sums of squares, the actual values of SS_{Tot} and SS_W can be computed more easily using the formulas:

$$SS_{Tot} = (n-1)s^2 \text{ and}$$

$$SS_W = \sum_{i=1}^{k} (n_i - 1)s_i^2.$$

Note that SS_W is the sum of the sums of squares for each sample. Also note that because $SS_{Tot} = SS_B + SS_W$, it is only necessary to calculate two of the three quantities using the formula. The third quantity may then be obtained by solving $SS_{Tot} = SS_B + SS_W$ for the desired value. For example, $SS_B = SS_{Tot} - SS_W$.

MS_B is the estimate of the between groups variance, and MS_W is the estimate of variance within groups (often called the error variance). These quantities are found by dividing the appropriate sum of squares by the appropriate degrees of freedom:

$$MS_B = \frac{SS_B}{df_B} \text{ where } df_B = k - 1, \text{ and}$$

$$MS_W = \frac{SS_W}{df_W} \text{ where } df_W = n - k.$$

The degrees of freedom associated with SS_{Tot} are $df_{Tot} = n - 1$. As with the sums of squares, $df_{Tot} = df_B + df_W$. However, the mean square between groups and mean square within groups do not sum to the mean square for total. In fact, the mean square for total is not a necessary quantity for ANOVA and thus is not calculated.

The F test statistic is constructed as the ratio of the two mean squares:

$$F_{calc} = \frac{MS_B}{MS_W},$$

Because the test statistic has an F distribution, the critical value is F_{α, df_B, df_W}. The decision rule is to reject H_0 if $F_{calc} > F_{\alpha, df_B, df_W}$.

When conducting a hypothesis test using analysis of variance, it is customary to show a summary table of the calculated values along with the components of the hypothesis test. The summary table is of the form:

Source	SS	df	MS	F
Between groups	$SS_B = \sum_{i=1}^{k} n_i(\bar{x}_i - \bar{x})^2$	$df_B = k - 1$	$MS_B = \dfrac{SS_B}{df_B}$	$F_{calc} = \dfrac{MS_B}{MS_W}$
Within groups	$SS_W = \sum_{i=1}^{k} (n_i - 1)s_i^2$	$df_W = n - k$	$MS_W = \dfrac{SS_W}{df_W}$	
Total	$SS_{Tot} = (n - 1)s^2$	$df_{Tot} = n - 1$		

Suppose that a researcher wants to determine if there are differences among three population means with a significance level of 0.05. The researcher takes independent random samples from each population and finds the following summary statistics:

$n = 45$	$n_1 = 15$	$n_2 = 15$	$n_3 = 15$
$\bar{x} = 5$	$\bar{x}_1 = 3$	$\bar{x}_2 = 8$	$\bar{x}_3 = 4$
$s = 4.106535811$	$s_1 = 2$	$s_2 = 5$	$s_3 = 3$

Note that the standard deviations of the samples are given in the table, as is often the case in textbook exercises, and one must square these values when doing calculations.

The hypotheses for the test are

$H_0 : \mu_1 = \mu_2 = \mu_3$ v. $H_1 :$ at least one pair of population means is not equal.

Because $df_B = k - 1 = 3 - 1 = 2$ and $df_W = n - k = 45 - 3 = 42$, the critical value and the decision rule are:

$F_{0.05, 2, 42} \approx F_{0.05, 2, 40} = 3.2317$, and

Reject H_0 if $F_{calc} > 3.2317$.

The sums of squares, mean squares, and test statistic are calculated and displayed in the summary table:

$$SS_B = \sum_{i=1}^{k} n_i(\bar{x}_i - \bar{x})^2 = (15)(3 - 5)^2 + (15)(8 - 5)^2 + (15)(4 - 5)^2 = 210$$

$$SS_W = \sum_{i=1}^{k} (n_i - 1)s_i^2 = (14)(2^2) + (14)(5^2) + (14)(3^2) = 532$$

$$SS_{Tot} = (n - 1)s^2 = (44)(3.571986969)^2 = 742$$

$$MS_B = \frac{SS_B}{df_B} = \frac{210}{2} = 105$$

$$MS_W = \frac{SS_W}{df_W} = \frac{532}{42} = 12.\overline{6}$$

$$F_{calc} = \frac{MS_B}{MS_W} = \frac{105}{12.\overline{6}} = 8.2895$$

Source	SS	df	MS	F
Between groups	210	2	105	8.2895
Within groups	532	42	12.$\overline{6}$	
Total	742	44		

Because 8.2895 > 3.2317, the decision is made to reject H_0. We do have sufficient evidence to conclude that there is a significant difference between at least one pair of the population means for $\alpha = 0.05$.

This test indicates that at least one pair of population means is significantly different, but not which pair(s). Multiple comparison tests are methods for determining which pair(s) of means are not the same. Frequently used multiple comparisons include the least significant difference (LSD), the Tukey's test, and the Scheffé test. Because of the ease of the calculation, the Scheffé test is presented here.

The Scheffé test is actually a series of tests that conducts pair-wise comparisons of the population means **after** it is determined that significant differences exist. In other words, each possible pair of means is tested for equality. In the previous example, the comparisons would be for μ_1 with μ_2, μ_1 with μ_3, and μ_2 with μ_3. The hypotheses, test statistic, critical value, and decision rule for each pair-wise test are, respectively:

$H_0 : \mu_i = \mu_j$ v. $H_1 : \mu_i \neq \mu_j$ for $i = 1, \ldots, k; j = 1, \ldots, k;$ and $i \neq j;$

$$F_S = \frac{(\bar{x}_i - \bar{x}_j)^2}{MS_W \left(\frac{1}{n_i} + \frac{1}{n_j} \right)};$$

$F' = (k-1) F_{\alpha, df_B, df_W};$ and

Reject H_0 if $F_S > F'$.

For the example,

$$F' = (k-1) F_{\alpha, df_B, df_W} = (2)(3.2317) = 6.4634$$

$$F_S = \frac{(\bar{x}_1 - \bar{x}_2)^2}{MS_W \left(\frac{1}{n_1} + \frac{1}{n_2} \right)} = \frac{(3-8)^2}{(12.\overline{6})\left(\frac{1}{15} + \frac{1}{15} \right)} = 14.8026 \text{ for } \mu_1 \text{ and } \mu_2,$$

$$F_S = \frac{(\bar{x}_1 - \bar{x}_3)^2}{MS_W \left(\frac{1}{n_1} + \frac{1}{n_3} \right)} = \frac{(3-4)^2}{(12.\overline{6})\left(\frac{1}{15} + \frac{1}{15} \right)} = 0.5921 \text{ for } \mu_1 \text{ and } \mu_3, \text{ and}$$

$$F_S = \frac{(\bar{x}_2 - \bar{x}_3)^2}{MS_W \left(\frac{1}{n_2} + \frac{1}{n_3} \right)} = \frac{(8-4)^2}{(12.\overline{6})\left(\frac{1}{15} + \frac{1}{15} \right)} = 9.4737 \text{ for } \mu_2 \text{ and } \mu_3.$$

The null hypothesis is rejected for μ_1 with μ_2 as well as for μ_2 with μ_3. There is sufficient evidence to conclude that μ_1 and μ_2 are significantly different ($\mu_1 \neq \mu_2$) and that μ_2 and μ_3 are significantly different ($\mu_2 \neq \mu_3$) at $\alpha = 0.05$. There is not sufficient evidence to conclude that μ_1 and μ_3 are significantly different ($\mu_1 = \mu_3$) at $\alpha = 0.05$.

FLASH REVIEW

An instructor believes that the average score of a comprehensive statistics exam will be different for students who took their statistics courses in three different departments at Connor College. The instructor takes random samples of 10 statistics students from each department and records the exam score for each student in the following table:

Student	1	2	3	4	5	6	7	8	9	10
Department A	97	69	83	66	78	55	82	73	70	92
Department B	88	67	77	60	82	95	92	52	100	75
Department C	71	78	63	47	75	69	90	81	54	80

1.   What is the independent variable?

2.   What is the response variable?

3.   Test the instructor's belief at the 0.05 level of significance. Be sure to include the summary table, hypotheses, decision rule, test statistic, decision, and conclusion.

4.   Is it appropriate to do a Scheffé multiple comparison test? Justify your answer.

Section 12.2—Two-Way Analysis of Variance

FLASH SUMMARY

Two-way analysis of variance is used when groups are classified on two factors. For example, a researcher might want to determine if there is a difference in average GPA for different combinations of student status (traditional v. nontraditional) and gender. The two factors are denoted A and B; the factor A has a levels, and the factor B has b levels. The combinations of levels (also called treatment combinations) are denoted $A_i B_j$ where $i = 1, \ldots, a$ and $j = 1, \ldots, b$. Then there are ab populations of interest, one for each treatment combination. The observations are often displayed in a table:

	B_1	B_2
A_1	$x_{11k_{11}}$ where $k_{11} = 1, \ldots, n_{11}$	$x_{12k_{12}}$ where $k_{12} = 1, \ldots, n_{12}$
A_2	$x_{21k_{21}}$ where $k_{21} = 1, \ldots, n_{21}$	$x_{22k_{22}}$ where $k_{22} = 1, \ldots, n_{22}$

It is obvious from the notation in the table that the calculation of the necessary values for the test statistic are tedious, and these values are almost always calculated using a computer software program. In this section, computations are not be performed; rather, hypothesis testing will be done using a summary table with pre-calculated values.

Assumptions for two-way analysis of variance are:

1.   the response variable is measured at the interval or ratio level;

2.   independent random samples are taken from each population;

3. the response variable is normally distributed in each population;

4. the population variances are equal; and

5. sample sizes are equal for the treatment combinations.

The requirement of equal sample sizes produces a balanced design. Although two-way ANOVA can be performed on unbalanced designs, the methods for doing so are beyond the scope of most introductory statistics courses.

The between-groups variation in two-way analysis of variance is partitioned into components for each of the factors A, B, and $A \times B$. Thus, three sets of null and alternative hypotheses are tested. The first two sets are:

$$H_{0_A}: \mu_{A_1} = \mu_{A2} = \cdots = \mu_{A_a} \text{ v. } H_{1_A}: \text{at least one pair of population means is not equal, and}$$

$$H_{0_B}: \mu_{B_1} = \mu_{B_2} = \cdots = \mu_{B_b} \text{ v. } H_{1_B}: \text{at least one pair of population means is not equal.}$$

These hypotheses are used to test the significance of the main effect of A and the main effect of B. A main effect is the effect of one factor averaged over (ignoring) the other. This is analogous to performing two separate one-way ANOVAs on the two factors but retains the level of significance for both at the same time. The third set of hypotheses tests the interaction effect of A and B.

An interaction effect, denoted $A \times B$, is the effect of both factors together. If the interaction effect is significant, then the effect of factor A is different for different levels of factor B. If the interaction effect is not significant, the effect of factor A is the same for all levels of factor B.

Interaction between factors A and B significant (Note that the lines intersect.)

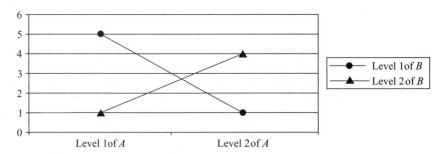

Interaction between factors A and B not significant (Note that the lines are parallel.)

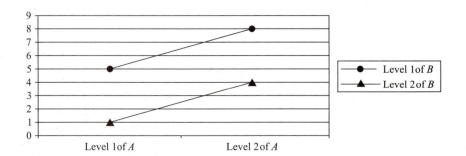

When the interaction is significant, the main effects are not interpreted because it is not appropriate to average over the levels of factor A if the effect is different for different levels of B. The null hypothesis for the interaction effect sets the means for all treatment combinations equal to one another, whereas the alternatives states that at least one pair of population means for $A \times B$ is not equal. For example, let $a = 3$ and $b = 2$; then the null and alternative hypotheses are:

$$H_{0_{A \times B}}: \mu_{A_1 B_1} = \mu_{A_1 B_2} = \mu_{A_2 B_1} = \mu_{A_2 B_2} = \mu_{A_3 B_1} = \mu_{A_3 B_2} \text{ v.}$$

$H_{1_{A \times B}}$: at least one pair of population means is not equal.

Multiple comparison tests can be conducted on factors with more than two levels if significant differences are found.

The test statistics for the three hypothesis tests are:

$$F_{A_{calc}} = \frac{MS_A}{MS_W},$$

$$F_{B_{calc}} = \frac{MS_B}{MS_W}, \text{ and}$$

$$F_{A \times B_{calc}} = \frac{MS_{A \times B}}{MS_W}.$$

Note that in this section, MS_B is the mean square for factor B rather than the mean square between. The between groups values of $SS_{Bet} = SS_A + SS_B + SS_{A \times B}$ and $df_{Bet} = df_A + df_B + df_{A \times B}$ are sometimes computed to verify that the sums of squares and degrees of freedom for the factors add up to these values. The critical values are F_{α, df_A, df_w}, F_{α, df_B, df_w}, and $F_{\alpha, df_{A \times B}, df_w}$, respectively. The associated decision rules are to reject H_0 if $F_{A_{calc}} > F_{\alpha, df_A, df_w}$, $F_{B_{calc}} > F_{\alpha, df_B, df_w}$, and $F_{A \times B_{calc}} > F_{\alpha, df_{A \times B}, df_w}$.

The ANOVA summary table for two-way ANOVA is similar to the table for one-way ANOVA, with the exception that between groups variance is partitioned into variance components for each of the factors A, B, and $A \times B$.

Source	SS	df	MS	F
Between groups	SS_{Bet}	$df_{Bet} = df_A + df_B + df_{A \times B}$		
A	SS_A	$df_A = a - 1$	$MS_A = \frac{SS_A}{df_A}$	$F_{A_{calc}} = \frac{MS_A}{MS_W}$
B	SS_B	$df_B = b - 1$	$MS_B = \frac{SS_B}{df_B}$	$F_{B_{calc}} = \frac{MS_B}{MS_W}$
$A \times B$	$SS_{A \times B}$	$df_{A \times B} = (a - 1)(b - 1)$	$MS_{A \times B} = \frac{SS_{A \times B}}{df_{A \times B}}$	$F_{A \times B_{calc}} = \frac{MS_{A \times B}}{MS_W}$
Within groups	SS_W	$df_W = n - ab$	$MS_W = \frac{SS_W}{df_W}$	
Total	SS_{Tot}	$df_{Tot} = n - 1$		

Suppose a researcher claims that there is a difference in the average age of NRA members classified according to political party preference (Republican, Democrat, Independent) and gender (male, female) at the 0.05 level of significance. Then factor A is political party preference and factor B is gender. The ANOVA summary table for 18 subjects was calculated:

Source	SS	df	MS	F
Between groups	69.68	5		
Party	13.13	2	6.565	0.1337
Gender	38.22	1	38.22	0.7783
Party × Gender	18.33	2	9.165	0.1866
Within groups	589.29	12	49.1075	
Total	658.97	17		

The hypothesis test on party by gender is constructed first:

Hypotheses: $H_{0_{A \times B}}: \mu_{A_1 B_1} = \mu_{A_1 B_2} = \mu_{A_2 B_1} = \mu_{A_2 B_2} = \mu_{A_3 B_1} = \mu_{A_3 B_2}$ v.

$H_{1_{A \times B}}$ at least one pair of population means for $A \times B$ is not equal

Test statistic: $F_{A \times B_{calc}} = 0.1866$

Critical value: $F_{\alpha, df_{A \times B}, df_W} = F_{0.05, 2, 12} = 3.8853$

Decision rule: Reject $H_{0_{A \times B}}$ if $F_{F \times B_{calc}} > 3.8853$

Decision: Fail to reject $H_{0_{A \times B}}$ because $0.1866 < 3.8853$

Conclusion: There is not sufficient evidence to conclude that the average age of NRA members is significantly different for combinations of political party preference and gender at $\alpha = 0.05$.

Because the interaction effect was not significant, the tests for the main effects of political party preference and gender are conducted:

Political Party Preference

Hypotheses: $H_{0_A}: \mu_{A_1} = \mu_{A_2} = \mu_{A_3}$ v.

H_{1_A}: at least one pair of population means for political party is not equal

Test statistic: $F_{A_{calc}} = 0.1337$

Critical value: $F_{\alpha, df_A, df_W} = F_{0.05, 2, 12} = 3.8853$

Decision rule: Reject H_{0_A} if $F_{A_{calc}} > 3.8853$

Decision: Fail to reject H_{0_A} because $0.1337 < 3.8853$

Conclusion: There is not sufficient evidence to conclude that the average age of NRA members is significantly different between Republicans, Democrats, and Independents at $\alpha = 0.05$.

Gender

Hypotheses: $H_{0_B}: \mu_{B_1} = \mu_{B_2}$ v.

H_{1_B} at least one pair of population means for gender is not equal
(Note that this hypothesis is equivalent to $H_{1_B}: \mu_{B_1} \neq \mu_{B_2}$.)

Test statistic: $F_{B_{calc}} = 0.7783$

Critical value: $F_{\alpha, df_B, df_W} = F_{0.05, 1, 12} = 4.7472$

Decision rule: Reject H_{0_B} if $F_{B_{calc}} > 4.7472$

Decision: Fail to reject H_{0_B} because $0.7783 < 4.7472$

Conclusion: There is not sufficient evidence to conclude that the average age of NRA members is significantly different between males and females at $\alpha = 0.05$.

FLASH REVIEW

1.   Complete the following ANOVA summary table:

Source	SS	df	MS	F
Between groups	87269	11		
A	52635	3		8.2467
B		2	1507	
A × B	31620		5270	2.4771
Within groups	102121	48	2127.520833	
Total	189390	59		

2.   Conduct a hypothesis test to determine if there is a significant interaction at $\alpha = 0.05$.

3.   Is it appropriate to conduct tests for the main effects of A and B? Justify your answer.

Chapter 9—Fundamentals of Hypothesis Testing

1. p, hypothesis test, $>$

2. ρ, confidence interval

3. $\mu_1 - \mu_2$, hypothesis test, $\neq$

Chapter 10—Section 10.1, Population Mean

1. a. $\bar{X} = 5.67$,

    $s = 1.866696428$,

    $$s_{\bar{X}} = \frac{s}{\sqrt{n}} = \frac{1.866696428}{\sqrt{10}} = 0.590301241,$$

    Hypotheses: $H_0 : \mu \leq 4$ v. $H_1 : \mu > 4$

    Test statistic: $t_{calc} = \dfrac{\bar{X} - \mu_0}{s_{\bar{X}}} = \dfrac{5.67 - 4}{0.590301241} = 2.829$

    Critical value: $t_{\alpha, df} = t_{0.01, 9} = 2.821$

    Decision rule: Reject H_0 if $t_{calc} > 2.821$

    Decision: Reject H_0 because $2.829 > 2.821$

    Conclusion: There is sufficient evidence to conclude that the average number of hours the instructor's students spend studying for the final exam is significantly greater than four hours for $\alpha = 0.01$.

    b. Because $2.821 < 2.829 < 3.250$, then $0.005 < p$-value < 0.01.

2. a. $s_{\bar{X}} = \dfrac{s}{\sqrt{n}} = \dfrac{9500}{\sqrt{50}} = 1343.502884,$

    Hypotheses: $H_0 : \mu \geq 53000$ v. $H_1 : \mu < 53000$

    Test statistic: $z_{calc} = \dfrac{\bar{X} - \mu_0}{s_{\bar{X}}} = \dfrac{51000 - 53000}{1343.502884} = -1.489$

    Critical value: $-z_\alpha = -z_{0.05} = -1.645$

    Decision rule: Reject H_0 if $Z_{calc} < -1.645$

    Decision: Fail to reject H_0 because $-1.489 > -1.645$

    Conclusion: There is not sufficient evidence to conclude that average cost of a three bedroom home in Cole County is significantly less than $53,000 for $\alpha = 0.05$.

    b. p-value$= P(Z < -1.49) = 0.0681$

3. a. $\sigma_{\bar{X}} = \dfrac{\sigma}{\sqrt{n}} = \dfrac{15}{\sqrt{25}} = 3,$

    Hypotheses: $H_0: \mu = 100$ v. $H_1 : \mu \neq 100$

    Test statistic: $z_{calc} = \dfrac{\bar{X} - \mu_0}{\sigma_{\bar{X}}} = \dfrac{117 - 100}{3} = 5.667$

    Critical value: $\pm z_{\frac{\alpha}{2}} = \pm z_{0.05} = 1.645$

    Decision rule: Reject H_0 if $\left| z_{calc} \right| > 1.645$

Decision: Reject H_0 because $5.667 > 1.645$

Conclusion: There is sufficient evidence to conclude that the average IQ of students enrolled at Connor College is significantly different than 100 points for $\alpha = 0.10$.

b. Yes, the null hypothesis would be rejected because 100 is not in the interval.

Chapter 10—Section 10.2, Population Proportion

1. **a.** $\hat{p} = \dfrac{24}{200} = 0.12$,

$$\sigma_{P_0} = \sqrt{\dfrac{p_0(1 - p_0)}{n}} = \sqrt{\dfrac{(0.10)(0.90)}{200}} = 0.021213203;$$

Hypotheses: $H_0 : p \leq 0.10$ v. $H_1 : p > 0.10$

Test statistic: $z_{calc} = \dfrac{\hat{p} - p_0}{\sigma_{P_0}} = \dfrac{0.12 - 0.10}{0.021213203} = 0.94$

Critical value: $z_\alpha = z_{0.10} = 1.28$

Decision rule: Reject H_0 if $Z_{calc} > 1.28$

Decision: Fail to reject H_0 because $0.94 < 1.28$

Conclusion: There is not sufficient evidence to conclude that the proportion of left-handed students at Connor College is significantly greater than 0.10 for $\alpha = 0.10$.

b. p-value $= P(Z > 0.94) = 0.1736$

2. **a.** $\hat{p} = \dfrac{720}{1000} = 0.72$,

$$\sigma_{P_0} = \sqrt{\dfrac{p_0(1 - p_0)}{n}} = \sqrt{\dfrac{(0.68)(0.32)}{1000}} = 0.014751271,$$

Hypotheses: $H_0: p = 0.68$ v. $H_1: p \neq 0.68$

Test statistic: $z_{calc} = \dfrac{\hat{p} - p_0}{\sigma_{P_0}} = \dfrac{0.72 - 0.68}{0.014751271} = 2.712$

Critical value: $\pm z_{\frac{\alpha}{2}} = \pm z_{0.005} = \pm 2.575$

Decision rule: Reject H_0 if $\left| z_{calc} \right| > 2.575$

Decision: Reject H_0 because $2.712 > 2.575$

Conclusion: There is sufficient evidence to conclude that the proportion of people voting for the campaign manager's candidate in a poll one month prior to election day is significantly different than 0.68 for $\alpha = 0.01$.

b. p-value $= (2)P(Z > 2.71) = (2)(0.0034) = 0.0068$

Chapter 10—Section 10.3, Linear Relationships Between Two Variables

1. $s_r = \sqrt{\dfrac{1 - r^2}{n - 2}} = \sqrt{\dfrac{1 - (0.970851506)^2}{8}} = 0.084740304$,

Hypotheses: $H_0 : \rho = 0$ v. $H_1 : \rho \neq 0$

Test statistic: $t_{calc} = \dfrac{r}{s_r} = \dfrac{0.970851506}{0.084740304} = 11.457$

Critical value: $\pm t_{\frac{\alpha}{2}, df} = \pm t_{0.025, 8} = \pm 2.306$

Decision rule:	Reject H_0 if $\left| t_{calc} \right| > 2.306$
Decision:	Reject H_0 because $11.457 > 2.306$
Conclusion:	There is sufficient evidence to conclude that there is a significant linear relationship between the number of hours that students study for the final exam in statistics and the students' final exam grades at $\alpha = 0.05$.

2.

Hypotheses:	$H_0: \beta_1 \leq 0$ v. $H_1 : \beta_1 > 0$
Test statistic:	$t_{calc} = \dfrac{b}{s_b} = \dfrac{0.105}{0.055} = 1.909$
Critical value:	$t_{\alpha, df} = t_{0.01,13} = 2.650$
Decision rule:	Reject H_0 if $t_{calc} > 2.650$
Decision:	Fail to reject H_0 because $1.909 < 2.650$
Conclusion:	There is not sufficient evidence to conclude that there is a significant positive slope for the regression equation between students' ACT scores and their GPAs at the end of their freshman year at $\alpha = 0.01$.

Chapter 11—Section 11.1, Difference Between Two Population Variances

1.

Hypotheses:	$H_0 : \sigma_1^2 = \sigma_2^2$ v. $H_1 : \sigma_1^2 \neq \sigma_2^2$
Test statistic:	$F_{calc} = \dfrac{s_N^2}{s_D^2} = \dfrac{6.7^2}{6.5^2} = 1.0625$
Critical value:	$F_{\frac{\alpha}{2}, df_N, df_D} = F_{0.05,13,15} \approx F_{0.05,12,15} = 2.4753$
Decision rule:	Reject H_0 if $F_{calc} > 2.4753$
Decision:	Fail to reject H_0 because $1.0625 < 2.4753$
Conclusion:	There is not sufficient evidence to conclude that the variance of television-watching time for males is significantly different than the variance of television-watching time for females at $\alpha = 0.10$.

2.

Hypotheses:	$H_0 : \sigma_1^2 = \sigma_2^2$ v. $H_1 : \sigma_1^2 \neq \sigma_2^2$
Test statistic:	$F_{calc} = \dfrac{s_N^2}{s_D^2} = \dfrac{35^2}{12^2} = 8.5069$
Critical value:	$F_{\frac{\alpha}{2}, df_N, df_D} = F_{0.025,14,14} \approx F_{0.025,12,14} = 3.0502$
Decision rule:	Reject H_0 if $F_{calc} > 3.0502$
Decision:	Reject H_0 because $8.5069 > 3.0502$
Conclusion:	There is sufficient evidence to conclude that the variance of amount spent on clothing in one month for the 20 to 35 age group is significantly different than the variance of amount spent on clothing in one month for the 50 to 65 age group at $\alpha = 0.05$.

Chapter 11—Section 11.2, Difference Between Two Population Means

1. First a test for equality of variances must be conducted:

Hypotheses:	$H_0 : \sigma_1^2 = \sigma_2^2$ v. $H_1 : \sigma_1^2 \neq \sigma_2^2$

Test statistic: $F_{calc} = \dfrac{s_N^2}{s_D^2} = \dfrac{10^2}{9^2} = 1.2346$

Critical value: $F_{\frac{\alpha}{2}, df_N, df_D} = F_{0.05, 12, 14} = 2.5342$

Decision rule: Reject H_0 if $F_{calc} > 2.5342$

Decision: Fail to reject H_0 because $1.2346 < 2.5342$

Conclusion: There is not sufficient evidence to conclude that the variance of final exam scores for the small semester is significantly different than the variance of final exam scores for the spring semester at $\alpha = 0.10$.

The test on $\mu_1 - \mu_2$ will be conducted assuming equal variances:

$$s_{pooled}^2 = \dfrac{(n_1 - 1)s_1^2 + (n_2 - 1)s_2^2}{n_1 + n_2 - 2} = \dfrac{(12)(10^2) + (14)(9^2)}{13 + 15 - 2} = 89.76923077,$$

Hypotheses: $H_0 : \mu_1 - \mu_2 = 0 \text{ v. } H_1 : \mu_1 - \mu_2 \neq 0$

Test statistic: $t_{calc} = \dfrac{(\bar{X}_1 - \bar{X}_2) - D_0}{\left(s_{pooled}\sqrt{\dfrac{1}{n_1} + \dfrac{1}{n_2}}\right)} = \dfrac{76 - 68}{\left(\sqrt{89.76923077} \cdot \sqrt{\dfrac{1}{13} + \dfrac{1}{15}}\right)} = 2.228$

Critical value: $\pm t_{\frac{\alpha}{2}, df} = \pm t_{0.025, 26} = \pm 2.056$

Decision rule: Reject H_0 if $|t_{calc}| > 2.056$

Decision: Reject H_0 because $2.228 > 2.056$

Conclusion: There is sufficient evidence to conclude that the average final exam score for the fall semester is significantly different than the average final exam score for the spring semester at $\alpha = 0.05$.

2. Differences (Before − After): $-2, 1, 6, -2, 7, 8, 6, 3$;

$\bar{X}_D = 3.375$,

$s_D = 3.997767234$,

$s_{\bar{X}_D} = \dfrac{s_D}{\sqrt{n_D}} = \dfrac{3.997767234}{\sqrt{8}} = 1.41342416$,

Hypotheses: $H_0 : \mu_D \leq 0 \text{ v. } H_1 : \mu_D > 0$

Test statistic: $t_{calc} = \dfrac{\bar{X}_D - D_0}{s_{\bar{X}_D}} = \dfrac{3.375}{1.41342416} = 2.389$

Critical value: $t_{\alpha, df_D} = t_{0.05, 7} = 1.895$

Decision rule: Reject H_0 if $t_{calc} > 1.895$

Decision: Reject H_0 because $2.389 > 1.895$

Conclusion: There is sufficient evidence to conclude that the average golf score before the workshop is significantly greater than the average golf score after the workshop for $\alpha = 0.01$.

Chapter 11—Section 11.3, Difference Between Population Proportions

1. a. $\hat{p}_1 = \dfrac{25}{100} = 0.25$, $\hat{p}_2 = \dfrac{15}{100} = 0.15$,

$$s_{\hat{p}_1 - \hat{p}_2} = \sqrt{\dfrac{\hat{p}_1(1 - \hat{p}_1)}{n_1} + \dfrac{\hat{p}_2(1 - \hat{p}_2)}{n_2}}$$

$$= \sqrt{\dfrac{(0.25)(0.75)}{100} + \dfrac{(0.15)(0.85)}{100}} = 0.05612486,$$

Hypotheses: $H_0: p_1 - p_2 \leq 0$ v. $H_1: p_1 - p_2 > 0$

Test statistic: $z_{calc} = \dfrac{(\hat{p}_1 - \hat{p}_2) - D_0}{s_{\hat{p}_1 - \hat{p}_2}} = \dfrac{0.25 - 0.15}{0.05612486} = 1.78$

Critical value: $z_\alpha = z_{0.01} = 2.33$

Decision rule: Reject H_0 if $z_{calc} > 2.33$

Decision: Fail to reject H_0 because $1.78 < 2.33$

Conclusion: There is not sufficient evidence to conclude that the proportion of seniors who have completed a course in statistics is significantly higher than the proportion of juniors at $\alpha = 0.01$.

   b. p-value $= P(Z > 1.78) = 0.0375$

Chapter 12—Section 12.1, One-way Analysis of Variance

1. The independent variable is department.
2. The response variable is score on the comprehensive statistics exam.
3.

$n = 30$	$n_1 = 10$	$n_2 = 10$	$n_3 = 10$
$\bar{x} = 75.3\overline{6}$	$\bar{x}_1 = 76.5$	$\bar{x}_2 = 78.8$	$\bar{x}_3 = 70.8$
$s^2 = 189.8954023$	$s_1^2 = 157.6\overline{1}$	$s_2^2 = 245.5\overline{1}$	$s_3^2 = 171.0\overline{6}$

$$SS_B = \sum_{i=1}^{k} n_i(\bar{x}_i - \bar{x})^2 = (10)(76.5 - 75.3\overline{6})^2 + (10)(78.8 - 75.3\overline{6})^2$$
$$+ (10)(70.8 - 75.3\overline{6})^2 = 339.2\overline{6},$$

$$SS_W = \sum_{i=1}^{k} (n_i - 1)s_i^2 = (9)(157.6\overline{1}) + (9)(245.5\overline{1}) + (9)(171.0\overline{6}) = 5167.7,$$

$$SS_{Tot} = (n - 1)s^2 = (29)(189.8954023) = 5506.9\overline{6},$$

$$df_B = k - 1 = 3 - 1 = 2$$

$$df_W = n - k = 30 - 3 = 27$$

$$df_{Tot} = n - 1 = 30 - 1 = 29$$

$$MS_B = \frac{SS_B}{df_B} = \frac{339.2\overline{6}}{2} = 169.6\overline{3},$$

$$MS_W = \frac{SS_W}{df_W} = \frac{5167.7}{27} = 191.3962963,$$

$$F_{calc} = \frac{MS_B}{MS_W} = \frac{169.6\overline{3}}{191.3962963} = 0.8863,$$

Source	SS	df	MS	F
Between groups	$339.2\overline{6}$	2	$169.6\overline{3}$	0.8863
Within groups	5167.7	27	191.3963	
Total	$5506.9\overline{6}$	29		

Hypotheses:	$H_0 : \mu_1 = \mu_2 = \mu_3$ v.
	H_1 : at least one pair of population means is not equal
Test statistic:	$F_{calc} = 0.8863$
Critical value:	$F_{\alpha, df_N, df_D} = F_{0.05, 2, 27} = 3.3541$
Decision rule:	Reject H_0 if $F_{calc} > 3.3541$
Decision:	Fail to reject H_0 because $0.8863 < 3.3541$
Conclusion:	There is not sufficient evidence to conclude that there is a significant difference between at least one pair of comprehensive exam score means for $\alpha = 0.05$.

4. It is not appropriate to do a Scheffé multiple comparison test because a significant difference was not found among the population means.

Chapter 12—Section 12.2, Two-Way Analysis of Variance

1. $MS_A = \dfrac{SS_A}{df_A} = \dfrac{52635}{3} = 17{,}545,$

$SS_B = SS_{Bet} - SS_A - SS_{A \times B} = 87269 - 52635 - 31620 = 3014$ or

$SS_B = df_B \cdot MS_B = (2)(1507) = 3014,$

$F_{B_{calc}} = \dfrac{MS_B}{MS_W} = \dfrac{1507}{2127.520833} = 0.7083$

$df_{A \times B} = (a-1)(b-1) = (3)(2) = 6$ or $df_{A \times B} = df_{Bet} - df_A - df_B = 11 - 3 - 2 = 6,$

Source	SS	df	MS	F
Between groups	87269	11		
A	52635	3	17545	8.2467
B	3014	2	1507	0.7083
A × B	31620	6	5270	2.4771
Within groups	102121	48	2127.520833	
Total	189390	59		

2.

Hypotheses:	$H_{0_{A \times B}} : \mu_{A_1 B_1} = \mu_{A_1 B_2} = \mu_{A_1 B_3} = \mu_{A_2 B_1} = \mu_{A_2 B_2} = \mu_{A_2 B_3} = \mu_{A_3 B_1}$
	$= \mu_{A_3 B_2} = \mu_{A_3 B_3}$ v. $= \mu_{A_4 B_1} = \mu_{A_4 B_2} = \mu_{A_4 B_2}$ v.
	$H_{1_{A \times B}}$: at least one pair of population means for $A \times B$ is not equal
Test statistic:	$F_{A \times B_{calc}} = 2.4771$
Critical value:	$F_{\alpha, df_{A \times B}, df_W} = F_{0.05, 6, 48} \approx F_{0.05, 6, 40} = 2.3359$
Decision rule:	Reject $H_{0_{A \times B}}$ if $F_{A \times B_{calc}} > 2.3359$
Decision:	Reject $H_{0_{A \times B}}$ because $2.4771 > 2.33559$
Conclusion:	There is sufficient evidence to conclude that the average is significantly different for at least one pair of combinations of factors A and B at $\alpha = 0.05$.

Note: Because 12 means are being compared, $\binom{12}{2} = 66$ multiple comparison tests are required to determine which pairs of means are significantly different.

3. No, it would not be appropriate to test the main effects because the interaction is significant.

FLASH TEST

The following pages contain a practice test so that you may assess your understanding of the material presented in Unit 4. Answers and explanations follow the exam. For any questions you miss, be sure to review the explanation carefully and reread the appropriate portion of the section to which the question applies. If you still do not understand the correct answer, review the concept in your text and/or ask your instructor for assistance.

TRUE/FALSE (3 points each)

_____ 1. The F test statistics are constructed as the ratio of two variance components.

_____ 2. If $H_0 : \rho = 0$ is rejected at $\alpha = 0.05$, then $H_0 : \beta_1 = 0$ will also be rejected at $\alpha = 0.05$ for the same data set.

_____ 3. Sample sizes must be equal for all hypothesis tests on the difference between two population means.

_____ 4. Multiple comparison tests are only appropriate following a hypothesis test using one-way analysis of variance in which the null hypothesis is rejected.

_____ 5. A Type II error can only be made when the null hypothesis is rejected.

MULTIPLE CHOICE (3 points each)

_____ 6. Which of the following is the appropriate standard error term calculation for the test statistic of a hypothesis test on $\mu_1 - \mu_2$, if $n_1 = 10$, $n_2 = 15$, and it is assumed that $\sigma_1^2 \neq \sigma_2^2$?

A. $\sqrt{\dfrac{\sigma_1^2}{n_1} + \dfrac{\sigma_2^2}{n_2}}$ C. $s_{pooled} \sqrt{\dfrac{1}{n_1} + \dfrac{1}{n_2}}$

B. $\sqrt{\dfrac{s_1^2}{n_1} + \dfrac{s_2^2}{n_2}}$ D. cannot determine from the information given

_____ 7. The critical value for a hypothesis test on the interaction effect in a two-way ANOVA depends on which of the following df terms?

A. $df_{A \times B}$ and df_A C. $df_{A \times B}$ and df_W

B. $df_{A \times B}$ and df_B D. $df_{A \times B}$ and df_{Tot}

_____ 8. An educator claims that a new study program can decrease the average amount of stress students feel during testing. The stress level of a sample of 20 students is measured during testing both before and after completing the program. The differences were found (Before – After). The appropriate alternative hypothesis is:

A. $H_1 : \mu_D = 0$ C. $H_1 : \mu_D > 0$

B. $H_1 : \mu_D \neq 0$ D. $H_1 : \mu_D < 0$

_____ 9. If the null hypothesis is rejected, a _____ error might have been made, and the probability of making this type of error is _____.

A. Type I, α C. Type II, β

B. Type I, p-value   D. none of these

_____ 10. Which of the following is the appropriate decision rule for a two-tailed hypothesis test on $\mu_1 - \mu_2$ when sample sizes are large?

A. Reject H_0 if $\left| t_{calc} \right| > t_{\frac{\alpha}{2}, df}$ C. Reject H_0 if $t_{calc} > t_{\alpha, df}$

B. Reject H_0 if $\left| z_{calc} \right| > z_{\frac{\alpha}{2}}$ D. Reject H_0 if $z_{calc} > z_\alpha$

_____ 11. Which of the following is the appropriate calculation for the degrees of freedom term for a hypothesis test on $\mu_1 - \mu_2$ when it is assumed that $\sigma_1^2 = \sigma_2^2$?

A. $n - 1$ B. $n_D - 1$ C. $n - 2$ D. $n_1 + n_2 - 2$

_____ 12. A researcher claims that the average credit card debt for U.S. residents is significantly different among those whose highest academic degree is a B.S., whose is an M.S., and a Ph.D. The appropriate test statistic for the hypothesis test is:

A. F_{calc} C. z_{calc}

B. t_{calc} D. cannot determine from the information given

_____ 13. A researcher claims that the average score of males on a manual dexterity test is significantly higher than the average for females. A random sample of 15 males and a random sample of 15 females are selected. Assume $\sigma_1^2 = \sigma_2^2$? The appropriate test statistic for the hypothesis test is:

A. F_{calc} C. z_{calc}

B. t_{calc} D. cannot determine from the information given

_____ 14. A researcher claims that the percent of undergraduates completing a B.S. degree in four years has decreased from last year's figure of 38%. The appropriate test statistic for the hypothesis test is:

A. F_{calc} C. z_{calc}

B. t_{calc} D. cannot determine from the information given

_____ 15. A researcher claims that there is a significant positive linear relationship between IQ score and typing speed. The appropriate test statistic for the hypothesis test is:

A. F_{calc} C. z_{calc}

B. t_{calc} D. cannot determine from the information given

SHORT ANSWER (3 points each)

16. A researcher conducted a hypothesis test to determine if the average score for males on a manual dexterity test is significantly higher than the average score for females. The null hypothesis was rejected at 0.05 level of significance. State the appropriate conclusion for the hypothesis test.

17. Explain how the p-value of a hypothesis test can be used to make the decision to reject H_0 or fail to reject H_0.

18. A recruiter at Connor College wants to determine if the average distance (in miles) that commuter students drive to campus has increased from the average five years ago at the 0.10 level of significance. The recruiter takes a random sample of 100 commuter students and finds the mean to be 30 miles with a standard deviation of five miles. State the appropriate test statistic formula for this hypothesis test. Justify your answer by stating the questions you would ask (in order) and the answers to those questions.

19. The school nurse at Connor College claims that the average weight (in pounds) of male students is significantly different than the national average of 170 pounds at the 0.05 level of significance. The nurse has already calculated a 95% confidence interval from a random sample to be (152.8, 187.6). Based on this interval, should the null hypothesis be rejected? Justify your answer.

20. For a test of $H_0 : \mu = \mu_0$ v. $H_1 : \mu \neq \mu_0$, z_{calc} for a large sample and t_{calc} for a small sample produce exactly the same value. Explain why the two different test statistics are necessary.

CALCULATIONS (5 points each)

21. A Republican candidate wants to determine if there is a significant difference in the proportions of registered Republicans between two small towns. He takes a random sample of 200 registered voters in each town and finds the proportions of Republicans to be 0.37 and 0.28 in Town 1 and Town 2, respectively. Find the value of the test statistic the candidate should use.

22. A hypothesis test of $H_0 : \mu = \mu_0$ v. $H_1 : \mu \neq \mu_0$ is conducted, and the value of the test statistic is $z_{calc} = 1.37$. Find the p-value for the test.

23. An administrator wants to determine if the average age of professors is significantly different between four colleges at a large university. She took a random sample of seven professors from each college. Complete the following partial ANOVA summary table by filling in the values for the shaded areas.

Source	SS	df	MS
Between groups		3	241
Within groups	2328	24	
Total		27	

24. Using the table in Problem 23, calculate the value of the test statistic, and state the critical value for a significance level of 0.05.

25. A consumer claims that the average price of items at Discount Drug is significantly higher than the average price of items at Drugs for Less. He randomly selects eight items from a list and purchases one of each item at Discount Drug and at Drugs for Less. He records the price of each item at each store and finds the differences (Drug Discount − Drugs for Less). The mean difference in price was $\bar{X}_D = 0.17$ with a standard deviation of $s_D = 0.2$. Test the consumer's claim at $\alpha = 0.05$.

26. A researcher is interested in differences in average credit card debt between genders and highest academic degree earned (B.S., M.S., Ph.D). Debt was measured in thousands of dollars on 48 subjects, and the following summary table was constructed:

Source	SS	df	MS	F
Between groups	23310	5		
Gender	7550	1	7550	7.4384
Degree	10580	2	5290	5.2118
Gender × Degree	5180	2	2590	2.5517
Within groups	42630	42	1015	
Total	65940	47		

Test to determine if the main effect of academic degree is significant at the 0.01 level of significance.

27. An instructor wants to determine if there is a significant difference between his 8 AM class and 3 PM class in the amount of time it takes students to complete an exam. He takes a random sample of size 10 from each class. The 8 AM class took an average of 42 minutes to complete the exam with a standard deviation of 5.2; the 3 PM class took an average of 38 minutes to complete the exam with a standard deviation of 7.6. Conduct a hypothesis test to determine if the population variances are equal at $\alpha = 0.05$.

28. The instructor in Problem 27 is going to conduct a hypothesis test of $H_0 : \mu_1 - \mu_2 = 0$ v. $H_1 : \mu_1 - \mu_2 \neq 0$. State the appropriate decision rule for $\alpha = 0.01$.

Answers to the practice test begin on the next page.

TRUE/FALSE

1. T; the F test statistic for equality of two population variances is the ratio of the two sample variances, and the F test statistic for ANOVA is the ratio of a between-groups variance estimate to a within-groups variance estimate

2. T; both tests are concerned with the existence of a linear relationship between X and Y; in fact, both test statistics will yield exactly the same value

3. F; sample sizes must be equal for dependent samples because the data are paired but need not be equal for independent samples

4. T; multiple comparison tests help determine which pairs of means are significantly different; if the null hypothesis is not rejected, there are no significant differences between any pairs

5. F; a Type II error is made when a false null hypothesis is **not** rejected

MULTIPLE CHOICE

6. B; A is used when the values of σ_1 and σ_2 are known, C is used when $\sigma_1^2 = \sigma_2^2$

7. C; $F_{calc} = \dfrac{MS_{A \times B}}{MS_W}$ so $df_{A \times B} = $ degrees of freedom for the numerator and

   $df_W = $ degrees of freedom for the denominator

8. C; the direction of subtraction is Before $-$ After, and a decrease is claimed, thus Before $>$ After, and Before $-$ After > 0

9. A; a Type I error occurs when a true H_0 is rejected; the level of significance is the probability of making a Type I error

10. B; the samples are large so the test statistic is a z_{calc}, and $\dfrac{\alpha}{2}$ is used for a two-tailed test

11. D; A is for μ, B is for μ_D, and C is for ρ or β_1

12. A; there are three population means, thus a one-way ANOVA is appropriate

13. B: there are two population means and small samples, thus a t test is appropriate

14. C; there is one population proportion, thus a z test is appropriate

15. B; a linear relationship is hypothesized, thus a t test is appropriate

SHORT ANSWER

16. There is sufficient evidence to conclude that the average score for males on the manual dexterity test is significantly greater that the average score for females at $\alpha = 0.05$.

17. The decision may be made by comparing the p-value to α and rejecting H_0 if p-value $< \alpha$.

18. The appropriate test statistic formula is $z_{calc} = \dfrac{\overline{X} - \mu_0}{s_{\overline{X}}}$

    Q1: Is the value of σ known?   A1: No

    Q2: Is $n \geq 30$?   A2: Yes

19. The null hypothesis should **not** be rejected because 170 is in the interval.

20. For large n, the quantity $\dfrac{\overline{X} - \mu_0}{s_{\overline{X}}}$ has approximately a standard normal distribution, and the test statistic will be compared to a value from the standard normal distribution. For small n, the quantity $\dfrac{\overline{X} - \mu_0}{s_{\overline{X}}}$ has a t distribution, and the critical value comes from the t distribution with $n - 1$ degrees of freedom.

CALCULATIONS

21. $s_{\hat{p}_1 - \hat{p}_2} = \sqrt{\dfrac{\hat{p}_1(1 - \hat{p}_1)}{n_1} + \dfrac{\hat{p}_2(1 - \hat{p}_2)}{n_2}} = \sqrt{\dfrac{(0.37)(0.64)}{200} + \dfrac{(0.28)(0.72)}{200}}$

$\qquad = 0.0466208,$

$\qquad z_{calc} = \dfrac{(\hat{p}_1 - \hat{p}_2) - D_0}{s_{\hat{p}_1 - \hat{p}_2}} = \dfrac{0.37 - 0.28}{0.0466208} = 1.930$

22. p-value $= (2)\mathrm{P}(Z > 1.37) = (2)(0.0853) = 0.1706$

23. $SS_B = (df_B)(MS_B) = (3)(241) = 723,$

$\qquad MS_w = \dfrac{SS_W}{df_W} = \dfrac{2328}{24} = 97,$

$\qquad SS_{Tot} = SS_B + SS_W = 723 + 2328 = 3051$

Source	SS	df	MS
Between groups	723	3	241
Within groups	2328	24	97
Total	3051	27	

24. $F_{calc} = \dfrac{MS_B}{MS_w} = \dfrac{241}{97} = 2.4845,$

$\qquad F_{\alpha, df_B, df_W} = F_{0.05, 3, 24} = 3.0088$

25. $s_{\overline{X}_D} = \dfrac{s_D}{\sqrt{n_D}} = \dfrac{.2}{\sqrt{8}} = 0.070710678,$

Hypotheses:	$H_0 : \mu_D \leq 0$ v. $H_1 : \mu_D > 0$
Test statistic:	$t_{calc} = \dfrac{\overline{X}_D - D_0}{s_{\overline{X}_D}} = \dfrac{0.17}{0.070710678} = 2.404$
Critical value:	$t_{\alpha, df_D} = t_{0.05, 7} = 1.895$
Decision rule:	Reject H_0 if $t_{calc} > 1.895$
Decision:	Reject H_0 because $2.404 > 1.895$
Conclusion:	There is sufficient evidence to conclude that the average price of items at Discount Drug is significantly greater than the average at Drugs for Less for $\alpha = 0.05$.

26.

Hypotheses:	$H_0 : \mu_1 = \mu_2 = \mu_3$ v.
	H_1: at least one pair of population means is not equal
Test statistic:	$F_{B_{calc}} = 5.2118$
Critical value:	$F_{\alpha, df_B, df_W} = F_{0.01, 2, 42} \approx F_{0.01, 2, 40} = 5.1785$
Decision rule:	Reject H_0 if $F_{B_{calc}} > 5.1785$
Decision:	Reject H_0 because $5.2118 > 5.1785$
Conclusion:	There is sufficient evidence to conclude that there is a significant difference in average credit card debt among U.S. residents with B.S., M.S., and Ph.D. degrees for $\alpha = 0.01$.

27.

Hypotheses:	$H_0 : \sigma_1^2 = \sigma_2^2$ v. $H_1 : \sigma_1^2 \neq \sigma_2^2$
Test statistic:	$F_{calc} = \dfrac{s_N^2}{s_D^2} = \dfrac{7.6^2}{5.2^2} = 2.1361$
Critical value:	$F_{\frac{\alpha}{2}, df_N, df_D} = F_{0.025, 9, 9} = 4.0260$
Decision rule:	Reject H_0 if $F_{calc} > 4.0260$
Decision:	Fail to reject H_0 because $2.1361 < 4.0260$
Conclusion:	There is not sufficient evidence to conclude that the variance of time needed to complete the exam for the 8 AM class is significantly different than the variance of time needed to complete the exam for the 3 PM class at $\alpha = 0.05$.

28. The samples are small, and population variances are assumed to be equal thus,

$$df = n_1 + n_2 - 2 = 10 + 10 - 2 = 18, \text{ and}$$

$$t_{\frac{\alpha}{2}, df} = t_{0.005, 18} = 2.878.$$

Decision rule: Reject H_0 if $|t_{calc}| > 2.878$

FLASH FOCUS

After completing this unit, you will be able to:

✓ Understand basic terms associated with nonparametric tests

✓ Determine the appropriate hypothesis test for nominal and ordinal level data

✓ Conduct nonparametric hypothesis tests

The following table lists the core concepts in this unit along with definitions and/or explanations. Space is provided to add concepts discussed by your instructor.

Core Concepts in Unit 5

Chapter 13—Tests with Nominal Level Data	
Concept	**Definition and/or Explanation**
Nonparametrics	statistical methods used when assumptions for parametric procedures are not met
Multinomial experiment	an extension of a binomial experiment in which there are more than two possible outcomes
χ^2 Goodness-of-fit test	a hypothesis test to determine if a specified multinomial distribution is appropriate
Expected frequency	the number of observations expected in a particular category or combination of categories
Observed frequency	the number of observations from the sample in a particular category or combination of categories
χ^2 test of independence	a hypothesis test to determine if two variables measured at the nominal level are independent
Contingency table	a method of displaying observed frequencies categorized on two variables
Row marginal	the number of observations in a row of a contingency table
Column marginal	the number of observations in a column of a contingency table

Chapter 14—Tests with Ordinal Level Data	
Tied ranks	when two or more observations have the same value, the ranks that would be assigned are averaged, and this average rank is associated with each of the values
Spearman rank correlation coefficient	the point estimate of the population correlation coefficient for ranked data, ρ_S
Wilcoxon signed-ranks test	a hypothesis test on the difference of two population distributions for paired ranked data
Wilcoxon rank sum test	a hypothesis test on the difference of two population distributions for independent samples for ranked data
Kruskal–Wallis test	a hypothesis test on the difference of more than two population distributions for ranked data

 FLASH LINK

The following table lists Web sites that may be helpful in studying the material in Unit 5. Space is provided to add other Web sites suggested in your text or by your instructor or those you find on your own. Key to resource type: D, definitions; E, examples; X, exercises; C, calculation; M, demonstration; GOF, goodness-of-fit.

Chapter	Resource Type	URL
13	D (GOF, independence)	http://www2.chass.ncsu.edu/garson/pa765/chisq.htm
13	D, E (independence)	http://www.psychstat.smsu.edu/introbook/SBK28.htm
13	D, E (GOF, independence)	http://www.anu.edu.au/nceph/surfstat/surfstat-home
13	D, E, X (GOF, independence)	http://davidmlane.com/hyperstat/chi_square.html
13	D, E, X (GOF, independence)	http://www.bmj.com/collections/statsbk/8.shtml
13	D, E, M (GOF)	http://www.ruf.rice.edu/~lane/stat_sim/chisq_theor
13	M	http://www.stat.uiuc.edu/~stat100/java/chisquare/ChiSquareApplet.html

(continued)

13	X	http://occ.awlonline.com/bookbind/pubbooks/weiss2_awl/chapter11/deluxe.html
13-14	X	http://occ.awlonline.com/bookbind/pubbooks/triola_awl/chapter10/deluxe.html (also chapter13)
14	D, E, X (Spearman, rank sum)	http://www.bmj.com/collections/statsbk/10.shtml (also 11)

CHAPTER 13—Tests with Nominal Level Data

FLASH SUMMARY

Nonparametrics are statistical methods used when assumptions for parametric methods are violated. These assumption violations are that:

1. data are measured at the nominal or ordinal level,
2. the distribution of the response variable is not normal, and
3. the population variances in analysis of variance are unequal.

There is a multitude of nonparametric methods; six of them are discussed in this unit. Nonparametric methods covered in this unit address hypothesized distributions and relationships between variables.

Commonly used nonparametric tests for nominal level data utilize χ^2 distributions. The first of these is appropriate for a multinomial experiment. A multinomial experiment is an extension of a binomial experiment in which there are more than two possible outcomes. The assumptions of a binomial hold except that are more than two possible outcomes, and the probability for each outcome is specified. This test is called a χ^2 goodness-of-fit (GOF) test, which allows the researcher to hypothesize values of proportions for each of the possible outcomes (often called categories). Rather than examining the difference between two population proportions, the GOF test examines differences among more than two population proportions or the difference between the proportions and the associated hypothesized values. The test allows a decision to be made about whether the hypothesized multinomial distribution is a good fit for the population based on the sample data.

The null and alternative hypotheses for the GOF test are:

$H_0 : p_1 = p_{1_0}, p_2 = p_{2_0}, \ldots, p_k = p_{k_0}$ v.

H_1: at least one of the proportions differs from its hypothesized value

where k = the number of possible outcomes. If the hypothesized values for all proportions are equal, the hypotheses can be stated as

$H_0 : p_1 = p_2 = \cdots = p_{k_0}$ v. H_1 : at least one pair of proportions is not equal.

Because the proportion for each category has been hypothesized, the expected frequency in each category can be calculated. The expected frequencies are denoted E_i and are calculated by:

$$E_i = n \cdot p_{i_0}$$

where n is the sample size, and p_{i_0} is the hypothesized value for the ith category. The observed frequency for the ith category, O_i, is the number of observations from the sample that fall into that category. If the observed frequencies differ greatly from the expected frequencies, the researcher would conclude that the hypothesized distribution is not appropriate for the population. The test statistic is:

$$\chi^2_{calc} = \sum_{i=1}^{k} \frac{(O_i - E_i)^2}{E_i} \text{ with } df = k - 1.$$

The critical value from the χ^2 distribution with $df = k-1$ is $\chi^2_{\alpha, df}$, and the decision rule is to reject H_0 if $\chi^2_{calc} > \chi^2_{\alpha, df}$.

Suppose a researcher believes that the proportion of students at Connor College who are registered Republicans is 0.62, the proportion who are registered Democrats is 0.26, and the proportion who are registered Independents is 0.12. Note that the sum of the hypothesized proportions must equal one. To test his claim, a random sample of 150 students is taken. Seventy-two are Republicans (Category 1), 60 are Democrats (Category 2), and 18 are Independents (Category 3). The expected frequencies are:

$E_1 = (150)(.62) = 93,$

$E_2 = (150)(.26) = 39,$ and

$E_3 = (150)(.12) = 18.$

Note that the sum of both the observed and expected frequencies must equal the sample size. The test statistic is calculated to be:

$$\chi^2_{calc} = \sum_{i=1}^{k} \frac{(O_i - E_i)^2}{E_i} = \frac{(72 - 93)^2}{93} + \frac{(60 - 39)^2}{39} + \frac{(18 - 18)^2}{18} = 16.050$$

Then the hypothesis test of the researcher's claim at the 0.05 level of significance would be conducted as follows:

Hypotheses: $H_0 : p_1 = 0.62, p_2 = 0.26, p_3 = 0.12$ v.

H_1 : at least one of the proportions differs from its hypothesized value

Test statistic: $\chi^2_{calc} = 16.050$

Critical value: $\chi^2_{\alpha, df} = \chi^2_{0.05, 2} = 5.991$

Decision rule: Reject H_0 if H_0 if $\chi^2_{calc} > 5.991$

Decision: Reject H_0 because $16.050 > 5.991$

Conclusion: There is sufficient evidence to conclude that at least one of the proportions differs significantly from its hypothesized value at $\alpha = 0.05$.

This means that the hypothesized multinomial distribution is not appropriate for the population based on information from the sample.

The second χ^2 test deals with relationships between two variables measured at the nominal level and is called a χ^2 test of independence. Observations are categorized on two variables, X and Y. This test allows a researcher to make a decision about whether the variables X and Y are independent (the category of X of an observation does not depend on the category of Y) or dependent.

X and Y are independent

X		Y	
		1	2
	1	25	25
	2	25	25

X and Y are dependent

X		Y	
		1	2
	1	50	0
	2	0	50

Assumptions for the test are:

1. sampling is random, and

2. the expected frequency in each cell is at least five.

The observed frequencies are placed in a contingency table in which each observation fits into one and only one combination of categories for X and Y. The size of the contingency table is denote by $r \times c$ where r is the number of rows (number of categories for X), and c is the number of columns (number of categories for Y). Each row/column combination is called a cell, and the observed frequency for a cell is denoted O_{ij} where i the number of the row and j is the number of the column. The sum of the observed frequencies in a row is called the row marginal, and the sum of the observed frequencies in a column is called a column marginal. The row marginal for row i will be denoted r_i, and the column marginal for column j will be denoted c_j. Both the row marginals and the column marginals must add to n. For example, a 3×4 contingency table would be constructed as follows:

		Y				
		1	2	3	4	Row Marginal
X	1	O_{11}	O_{12}	O_{13}	O_{14}	r_1
	2	O_{21}	O_{22}	O_{23}	O_{24}	r_2
	3	O_{31}	O_{32}	O_{33}	O_{34}	r_3
	Column Marginal	c_1	c_2	c_3	c_4	n

The expected frequencies are calculated by

$$E_{ij} = \frac{r_i \cdot c_j}{n}.$$

The hypotheses for the test are

H_0: X and Y are independent v. H_1: X and Y are dependent,

and the test statistic is

$$\chi^2_{calc} = \sum_{j=1}^{c} \sum_{i=1}^{r} \frac{(O_{ij} - E_{ij})^2}{E_{ij}} \text{ with } df = (r-1)(c-1).$$

The critical value from the χ^2 distribution with $(r-1)(c-1)$ degrees of freedom is $\chi^2_{\alpha, df}$ and the decision rule is to reject H_0 if $\chi^2_{calc} > \chi^2_{\alpha, df}$.

A researcher wants to determine if there is a relationship between political party preference and gender for NRA members at $\alpha = 0.025$. He takes a random sample of 150 NRA members and categorizes them in the following contingency table:

Political Party Preference

Gender		Republican	Democrat	Independent	Row Marginal
	Male	39	38	8	85
	Female	20	40	5	65
	Column Marginal	59	78	13	$n = 150$

The expected frequencies and test statistic are calculated:

$$E_{11} = \frac{r_i \cdot c_i}{n} = \frac{(85)(59)}{150} = 33.4\overline{3},$$

$$E_{12} = \frac{r_1 \cdot c_2}{n} = \frac{(85)(78)}{150} = 44.2,$$

$$E_{13} = \frac{r_1 \cdot c_3}{n} = \frac{(85)(13)}{150} = 7.3\overline{6},$$

$$E_{21} = \frac{r_2 \cdot c_1}{n} = \frac{(65)(59)}{150} = 25.5\overline{6},$$

$$E_{22} = \frac{r_2 \cdot c_2}{n} = \frac{(65)(78)}{150} = 33.8,$$

$$E_{23} = \frac{r_2 \cdot c_3}{n} = \frac{(65)(13)}{150} = 5.6\overline{3}; \text{ and}$$

$$\chi^2_{calc} = \sum_{j=1}^{c} \sum_{i=1}^{r} \frac{(O_{ij} - E_{ij})^2}{E_{ij}} = \frac{(39 - 33.4\overline{3})^2}{33.4\overline{3}} + \frac{(38 - 44.2)^2}{44.2} + \frac{(8 - 7.3\overline{6})^2}{7.3\overline{6}}$$

$$+ \frac{(20 - 25.5\overline{6})^2}{25.5\overline{6}} + \frac{(40 - 33.8)^2}{33.8} + \frac{(5 - 5.6\overline{3})^2}{5.6\overline{3}}$$

$$= 4.272$$

with $df = (r - 1)(c - 1) = (1)(2) = 2$. The hypothesis test is conducted:

Hypotheses: H_0: Gender and political party preference are independent v.

                  H_1: Gender and political party preference are dependent

Test statistic: $\chi^2_{calc} = 4.272$

Critical value: $\chi^2_{\alpha, df} = \chi^2_{0.025,2} = 7.378$

Decision rule: Reject H_0 if $\chi^2_{calc} > 7.378$

Decision: Fail to reject H_0 because $4.272 < 7.378$

Conclusion: There is not sufficient evidence to conclude that gender and political party preference are dependent at $\alpha = 0.025$.

 ## FLASH REVIEW

1. An instructor claims that 20% of students at Connor College have blonde hair, 40% have brown hair, 15% have black hair, 15% have red hair, and 10% have hair of another color. A random sample of 100 students was categorized by hair color and the results displayed in the following table:

Blonde	Brown	Black	Red	Other
17	47	14	13	7

Test the instructors claim at the 0.10 level of significance.

2. A researcher wants to determine if categorization of freshmen by math ACT (low is < 19, high is ≥ 19), and student success in college algebra (pass/fail) are independent. A random sample of 500 freshman who took college algebra was taken and categorized in the following table:

	Pass	Fail
Low ACT	94	58
High ACT	281	67

Determine if math ACT category and success in college algebra are independent at the 0.01 level of significance.

CHAPTER 14—Tests with Ordinal Level Data

FLASH SUMMARY

Nonparametric methods for ordinal level data are obviously used when data are measured at the ordinal level. They are also used when data are measured at the interval or ratio level, but assumptions about distributions such as normality or equal variances are violated. Nonparametric methods discussed in this chapter include tests for rank correlations, differences between two population distributions for paired data, differences between two population distributions for independent samples, and differences among more than two population distributions. These tests are analogous to the parametric tests on ρ, μ_D, and $\mu_1 - \mu_2$ and to one-way analysis of variance, respectively. The Spearman rank correlation coefficient, r_S, is the point estimate of the population correlation coefficient for ranked data, ρ_S. The Spearman coefficient is the ranked data equivalent to Pearson's r and is used when X or Y or both are measured at the ordinal level or when the assumption of normality is not met. The hypothesis test allows a decision to made about whether a relationship exists between the two variables. The null and alternative hypotheses are:

$$H_0: \rho_S = 0 \text{ v. } H_1: \rho_S \neq 0.$$

Only two-tailed tests are considered in this unit.

The test statistic is based on the differences of the ranks for X and Y for each observation. Observations are ranked on X and ranked separately on Y. However, the pairings must be maintained. Observations can be ranked in either ascending or descending order as long as the same order is used for both variables. If two or more observations have equal value, the average of the ranks that would be assigned is calculated, and this average is the rank associated with each of the observations. These are called tied ranks. The differences between the ranks, denoted d, are then used to calculate the test statistic:

$$r_{S_{calc}} = 1 - \frac{6\sum d^2}{n(n^2 - 1)} \text{ where } n \text{ is the number of paired observations.}$$

This formula is appropriate only when there are few tied ranks. If there are many tied ranks in the data, the formula for Pearson's r is used with the ranks substituted for the raw scores. A special table for critical values, $\pm r_{S\frac{\alpha}{2},n}$, is found in most texts and applies to small samples. Be sure to read the instructions for using the table. If the sample size is large, the critical value is $\pm r_{S\frac{\alpha}{2},n} = \pm \dfrac{z_{\frac{\alpha}{2}}}{\sqrt{n - 1}}$. The decision rule is to reject H_0 if

$$|r_{S_{calc}}| > r_{S\frac{\alpha}{2},n}.$$

Suppose Eric wants to explore the linear relationship between the age of students at Connor College (X) and the amount of time students spend socializing during finals week (Y). He takes a random sample of 10 students and records their ages and socialization time. Assume socialization time is not normally distributed. To determine if a significant relationship exists between age and socialization time, the observations are ranked separately on the two variables (in ascending order) and the differences in the ranks calculated:

Student	1	2	3	4	5	6	7	8	9	10
Age	19	20	20	21	23	25	26	29	32	40
Rank for Age	**1**	**2.5**	**2.5**	**4**	**5**	**6**	**7**	**8**	**9**	**10**
Social time	15.2	8.3	11.7	12.2	8.2	7.5	5.4	7.6	2.3	1.5
Rank for Social time	**10**	**7**	**8**	**9**	**6**	**4**	**3**	**5**	**2**	**1**
Difference in Ranks	**−9**	**−4.5**	**−5.5**	**−5**	**−1**	**2**	**4**	**3**	**7**	**9**

Note that the sign of the difference can be ignored because the differences will be squared. Because there is only one tie in ranks, the calculated value of the test statistic is

$$r_{S_{calc}} = 1 - \frac{6\sum d^2}{n(n^2 - 1)}$$

$$= 1 - \frac{6(9^2 + 4.5^2 + 5.5^2 + 5^2 + 1^2 + 2^2 + 4^2 + 3^2 + 7^2 + 9^2)}{10(10^2 - 1)}$$

$$= -0.918.$$

The test to determine if a significant relationship between age and socialization time exists at the 0.05 level of significance is as follows:

Hypotheses: $H_0 : \rho_S = 0$ v. $H_1 : \rho_S \neq 0$

Test statistic: $r_{S_{calc}} = -0.918$

Critical value: $r_{S_{\frac{\alpha}{2}, n}} = r_{S_{0.025, 10}} = 0.648$

Decision rule: Reject H_0 if H_0 if $|r_{S_{calc}}| > 0.648$

Decision: Reject H_0 because $0.918 > 0.648$

Conclusion: There is sufficient evidence to conclude that there is a significant relationship between age and socialization time at $\alpha = 0.05$.

The Wilcoxon signed-ranks test is analogous to a t test on the difference between means for paired samples. Assumptions for the test are that:

1. a random sample is selected, and

2. the population of differences of ranks is symmetric.

The null and alternative hypotheses are:

H_0: the two populations have the same distribution v.

H_1: the two populations have different distributions.

As with the t test, the differences between the paired measurements are calculated. The absolute value of these differences are then ranked from lowest to highest, and the sign of the difference is attached to the rank. Pairs for which $d = 0$ are deleted from the data set. The absolute value of the sum of the negative ranks is compared with the sum of the positive ranks. For small samples, the smaller of these two values is the test statistic, denoted T_{calc}. The critical value is found in a table of T values, and the decision rule is to reject H_0 if $T_{calc} \leq T_{\frac{\alpha}{2},n}$ where n is the number of pairs for which $d \neq 0$. Note that the table for T values is not the same as the t distribution table and that the sign in the decision rule is different than for most tests. For large samples, the test statistic T_{calc} is transformed to a z value.

Consider the example from Unit 3 in which a random sample of 10 students was selected to compare the difference in the average scores on Exam 1 and Exam 2. Suppose exam scores are not normally distributed. Then the distributions of the two populations rather than the averages will be compared. Because the samples are dependent, a Wilcoxon signed-ranks test can be conducted. The exam scores, differences, absolute value of differences, ranks, and signed ranks are recorded in the following table:

Student	1	2	3	4	5	6	7	8	9	10
Exam 1	56	71	76	68	76	85	83	81	90	98
Exam 2	54	65	78	71	75	79	86	88	86	95
Difference	2	6	−2	−3	1	6	−3	−7	4	3
|Difference|	2	6	2	3	1	6	3	7	4	3
Rank	2.5	8.5	2.5	5	1	8.5	5	10	7	5
Signed Rank	2.5	8.5	−2.5	−5	1	8.5	−5	−10	7	5

The sum of the positive ranks is 32.5 and the sum of the absolute value of the negative ranks is 22.5. The value of the test statistic is the smaller of the two sums; hence, $T_{calc} = 22.5$

The hypothesis test for the difference of the two population distributions at the 0.05 level of significance is as follows:

Hypotheses: H_0: Scores for Exam 1 and Exam 2 have the same distribution v.

H_1: Scores for Exam 1 and Exam 2 have different distributions

Test statistic: $T_{calc} = 22.5$

Critical value: $T_{\frac{\alpha}{2},n} = T_{0.025,10} = 8$

Decision rule: Reject H_0 if $T_{calc} \leq 8$

Decision: Fail to reject H_0 because $22.5 > 8$

Conclusion: There is not sufficient evidence to conclude that the distribution of scores for Exam 1 is significantly different than the distribution of scores for Exam 2 at $\alpha = 0.05$.

The Wilcoxon rank sum test is analogous to a t test on the difference between means for independent samples. Assumptions for the test are that:

1. two independent random samples are selected, and

2. $n_1 > 10$ and $n_2 > 10$.

The null and alternative hypotheses are

H_0: the two populations have the same distribution v.

H_1: the two populations have different distributions.

To calculate the test statistic, all observations from both samples are combined into one data set while keeping track of group membership. The observations are then ranked in ascending order. The value R is the sum of the ranks for one of the samples.

Although it does not matter which sample is selected to produce R, Sample 1 is used in this unit for consistency. Then the test statistic is:

$$z = \frac{R - \mu_R}{\sigma_R} \text{ where}$$

$$\mu_R = \frac{n_1 (n_1 + n_2 + 1)}{2} \text{ and}$$

$$\sigma_R = \sqrt{\frac{n_1 n_2 (n_1 + n_2 + 1)}{12}}.$$

Note that n_1 is the sample size associated with the sample that produced R. The critical values come from the standard normal table, and the decision rule is to reject H_0 if $|z_{calc}| > z_{\frac{\alpha}{2}}$.

Suppose a researcher wants to compare the annual income of students who graduate from Connor College with students who graduate from the state university. A random sample of 15 Connor College graduates and a random sample of 20 graduates from the state university are selected. The researcher has determined that income is not normally distributed in the populations. Thus, the distributions of the two populations will be compared at the 0.10 level of significance. The annual income of the students three years after graduation is recorded in thousands of dollars:

Connor College: 31.6, 33.4, 14.7, 30.5, 36.1, 33.6, 31.3, 35.6, 57.0, 37.8, 20.5, 28.1, 34.9, 33.7, 40.3

State University: 58.5, 31.1, 36.4, 24.3, 46.2, 30.5, 39.5, 51.5, 41.2, 22.2, 36.4, 72.8, 41.6, 28.8, 32.4, 36.3, 56.4, 44.5, 33.4, 37.4

The observations are collapsed into one data set and ranked from lowest to highest.

Income	Rank	Income	Rank
31.6	11	58.5	34
33.4	13.5	31.1	9
14.7	1	36.4	21.5
30.5	7.5	24.3	4
36.1	19	46.2	30
33.6	15	30.5	7.5
31.3	10	39.5	25
35.6	18	51.5	31
57.0	33	41.2	27
37.8	24	22.2	3
20.5	2	36.4	21.5
28.1	5	72.8	35
34.9	17	41.6	28
33.7	16	28.8	6
40.3	26	32.4	12
		36.3	20
		56.4	32

(continued)

		44.5	29
		33.4	13.5
		37.4	23
	Σ Ranks = 218		

Then $R = 218$,

$$\mu_R = \frac{n_1(n_1 + n_2 + 1)}{2} = \frac{(15)(15 + 20 + 1)}{2} = 270 \text{ and}$$

$$\sigma_R = \sqrt{\frac{n_1 n_2 (n_1 + n_2 + 1)}{12}} = \sqrt{\frac{(15)(20)(15 + 20 + 1)}{12}} = 30.$$

The hypothesis test is conducted:

Hypotheses: H_0: Annual income for Connor College graduates and annual income for the state university graduates have the same distribution v.

H_1: Annual income for Connor College graduates and annual income for the state university graduates have different distributions

Test statistic: $z = \dfrac{R - \mu_R}{\sigma_R} = \dfrac{218 - 270}{30} = -1.733$

Critical value: $\pm z_{\frac{\alpha}{2}} = \pm z_{0.05} = \pm 1.645$

Decision rule: Reject H_0 if $|z_{calc}| > 1.645$

Decision: Reject H_0 because $1.733 > 1.645$

Conclusion: There is sufficient evidence to conclude that the distribution of annual income for Connor College graduates is significantly different than the distribution of annual income for the state university graduates at $\alpha = 0.10$.

Using the sum of ranks for the second sample should yield the same decision. The Mann–Whitney U test is an equivalent test to the Wilcoxon rank sum test that is presented in some texts.

The Kruskal–Wallis test is the ranked data equivalent of a one-way analysis of variance. This test compares the population distributions rather than the population means. Assumptions for the Kruskal–Wallis test are that:

1. at least three independent random samples are selected, and

2. the sample size is greater than or equal to five for each group.

The null and alternative hypotheses are

H_0: the populations have the same distribution v.

H_1: the populations have different distributions.

As in the Wilcoxon rank sum test, the observations from all samples are combined into one data set and then ranked from lowest to highest. The sum of the ranks for each sample is then calculated. The test statistic is

$$H_{calc} = \frac{12}{n(n + 1)} \left(\frac{R_1^2}{n_1} + \frac{R_2^2}{n_2} + \cdots + \frac{R_k^2}{n_k} \right) - 3(n + 1) \text{ with } df = k - 1,$$

where n is the size of the combined sample, n_i is the size of the ith sample, R_i is the sum of the ranks of the ith sample, k is the number of samples ($k \geq 3$), and $i = 1, \ldots, k$. This test statistic has approximately a χ^2 distribution with $k - 1$ degrees of freedom, thus the critical value is $\chi^2_{\alpha,df}$, and the decision rule is to reject H_0 if $\chi^2_{calc} > \chi^2_{\alpha,df}$.

Suppose a company's personnel director wants to know if the distribution of number of days of sick leave taken by employees is different for four different branch offices at the 0.05 level of significance. A random sample of 10 employees is selected from each branch. The 40 employees selected are ranked on number of sick leave days from the least to the most, and the ranks are recorded by branch in the following table:

Employee	1	2	3	4	5	6	7	8	9	10	Sum
Branch 1	13	32	6	4	19	22.5	16	29.5	8	26	**176**
Branch 2	29.5	1	22.5	29.5	16	7	36	11	25	9.5	**187**
Branch 3	14	29.5	12	20	2	24	4	16	39	35	**195.5**
Branch 4	40	4	33	21	37	38	34	9.5	18	27	**261.5**

The value of the test statistic is calculated by

$$H_{calc} = \frac{12}{n(n+1)}\left(\frac{R_1^2}{n_1} + \frac{R_2^2}{n_2} + \cdots + \frac{R_k^2}{n_k}\right) - 3(n+1)$$

$$= \frac{12}{40(40+1)}\left(\frac{176^2}{10} + \frac{187^2}{10} + \frac{195.5^2}{10} + \frac{261.5^2}{10}\right) - 3(40+1) = 3.254$$

with $df = 4 - 1 = 3$. The hypothesis test is constructed as follows:

Hypotheses: H_0: Number of sick leave days for the four branch offices has the same distribution v.

H_1: Number of sick leave days for the four branch offices has different distributions

Test statistic: $\chi^2_{calc} = 3.254$

Critical value: $\chi^2_{\alpha, df} = \chi^2_{0.05,3} = 7.815$

Decision rule: Reject H_0 if $\chi^2_{calc} > 7.815$

Decision: Fail to reject H_0 because $3.254 < 7.815$

Conclusion: There is not sufficient evidence to conclude that distributions for number of sick leave days for the four branch offices are significantly different at $\alpha = 0.05$.

Nonparametric tests and analogous parametric tests

	Nonparametric Test	**Parametric Test**
Correlation coefficient	Spearman rank correlation coefficient (relationship between two variables)	Pearson product moment correlation coefficient (linear relationship between two variables)
Difference between two populations—dependent samples	Wilcoxon signed-rank test (difference between distributions)	dependent t test (difference between means)
Difference between two populations—independent samples	Wilcoxon rank sum test (difference between distributions)	z test or independent t test (difference between means)
Difference among more than two populations	Kruskal–Wallis test (difference between distributions)	one-way analysis of variance (difference between means)

1. A golf pro claims that golf scores for players before and after a golfing workshop have different distributions. He randomly selects eight golfers, records the score of a round they shot the day before the workshops, then records the score of a round they shot the day after the workshop was completed. The results are in the following table:

Player	1	2	3	4	5	6	7	8
Before	68	72	79	80	83	89	91	93
After	70	71	73	82	76	81	85	90

Assuming that golf scores are not normally distributed, test the golf pro's claim at the 0.10 level of significance.

2. A school superintendent wanted to compare the first grade reading programs at two elementary schools. Random samples of 15 students from each school were selected, the reading scores for the students were recorded, and then the group of 30 students was ranked from lowest score to highest score. The rankings for the students, by school, were as follows:

School 1: 1, 2, 4.5, 9, 9, 13, 14, 15.5, 15.5, 19, 21, 23, 24, 26, 30

School 2: 3, 4.5, 6, 7, 9, 11, 12, 17, 19, 19, 22, 25, 27, 28, 29

Determine, at the 0.01 level of significance, if the distribution of reading scores is the same for the two schools.

3. Daci did a project for an education class in which she explored a linear relationship between the number of hours that students study for the final exam in statistics (X) and the students' final exam grades (Y). She took a random sample of 10 statistics students and recorded the number of study hours and their final exam grade for each. Assuming grades are not normally distributed, determine if there is a significant relationship between hours studied and final exam grade at $\alpha = 0.05$.

Student	1	2	3	4	5	6	7	8	9	10
Hours	0	7.1	3.5	2.6	5.4	6.0	1.7	5.8	4.2	6.5
Grade	43	89	74	68	86	92	55	85	80	97

4. An instructor believes that the distributions of scores on a comprehensive statistics exam will be significantly different for students who took their statistics courses in three different departments at Connor College. The instructor takes random samples of 10 statistics students from each department, combines the students' scores, and records the rank for each student by department in the following table.

Student	1	2	3	4	5	6	7	8	9	10
Department A	8	15	2	10	3	17	24	5	14	1
Department B	17	5	9	21	5	11	19	12	27	23
Department C	7	17	29	30	20	28	25	13	26	22

Determine if the distributions of scores on the exam for the three departments are significantly different at the 0.10 level of significance.

Chapter 13—Tests with Nominal Level Data

1. $E_1 = (100)(.2) = 20, E_2 = (100)(.4) = 40, E_3 = (150)(.15) = 15,$
   $E_4 = (150)(.15) = 15, E_5 = (100)(.10) = 10,$

$$\chi_{calc}^2 = \sum_{i=1}^{k} \frac{(O_i - E_i)^2}{E_i}$$

$$= \frac{(17 - 20)^2}{20} + \frac{(47 - 40)^2}{40} + \frac{(14 - 15)^2}{15} + \frac{(13 - 15)^2}{15} + \frac{(7 - 10)^2}{10}$$

$$= 2.908$$

Hypotheses: $H_0: p_1 = 0.2, p_2 = 0.4, p_3 = 0.15, p_4 = .15, p_5 = .10$ v.

   $H_1:$ at least one of the proportions differs from its hypothesized value

Test statistic: $\chi_{calc}^2 = 2.908$

Critical value: $\chi_{\alpha,df}^2 = \chi_{0.10,4}^2 = 7.779$

Decision rule: Reject H_0 if $\chi_{calc}^2 > 7.779$

Decision: Fail to reject H_0 because $2.908 < 7.779$

Conclusion: There is not sufficient evidence to conclude that at least one of the proportions differs from its hypothesized value at $\alpha = 0.10$.

2. Marginals: $r_1 = 152, r_2 = 348, c_1 = 375, c_2 = 125;$

$$E_{11} = \frac{r_1 \cdot c_1}{n} = \frac{(152)(375)}{500} = 114, E_{12} = \frac{r_1 \cdot c_2}{n} = \frac{(152)(125)}{500} = 38,$$

$$E_{21} = \frac{r_2 \cdot c_1}{n} = \frac{(348)(375)}{500} = 261, E_{22} = \frac{r_2 \cdot c_2}{n} = \frac{(348)(125)}{500} = 87,$$

$$\chi_{calc}^2 = \sum_{j=1}^{c} \sum_{i=1}^{r} \frac{(O_{ij} - E_{ij})^2}{E_{ij}}$$

$$= \frac{(94 - 114)^2}{114} + \frac{(58 - 38)^2}{38} + \frac{(281 - 261)^2}{261} + \frac{(67 - 87)^2}{87}$$

$$= 20.165$$

Hypotheses: $H_0:$ Math ACT and success in college algebra are independent v.

   $H_1:$ Math ACT and success in college algebra are dependent

Test statistic: $\chi_{calc}^2 = 20.165$

Critical value: $\chi_{\alpha,df}^2 = \chi_{0.01,1}^2 = 6.635$

Decision rule: Reject H_0 if $\chi_{calc}^2 > 6.635$

Decision: Reject H_0 because $20.165 > 6.635$

Conclusion: There is sufficient evidence to conclude that math ACT and success in college algebra are dependent at $\alpha = 0.01$.

Chapter 14—Tests with Ordinal Level Data

1. Signed ranks: $-2.5, 1, 5.5, -2.5, 7, 8, 5.5, 4;$
   sum absolute value of negative ranks $= 5$, sum of positive ranks $= 31;$

Hypotheses: $H_0:$ Golf scores before and after the workshop have the same distribution v.

   $H_1:$ Golf scores before and after the workshop have different distributions

Test statistic: $T_{calc} = 5$

Critical value: $T_{\frac{\alpha}{2},n} = T_{0.05,8} = 6$

Decision rule: Reject H_0 if $T_{calc} \le 6$

Decision: Reject H_0 because $5 \le 6$

Conclusion: There is sufficient evidence to conclude that the distribution of golf scores before the workshop is significantly different than the distribution of golf scores after the workshop $\alpha = 0.10$.

2. R = sum of ranks for School 1 = 226.5;

$$\mu_R = \frac{n_1(n_1 + n_2 + 1)}{2} = \frac{(15)(15 + 15 + 1)}{2} = 232.5;$$

$$\sigma_R = \sqrt{\frac{n_1 n_2 (n_1 + n_2 + 1)}{12}} = \sqrt{\frac{(15)(15)(15 + 15 + 1)}{12}} = 24.1091269;$$

Hypotheses: H_0: Reading scores for School 1 and School 2 have the same distribution v.

H_1: Reading scores for School 1 and School 2 have different distributions

Test statistic: $z = \dfrac{R - \mu_R}{\sigma_R} = \dfrac{226.5 - 232.5}{24.1091269} = -0.249$

Critical value: $\pm z_{\frac{\alpha}{2},n} = \pm z_{0.005} = \pm 2.575$

Decision rule: Reject H_0 if $|z_{calc}| > 2.575$

Decision: Reject H_0 because $0.249 < 2.575$

Conclusion: There is not sufficient evidence to conclude that the distribution of reading scores for School 1 is significantly different than the distribution of reading scores for School 2 at $\alpha = 0.01$.

3. Ranks for hours (in order): 1, 10, 4, 3, 6, 8, 2, 7, 5, 9;
Ranks for grades (in order): 1, 8, 4, 3, 7, 9, 2, 6, 5, 10;
Difference in ranks (ignoring signs): 0, 2, 0, 0, 1, 1, 0, 1, 0, 1;

$$r_{S_{calc}} = 1 - \frac{6\sum d^2}{n(n^2 - 1)} = 1 - \frac{6(2^2 + 1^2 + 1^2 + 1^2 + 1^2)}{10(10^2 - 1)} = 0.952.$$

Hypotheses: $H_0 : \rho_S = 0$ v. $H_1 : \rho_S \ne 0$

Test statistic: $r_{S_{calc}} = 0.952$

Critical value: $r_{S\frac{\alpha}{2},n} = r_{S_{0.025,10}} = 0.648$

Decision rule: Reject H_0 if $|r_{S_{calc}}| > 0.648$

Decision: Reject H_0 because $0.952 > 0.648$

Conclusion: There is sufficient evidence to conclude that there is a significant relationship between number of study hours and final exam grade at $\alpha = 0.05$.

4. $R_1 = 99, R_2 = 149, R_3 = 217$;

$$H_{calc} = \frac{12}{n(n + 1)}\left(\frac{R_1^2}{n_1} + \frac{R_2^2}{n_2} + \cdots + \frac{R_k^2}{n_k}\right) - 3(n + 1)$$

$$= \frac{12}{30(30 + 1)}\left(\frac{99^2}{10} + \frac{149^2}{10} + \frac{217^2}{10}\right) - 3(30 + 1) = 9.053$$

Hypotheses: H_0: Exam scores for the three departments have the same distribution v.

H_1: Exam scores for the three departments have different distributions

Test statistic: $\chi^2_{calc} = 9.053$

Critical value: $\chi^2_{\alpha,df} = \chi^2_{0.10,2} = 4.605$

Decision rule: Reject H_0 if $\chi^2_{calc} > 4.605$

Decision: Reject H_0 because $9.053 > 4.605$

Conclusion: There is sufficient evidence to conclude that distributions of exam scores for the four departments are significantly different at $\alpha = 0.10$.

FLASH TEST

The following pages contain a practice test so that you may assess your understanding of the material presented in Unit 5. Answers and explanations follow the exam. For any questions you miss, be sure to review the explanation carefully and reread the appropriate portion of the section to which the question applies. If you still do not understand the correct answer, review the concept in your text and/or ask your instructor for assistance.

FLASH TEST FOR UNIT 5

TRUE/FALSE (3 points each)

_____ **1.** Critical values of χ^2 get larger as the sample sizes get larger.

_____ **2.** Sample sizes must be equal when conducting a Kruskal–Wallis test.

_____ **3.** Both the Spearman rank correlation coefficient and the χ^2 test for independence are concerned with the relationship between two random variables.

_____ **4.** T_{calc} is the test statistic used for a Wilcoxon rank sum test

_____ **5.** If $R = 126.5$, at least one set of tied ranks occurred in the data set.

MULTIPLE CHOICE (3 points each)

_____ **6.** The appropriate test to determine if a significant relationship exists between X and Y when the random variables are not normally distributed is:

A. χ^2 Goodness-of-Fit   C. test using Pearson's r

B. test using Spearman's r_s D. Wilcoxon rank sum test

_____ **7.** The decision rule for a Wilcoxon signed-ranks test is to reject H_0 if:

A. $|T_{calc}| > T_{\frac{\alpha}{2},n}$ C. $T_{calc} < T_{\frac{\alpha}{2},n}$

B. $T_{calc} \leq -T_{\frac{\alpha}{2},n}$ D. none of these

_____ **8.** The expected frequency of a cell in a χ^2 goodness-of-fit test is calculated by:

A. $n \cdot p_{i_0}$ C. $k - 1$

B. $\dfrac{r_i \cdot c_j}{n}$ D. none of these

_____ **9.** The calculated value of the test statistic for a Wilcoxon rank sum test is -1.82. The p-value is:

A. 0.0344   C. 0.4656

B. 0.0688   D. cannot determine from the information given

_____ **10.** The appropriate critical value for a Kruskal–Wallis test in which $n = 25$, $k = 5$, and $\alpha = 0.10$ is:

A. 7.779   B. 9.488   C. 11.071   D. 35.172

_____ **11.** A researcher claims that handedness (left, right, ambidextrous) and ethnicity (Caucasian, African American, Hispanic, other) are independent. The appropriate test statistic for the hypothesis test is:

A. T_{calc} B. H_{calc} C. χ^2_{calc} D. $r_{S_{calc}}$

_____ **12.** A researcher claims that the distribution of credit card debt for U.S. residents is significantly different among those whose highest academic degree is a B.S., an M.S., and whose is a Ph.D. The appropriate test statistic for the hypothesis test is:

A. T_{calc} B. H_{calc} C. χ^2_{calc} D. $r_{S_{calc}}$

_____ **13.** A researcher claims that there is a significant relationship between ranked income and ranked credit card debt of U.S. residents with a B.S. degree. The appropriate test statistic for the hypothesis test is:

A. T_{calc} B. H_{calc} C. χ^2_{calc} D. $r_{S_{calc}}$

_____ 14. A researcher claims that of U.S. residents with a Ph.D., 20% are left-handed, 75% are right-handed, and 5% are ambidextrous. The appropriate test statistic for the hypothesis test is:

A. T_{calc} B. H_{calc} C. χ^2_{calc} D. $r_{S_{calc}}$

_____ 15. Which of the following is an appropriate conclusion for a Wilcoxon rank sum test in which the null hypothesis is not rejected at $\alpha = 0.10$?

A. There is not sufficient evidence to conclude that the three population distributions are significantly different at $\alpha = 0.10$.

B. There is not sufficient evidence to conclude that the two population distributions are significantly different at $\alpha = 0.10$.

C. There is not sufficient evidence to conclude that the two variables are independent at $\alpha = 0.10$.

D. There is sufficient evidence to conclude that the two population distributions are significantly different at $\alpha = 0.10$.

SHORT ANSWER (3 points each)

16. Under what circumstances should a test utilizing the Spearman rank correlation coefficient be constructed instead of a test using the Pearson product moment correlation coefficient?

17. Suppose a researcher is conducting a multinomial experiment in which there are four possible outcomes. A χ^2 goodness-of-fit test will be used to determine if the four outcomes are equally likely. What are the two appropriate ways to state the null hypothesis?

18. The null hypothesis for a χ^2 test of independence between eye color and hair color of students at Connor College is rejected at the 0.10 level of significance. State the appropriate conclusion.

19. A nutritionist wants to determine if the distribution of weight for students who exercise is significantly different than the distribution of weight for students who do not exercise. A random sample of 15 students is selected from each group. Which Wilcoxon test is appropriate? Justify your answer.

20. How might the situation in Problem 19 be reworded so that a parametric test would be appropriate?

CALCULATIONS (5 points each)

21. Rank the following data set in ascending order:

Observation	40	49	36	56	45	40	38	49	58	37	62	40
Rank												

22. For the following 3×3 contingency table, fill in the shaded areas with the appropriate values.

X \ Y	1	2	3	Row Marginal
1	42		20	116
2		81	32	
3	27	50		135
Column Marginal	105	185	110	

23. For the contingency table in Problem 22, find the expected frequencies for cell 1, 3 and cell 3, 2.

24. An administrator wants to determine if the distribution of professors' ages among four colleges at a large university were the same. She took a random sample of size seven from each college, combined the 28 observations into one data set, ranked the ages from youngest to oldest, and displayed the results in the following table:

Professor	1	2	3	4	5	6	7
College 1	25	17.5	9	28	21	14	26
College 2	3	8	22	12	19	10	6
College 3	12	24	17.5	27	2	23	15
College 4	4	16	20	1	12	5	7

The hypotheses for her test are H_0: Professors' ages in the four colleges have the same distribution v. H_1: Professors' ages in the four colleges have different distributions. The decision rule is to reject H_0 if the test statistic is greater than 11.345. What is the appropriate **decision** for this test?

25. A Wilcoxon signed-ranks test is to be conducted (at $\alpha = 0.05$) in which the sum of the absolute value of the negative ranks is 156, and the sum of the positive ranks is 169. For the random sample of 25, three pairs had differences of zero. Calculate the test statistic and state the decision rule.

26. The owner of an ice cream store claims that 60% of elementary school children prefer ice cream cones, 32% prefer ice cream sundaes, and 8% prefer banana splits. A random sample of 250 elementary school children were asked their preference. The observed and expected frequencies are listed in the following table:

	Cone	Sundae	Banana Split
Observed frequency	170	50	30
Expected frequency	150	80	20

Test the owner's claim at the 0.01 level of signficance.

27. A hypothesis test is to be conducted using a Wilcoxon rank sum test. The following is the ranked data for two independent random samples of size 12 each.

Sample 1	10	4	14	5	1	13	16	19	6	22	21	9
Sample 2	18	12	3	11	17	24	2	7	15	20	23	8

Calculate the value of the test statistic.

28. An instructor claims that there is a significant relationship between a student's IQ score and his/her ranking in a statistics class. A random sample of eight students is selected. The rank of IQ score and class rank are recorded for each student.

Student	1	2	3	4	5	6	7	8
IQ rank	1	2	3	4	5	6	7	8
Class rank	1	2	4	7	3	5	6	8

Test the instructor's claim at the 0.05 level of significance.

Answers to practice test begin on the next page.

SOLUTIONS TO FLASH TEST FOR UNIT 5

TRUE/FALSE

1. F; critical values of χ^2 are based on number of groups, not sample sizes

2. F; the only assumption on the sample size for the Kruskal–Wallis test is that each sample must contain at least five observations

3. T; χ^2 test for independence is concerned with the relationship between two nominal level variables, whereas the Spearman rank correlation coefficient is concerned with the relationship between two ordinal level variables

4. F; T_{calc} is the test statistic used for a Wilcoxon signed-ranks test, z_{calc} is the test statistics used for a Wilcoxon rank sum test

5. T; if there are no tied ranks, R would be a whole number

MULTIPLE CHOICE

6. B; the χ^2 goodness-of-fit test deals with a multinomial distribution, Pearson's requires the assumption of normality, the Wilcoxon rank sum test deals with two populations and one variable

7. D; the decision rule is to reject H_0 if $T_{calc} \leq T_{\frac{\alpha}{2}, n}$

8. A; B is for the χ^2 test for independence, and C is degrees of freedom

9. B; the test statistic is a z, thus the p-value $= (2)P(Z < -1.82) = (2)(0.0344) = 0.0688$

10. A; $df = k - 1 = 4$, thus the critical value is $\chi^2_{\alpha, df} = \chi^2_{0.10, 4} = 7.779$

11. C; relationship between two nominal level variables, χ^2 test for independence

12. B; difference between distributions for more than two populations, Kruskal–Wallis test

13. D; relationship between two ordinal level variables, Spearman rank correlation coefficient

14. C; multinomial experiment, hypothesized values for proportions, χ^2 goodness-of-fit test

15. B; A is for Kruskal–Wallis, C is for χ^2 test for independence, D is appropriate when the null hypothesis is rejected

SHORT ANSWER

16. It is appropriate to use r_S instead of r when the data are measured at the ordinal level or the assumption of normality cannot be met.

17. 1) $H_0 : p_1 = 0.25, p_2 = 0.25, p_3 = 0.25, p_4 = 0.25$; if all outcomes are equally likely, the hypothesized proportion for each is $\dfrac{1}{4} = 0.25$.

    2) $H_0 : p_1 = p_2 = p_3 = p_4$; if the hypothesized value is the same for each proportion, the researcher is hypothesizing that the population proportions are equal.

18. There is sufficient evidence to conclude that eye color and hair color of students at Connor College are dependent at $\alpha = 0.10$.

19. The Wilcoxon rank sum is appropriate because samples are independent.

20. The situation could be reworded as follows: A nutritionist wants to determine if the average weight for students who exercise is significantly different than the average weight of students who do not exercise, assuming that weight is normally distributed.

CALCULATIONS

21.

Observation	40	49	36	56	45	40	38	49	58	37	62	40
Rank	5	8.5	1	10	7	5	3	8.5	11	2	12	5

22. First find n by adding column marginals, then find the marginal for Row 2 by subtracting the marginals for Row 1 and Row 3 from n. The cell values can then be found by subtraction.

		Y		
	1	2	3	Row Marginal
1	42	54	20	116
X 2	36	81	32	149
3	27	50	58	135
Column Marginal	105	185	110	400

23. $E_{13} = \dfrac{r_1 \cdot c_3}{n} = \dfrac{(116)(110)}{400} = 31.9$; $E_{32} = \dfrac{r_3 \cdot c_2}{n} = \dfrac{(135)(185)}{400} = 62.4375$

24. First sum the ranks for each group: $R_1 = 140.5$, $R_2 = 80$, $R_3 = 120.5$, $R_4 = 65$.

Then calculate the test statistic:

$$H_{calc} = \frac{12}{n(n+1)}\left(\frac{R_1^2}{n_1} + \frac{R_2^2}{n_2} + \cdots + \frac{R_k^2}{n_k}\right) - 3(n+1)$$

$$= \frac{12}{28(28+1)}\left(\frac{140.5^2}{7} + \frac{80^2}{7} + \frac{120.5^2}{7} + \frac{65^2}{7}\right) - 3(28+1) = 7.762.$$

The appropriate decision is to fail to reject H_0 because $7.762 < 11.345$.

25. The test statistic is $T_{calc} =$ the smaller of the two sums $= 156$. Because $d = 0$ for three pairs, $n = 25 - 3 = 22$, thus the critical value is $T_{\frac{\alpha}{2}, n} = T_{0.025, 22} = 66$.

26. $\chi^2_{calc} = \displaystyle\sum_{i=1}^{k} \frac{(O_i - E_i)^2}{E_i} = \frac{(170 - 150)^2}{150} + \frac{(50 - 80)^2}{80} + \frac{(30 - 20)^2}{20} = 18.917$;

Hypotheses: $H_0: p_1 = 0.60, p_2 = 0.32, p_3 = 0.08$ v.

H_1: at least one of the proportions differs from its hypothesized value

Test statistic: $\chi^2_{calc} = 18.917$

Critical value: $\chi^2_{\alpha,df} = \chi^2_{0.01,2} = 9.210$

Decision rule: Reject H_0 if $\chi^2_{calc} > 9.210$

Decision: Reject H_0 because $18.917 > 9.210$

Conclusion: There is sufficient evidence to conclude that at least one of the proportions differs from its hypothesized value at $\alpha = 0.05$.

27. R = the sum of the ranks for sample 1 = 140;

$$\mu_R = \frac{n_1(n_1 + n_2 + 1)}{2} = \frac{(12)(12 + 12 + 1)}{2} = 150;$$

$$\sigma_R = \sqrt{\frac{n_1 n_2 (n_1 + n_2 + 1)}{12}} = \sqrt{\frac{(12)(12)(12 + 12 + 1)}{12}} = 17.32050808;$$

$$z = \frac{R - \mu_R}{\sigma_R} = \frac{140 - 150}{17.32050808} = -0.577$$

28. The differences between the ranks (ignoring signs) are: 0, 0, 1, 3, 2, 1, 1, 0;

$$r_{S_{calc}} = 1 - \frac{6\sum d^2}{n(n^2 - 1)} = 1 - \frac{6(1^2 + 3^2 + 2^2 + 1^2 + 1^2)}{8(8^2 - 1)} = 0.810;$$

Hypotheses: $H_0: \rho_S = 0$ v. $H_1: \rho_S \neq 0$

Test statistic: $r_{S_{calc}} = 0.810$

Critical value: $r_{S_{\frac{\alpha}{2},n}} = r_{S_{0.025,8}} = 0.738$

Decision rule: Reject H_0 if $|r_{S_{calc}}| > 0.738$

Decision: Reject H_0 because $0.810 > 0.738$

Conclusion: There is sufficient evidence to conclude that there is a significant relationship between IQ scores and class rank at $\alpha = 0.05$.

INDEX

linear, between two variables, 70–76,
    109–11
    negative, 22
    positive, 22
Relative frequency, 12, 20
Relative frequency probability, 33, 39
Research hypothesis, 95, 99
Residual, 60
Response variables, 12, 17, 60, 70
Right-skewed distribution, 12, 20
Row marginal, 144, 148
Rules of probability. *see* Probability rules

S
Sample mean, 64
    sampling distribution of the, 47–48
Sample(s), 11, 14
    dependent, 60
    independent, 60
    paired, 60
    random, 62
    types of, 17–19
Sample space, 33, 37
Sampling
    cluster, 18–19
    random, 12
    simple random, 18
    systematic random, 18
Sampling distribution, 35
    online resources for, 36
    of the sample mean, 47–48
    standard deviation of, 48
Sampling error, 12
Satterwaite approximation, 80, 116–17
Scatterplots, 22
Scheffe test, 124
Significance level, 95
Simple event, 33, 37
Simple random sampling, 18
Slope
    point estimate of, 76
    of the population regression equation,
        109–12
    standard error of, 11
    test statistic of, 11
Spearman rank correlation coefficient, 145,
    150–51, 155
Standard deviation, 13, 25
Standard error, 35, 48
    of the estimate, 60, 63
    with pooled variance estimate, 81
    of the predicted value, 75
    of regression equation, 74

Statistics
    defined, 11
    as a field of study, 14–15
Stem-and-leaf plots, 20–21
Strong relationship, 22
Subjective probability, 34, 39
Sum of squares, in one way analysis of variance
        (ANOVA), 122–23
Symmetric distribution, 12, 20
Systematic random sampling, 18

T
Test statistic(s), 95, 98
    of correlation coefficient, 11
    f, 99, 122–23
    for population mean, 106
    of slope, 11
    t, 99, 155
    tables of, 96, 111
The Basic Practice of Statistics, 7–10
Tied ranks, 145, 150
Tree diagram, 37–38
Trial, 33, 37
Triola, M., 7–10
T test statistic, 99
    dependent, 155
    independent, 155
Two way analysis of variance (ANOVA),
        125–29, 155
    assumptions of, 125–26
    example of, 127–29
    interaction effect in, 126–27
    multiple comparison tests for, 127
    online resources for, 98
    purpose of, 125
    summary table for, 127
Type I error, 95, 101
Type II error, 101

U
Unbiased estimator, 64
Understandable Statistics, 7–10
Union, 33, 37
    calculating the probability of, 39

V
Variability
    measures of, 25
    online resources for, 13–14
Variable(s), 11
    binomial random, 35
    confounding, 17–18

NOTES